OUR GLORIOUS INHERITANCE

Volume Six . . . The Hope of Glory

by
MIKE SHREVE

An exhaustive study of the revelation of the titles of the children of God

---

DEEPER REVELATION BOOKS

"Holding forth the word of life . . ." Phil. 2:16

Published by: **Deeper Revelation Books** - an outreach of the ministry of Mike Shreve

Printed by: **Faith Printing Company**
4210 Locust Hill Rd.
Taylors, SC 29687-8911
803-895-3822

Cover design by: **Mike Shreve**
Artwork by: **Dale Thompson**, Imagination Art, Greenville, S.C. 803-232-5444

ISBN: 0-942507-12-6
ISBN: 0-942507-04-5 (8-Volume Set)
Our Glorious Inheritance Volume Six
Copyright © 1991 by Mike Shreve

All correspondence should be directed to:
Mike Shreve
P.O. Box 4260
Cleveland, TN 37320

A complete list of available tapes (audio and video) can be obtained upon request.

DEDICATION

Since this sixth volume of **OUR GLORIOUS INHERITANCE** is entitled *The Hope of Glory*, I dedicate its contents to Nancy Schmelling who recently graduated from *hope* to *glory*...and who showed us, in a heroic way, how to maintain *hope*, even when confronted by immeasurably dark circumstances of life. The courage, faith and strength her family displayed (her husband, John, and her sons, Jim and Ronnie) will be long remembered by all of us who loved them and united with them in prayer.

COVER ART

The main theme of this sixth volume of **OUR GLORIOUS IN-HERITANCE** is "the mystery...hid from ages and from generations...Christ in you, *the hope of glory*." (Col. 1:26-27) Great emphasis will be placed on two terms: *hope* and *glory*. A third major emphasis is *the ark of the covenant* (depicted on the front cover). This acacia wood box, inlaid and overlaid with gold, contained the tablets of stone given to Moses, the golden bowl full of manna, Aaron's rod that budded and the book of the law. Upon the lid of this ark, between the cherubim, the Shekinah glory of God manifested. Once a year, on the Day of Atonement, the high priest would sprinkle blood on this lid (also called the "mercy seat") to atone for the sins of Israel. **In the New Covenant era, this ark speaks of Jesus.** The glory of God rested upon Him, and in Him we find: the fulfillment of the Law, bread from heaven, resurrection life, and the Word made flesh. **The four articles in the ark relate to these four things.** Under the Old Will, this ark resided in the innermost sanctuary, the holy of holies: first, in the tabernacle, and later on, in the temple of Solomon. Under the New Will, believers become *"The Temple of God"* and our regenerated spirits become the holy of holies in which the *"God of glory"* dwells. He has atoned for our sins, sprinkled us with His blood, and mercifully enthroned Himself in our praise. The *glory* that initially *rested* upon Jesus now *rests* upon us. And all that the ark symbolized, in the former age, is presently taking place in the heart and life of every child of God. Because of these things, we have also been entitled: *His Abode, His Glory, His Habitation, His Rest* and *Lively Stones* that make up *His Temple* (just a few of the *titles* contained in this volume). Comprehending these names and *titles* should fill the heart of every covenant son and daughter of God with a full-of-*hope* insight into a *glory*-filled heritage and future.

EXPLANATION OF SPECIAL MARKINGS

● Bullets have been used on some *title-pages* to draw greater attention to the more important, or more highly emphasized *titles* in that particular chapter. Bullets and blocks (● and ■) have also been used, throughout the text, to signal that there is a major shift in the subject matter or the introduction of important material that should be more carefully noted.

Italic and **bold** print are also often used as a means of emphasis or to draw attention to certain words or ideas that weave their way through the fabric of an entire chapter or the book as a whole.

EXPLANATION OF THE TABLE OF CONTENTS

Each of the chapters listed in the table of contents contains one or more of the *titles* God has given us in His Word. Normally, only those names or *titles* which are related in meaning are gouped together into one chapter. Most are from the King James Version, some from other versions of the Bible. A few of the *titles* are English interpretations of Hebrew or Greek names or words; and a few are *titles* literally applied to the city of God, New Jerusalem, which is also called "the bride, the Lamb's wife." (Rev. 21:9) By association, we have also inherited these names, all of which will be designated as such in the final index. Usually, the main *title* of a chapter is listed first in the table of contents, with the subordinate, complementary *titles* following.

Only those *titles* which appear on the *title-pages* at the beginning of each chapter are listed in the main part of the table of contents. In a few chapters, there is an excessive amount of extra, lesser-important *titles* that are printed in small print, either on the last *title-page* or at the end of the chapter. When this takes place, a note will be placed in the table of contents.

There are hundreds of names, *titles* and descriptive appellations God has given to us in His Word. Many are interwoven, lending richness of meaning to each other. The author has attempted to group all of those *titles* which tend to convey a central theme in individual volumes, with many sub-groups in each book centered on this common theme. (In Volume Six this underlying theme is *The Hope of Glory*.) All eight volumes together will provide any believer with a rich and comprehensive picture of the fullness of **OUR GLORIOUS INHERITANCE.**

TABLE OF CONTENTS

THE PLACE WHERE HIS HONOUR DWELLS
THE STONES OF THE SANCTUARY
THE DESIRED OF ALL NATIONS
A BRAND PLUCKED OUT OF THE FIRE
THE PLACE OF HIS THRONE
NOTE: Four other associated *titles* are listed at the end
of the third *title-page* and over forty more associated
titles appear on the last page of this chapter.

The sixth volume in
an eight-volume series
on

The Revelation
of the
Titles of the Children
of God

THE
HOPE
OF
GLORY

*"To whom God would make known what is the riches of the glory of this mystery among the Gentiles; which is Christ in you, **THE HOPE OF GLORY.**"*

(Colossians 1:27)

INTRODUCTORY CHAPTER

THE HOPE OF GLORY

*"To whom God would make known what is
the riches of the glory of this mystery among
the Gentiles; which is Christ in you, THE
HOPE OF GLORY."*

(Colossians 1:27)

● **The main theme of this, and every other volume of OUR GLORIOUS
INHERITANCE, is quite evidently the study of all the hundreds of names
and *titles* the Everlasting Father has bestowed upon His offspring.**

Each volume has its own unique sub-theme, though, that weaves its way
through every chapter...uniting them all in a common design. The "fabric" of
Volume Six contains three of these interwoven sub-themes: one very sacred
object - *the ark of the covenant*, and two very edifying words - *hope* and *glory*.

God's Old Covenant people, newly delivered from Egypt and wandering
through the wilderness of Sin, had only one source of *hope* and *glory* - the
presence of God that went with them. Moses even pled with Jehovah:

> *"...If Thy presence go not [with us], carry
> us not up hence.*
> *For wherein shall it be known here that I
> and Thy people have found grace in Thy sight?*
> *is it not in that Thou goest with us? so shall we
> be separated, I and Thy people, from all the
> people that are upon the face of the earth."*

(Exodus 33:15-16 AV, NIV)

Moses knew that without the divine *glory* in their midst, the Israelites would
end up only minimally religious - or even irreligious - steeped in corruption
and overpowered by deception, like any other people.

Not only would they be without distinction, they would be without *hope*.
Their plight would doubtless be to wander aimlessly through life, having no
real direction through the arid wasteland and no protection against the dangers
encountered there. They had to have God's presence - which was itself a sure
sign of His grace (as the previously quoted scripture clearly indicates).

● **Unfortunately, there was no way for men's hearts, at that time, to be
properly sanctified for God's indwelling, that this *hope* might be perfectly
realized. So God had to institute a temporary, yet beautifully detailed and
highly symbolic, alternate plan.**

He presented Moses with the design for a sanctuary of worship: a place of
visitation and reconciliation. It was to be called "the tabernacle."

Within its white linen walls there would be **an outer court**, with a brazen
altar of sacrifice and a laver; **the holy place**, containing the golden lampstand,
the table of shewbread, and the altar of incense; and **the holy of holies**,
containing the ark of the covenant (depicted on the cover of this book).

Upon the lid of the ark - called "the mercy seat" - blood would be annually
sprinkled to atone for Israel's sin. Between the cherubim, just above the mercy

1

seat, the *Shekinah glory of God* would manifest and out of this *glory cloud*, God would speak.

So the ark was the abode of both the Spirit and Word of Almighty God. But there was a major drawback.

Only one man - the high priest - was ever allowed into this sacred chamber. He went in only one time year and he went in with fearful trembling.

The ordinary Israelite had no such intimacy with God.

Certain veils prevented his entrance and death would more than likely be his judgment if he dared to trespass.

Obviously, the way back to God - in perfection - had not yet been revealed.

God's people knew all about the articles contained in the ark: the tablets of stone, the book of the law, Aaron's rod that budded, and the golden bowl full of manna. But these objects were all out of sight and out of reach...as well as what they symbolized!

Furthermore, the people just could not live up to the law...and what should have been a blessing became a curse. For this cause, and many other reasons, God found fault with the Old Covenant and decided to bring to birth a New Covenant that would meet the need of His chosen:

> *"But this shall be the covenant that I will make with the house of Israel; After those days, saith the Lord, I WILL PUT MY LAW IN THEIR INWARD PARTS, AND WRITE IT IN THEIR HEARTS; and will be their God, and they shall be My people."*
>
> (Jeremiah 31:33)

Furthermore, He promised:

> *"And I will put My Spirit within you, and cause you to walk in My statutes..."*
>
> (Ezekiel 36:27)

These two prophecies alone show the beauty, the greatness and the value of what Jesus came to accomplish.

Because of the victory that was won on Calvary, in this dispensation, each believer becomes God's tabernacle - **the dwelling place of both the Word and the Spirit - HIS ABODE, HIS HABITATION, HIS REST** and **HIS TEMPLE** (some of the *titles* yet to be revealed in this volume).

Now, instead of residing in the ark, God's law resides within us. Instead of dwelling between the cherubim above the ark, God's Spirit (God's *glory*) rests upon us...and within our hearts.

So the "hidden man of the heart" has become, as it were, the new "holy of holies." **The ark of the covenant is now spiritual in essence and is positioned in this "inward man."** (I Peter 3:4, II Corinthians 4:16)

Because the law provided "a shadow of good things to come," this ancient article of furniture, with all the details of its construction, spoke symbolically of something far more profound that was yet to be, something that is presently happening deep in the heart of every yielded and believing child of God. (Hebrews 10:1)

2

Of course, such an outcome was God's plan from the beginning...yet mysteriously, He hid it from ages and generations.

But now we have received "the spirit of wisdom and revelation" in the knowledge of God that we might know *"the hope of His calling"* and *"the riches of the glory of His inheritance in the saints."* (Ephesians 1:17-18)

It is no longer the ark of the testimony in the holy of holies providing *hope* for God's people and a resting place for *His glory.*

IT IS "CHRIST IN YOU, *THE HOPE OF GLORY!"* (Colossians 1:27)

> *"For the law made nothing perfect, but the bringing in of a better hope did, by the which we draw nigh unto God."*
>
> (Hebrews 7:19)

This is the foundation of the revelation contained in this sixth volume of **OUR GLORIOUS INHERITANCE.**

THE DEFINITION OF HOPE

● Since several of the forthcoming chapters of this book have been designated to more fully bring out the revelation of the *ark* and the *glory,* in the remainder of this introductory chapter we will pursue instead the intriguing definition and heartwarming revelation of *hope.* *1

From a scriptural standpoint especially, **hope** means *desire married to expectation.* It is the happy anticipation of good...not only the *"desire for,"* but the *"expectation of "* God's blessings, God's provision, God's power and the fulfillment of His promises.

Tertullian, an early church father, offered the unique idea that:

> *"Hope is patience with the lamp lit."*

One of the main Hebrew words translated **hope** is *tiqvah.* It literally means *a cord (as an attachment)* and grows out of the primary root word *qavah* which means *to bind together.* When we fix our hearts on a certain goal or answer to prayer, we are *bound* to the same with *cords of hope.*

Interwoven together, *faith, hope, and charity* - which abide forever - make up a *"threefold cord* not quickly broken." (Eccl. 4:12, See I Cor. 13:13)

This spiritual *attitude-cord* binds our hearts to the heart of the prayer-answering God Himself. We are bound to Him with cords of faith and cords of *hope.* The very moment we are born again, there emerges this strong spiritual *attachment* or *bonding* between us that persists the rest of our days.

The Almighty maintains a certain longing and expectation toward us.

We cultivate a certain longing and expectation toward Him.

As we will soon see very clearly: in the end, these two are one.

God's *hope* and our *hope* blend together, for there is - *"one hope of [our] calling."* (Ephesians 4:4)

THE REASON FOR OUR TITLES

● Thoughtful, spiritual-minded parents often bestow meaningful names on their children at birth in the *hope* that those children will then grow into the fulfillment of their names and be a praise in the earth.

The Everlasting Father has set this precedent Himself...in an exceptional and excellent way...giving us over 800 names and *titles*, that we might be "for **A PEOPLE**, and for **A NAME**, and for **A PRAISE**, and for **A GLORY**" - "among all the people of the earth." (Jeremiah 13:11, Zephaniah 3:20)

God bestows all of these names and *titles* upon us in the *hope* that we will grow into their fulfillment, and thus, emerge in Christlikeness.

We probe into the revelation of these names and *titles* in the *hope* that we will discover who we are in God's plan, and thus, emerge in Christlikeness.

So again, there is *one hope of our calling* - and our names and *titles* reveal different facets of this holy and heavenly calling.

It should be remembered that every *title* we have received is a descriptive name that indicates position, office, responsibility or privilege. It is God's *hope* that we enjoy all of the privileges given to us as sons of God.

It is His *hope* that we fulfill all of the offices, responsibilities and spiritual positions for which we have been ordained.

But how can we lay hold to these things except we are aware of our God-given entitlements. Therefore, it is of exceeding importance that we learn our names and *titles* and strive daily to walk in their fulfillment.

Then we will be fruitful in this world and we will not be "ashamed before Him at His coming." (I John 2:28)

Seeing believers fulfill such a goal is the very purpose for the writing of this book.

HOPING AGAINST HOPE

It has been proven that an ordinary human being can live about forty days without food, about three days without water, and at maximum, about eight minutes without air. But no one can live (not really, not even for one moment) without *hope*.

The tragic truth of the matter is this: that prior to salvation, we were "strangers from the covenants of promise, *having no hope*, and without God in the world." Our lives had no meaning, our paths were aimless, as we wandered through the gross darkness of this "wilderness of sin." (Eph. 2:12)

● But then we met the gracious God who has been appropriately entitled *the hope of Israel, the hope of our fathers, the hope of His people, our hope* and *the God of hope.* (Jer. 14:8; 50:7, Jl. 3:16; I Tim. 1:1, Ro. 15:13)

In Him we discovered a wellspring of *hope* that never runs dry. And we soon learned the trueness of that oft-quoted statement:

> *"Without Christ, life is a hopeless end;*
> *But with Christ, life is **endless hope**!"*

4

Just as there was an endless supply of water in the Rock that followed the Israelites through the desert, so there is an endless supply of *hope* in our God...even when circumstances seem to be totally the opposite.

● In Romans 4:18, we find a perfect example as we read how Abraham - *"against hope believed in hope,* **that he might become the father of many nations, according to that which was spoken..."**

Another translation says - *"when hope seemed hopeless"* and still another - *"when hope was dead within him [he] went on hoping in faith."* (NEB, PME)

Abraham's body was dead.

Sarah's womb was dead.

So it was only logical, to a carnal minded person at least, that any *hope* for change was dead as well. But just as the beautiful quotation declares - "When you say a situation or a person is *hopeless,* you are slamming the door in the face of God. " - (Charles Allen)

Because Abraham kept *hoping,* the door to the supernatural was held open.

God came through the open door, granted a miracle and Sarah conceived.

Now if we are the children of Abraham, we will surely face severe tests and trials just like our spiritual foreparents...for they were examples to us.

Let us remind ourselves of this often.

But even when our lives seem barren; when we are surrounded with situations that testify impossibility and death - emotional death, mental death, spiritual death, or even physical death - we can reprove our own doubt-prone hearts with Psalm 42:11:

> *"Why art thou cast down, O my soul? and why art thou disquieted within me? HOPE THOU IN GOD: for I shall yet praise Him, who is the health of my countenance, and my God."*

In the darkness of midnight, we *hope* for the dawn; in the cold grip of winter, we *hope* for the spring; in the pain of travail, we *hope* for new birth; in the burying of seed, we *hope* for germination.

No matter what comes, we can dare to say - *"I shall yet praise Him."*

We know the future, and our destiny, rests securely in His hands.

Those who are chosen of God can have such trust and confidence (kindred words to *hope*); for having been through the flood and the fire, we have discovered that the Captain of our salvation is faithful and true.

● What boldness the apostle and epistle-writer communicated to the persecuted Roman church when he wrote:

> *"...we glory in tribulations also: knowing that tribulation worketh patience;*
> *And patience, experience; and experience, hope:*
> *And hope maketh not ashamed; because the love of God is shed abroad in our hearts by the Holy Ghost which is given unto us."*
> (Romans 5:3-5)

5

Experience works *hope* because the more valleys we face, the more we find our Saviour to always be the Lily of the valleys; the more fiery trials we go through, the more we discover He is always the "fourth Man in the fire," ready to bring us forth in victory.

The more *experiences*, such as these, that we have in life, the more we conclude that our God is always "beautiful for situation." (Psalm 48:2)

This is why *"hope maketh not ashamed."* (Romans 5:5)

Several other translations of this passage declare with one voice that this *"hope does not disappoint us."* (TEV, NIV, RSV)

● **This very statement shows the vast difference between the biblical use of the term *hope* as opposed to the present and common use of the word among those who are unenlightened.**

Normally and ironically, when someone of this world uses this word, it carries with it a strong, negative sense of impending disappointment. When a person says - "I *hope* so" - they are really saying - "I don't really expect this to work out" or "I'm really preparing for disappointment in this matter."

Not so in the positive, biblical sense of the word. As believers, our hope is not based on sense-knowledge, fleshly desire, or some mere stroke of luck.

Our *hope* is based on the infallible, unchangeable Word of God.

Six times Psalm 119 even mentions that our *hope* is in the Word of the Lord. (Psalm 119:43,49,74,81,114,147)

First, our *hope* is based on **the written Word** (which has become for us a sure foundation). Second, our *hope* is based on **the living Word** (God's Spirit-inspired communication toward us on a personal basis).

What we *hope* for, we fully expect to come to pass!

If we place our confidence in either the written or the living Word, we know we will not be *ashamed* or *disappointed*.

This is correct irregardless of how hopeless circumstances may look. "For the Scripture saith, Whosoever believeth on Him shall not be *ashamed*." (Romans 10:11)

One way or the other, God always comes through. He always causes us to triumph. He always vindicates His Word.

● Paul could write such words as those just mentioned because he had "been there." He was a man of experience...and as Romans 5:4 indicates, experience had worked *hope* into his spirit. Numerous experiences, both positive and negative, had instructed him in the faithfulness of God and the dependability of God's Word.

Once, in route to Rome, the ship on which he was sailing was hit by a fierce storm at sea. This "euroclydon" persisted for so many days that the one recording the incident concluded - "All *hope* that we should be saved was...taken away." (Acts 27:20)

But Paul had a direct communication from God on the matter - **a living Word**. So he boldly stood amid the crew and passengers declaring - "Sirs, be of good cheer: for I believe God." (Acts 27:25)

Paul, like Abraham, *"against hope believed in hope."* (Romans 4:18)

Sense-knowledge *hope* looked hopeless, but revelation-knowledge *hope* looked beyond the natural to the supernatural promise of God.

God came through just as Paul had *desired* and *expected*.

In like manner, when the storms of life rage against us, and the light of the

"Son" seems to be blotted out for days and weeks at a time, we can still be of good cheer and announce - "We believe God!"

The world may say our situation is hopeless, but still, *against hope we can believe in hope.* Whether we are depending on the written Word or the living Word, we will not be *ashamed.* Through Jesus, who is the sum of both the written and the living Word, we have:

> *"...access by faith into this grace wherein we stand, and rejoice in hope of the glory of God."*
>
> (Romans 5:2)

We can rejoice in persecutions.
We can rejoice in temptations.
We can rejoice in tribulations.
We can rejoice in trials.

We can always "rejoice in *hope of the glory* of God," for we have that abiding witness - "Christ in us, *the hope of glory.*"

We know that God will make all things work together for our good...for, as a forthcoming chapter of this volume will yet reveal, we are **"THE CALLED ACCORDING TO HIS PURPOSE."** (Romans 8:28)

We have been predestinated to be conformed to the image of God's dear Son. Everything that we face in life will serve to help us reach this goal.

THE HELMET OF HOPE

● In I Thessalonians 5:8, members of the last days' church especially are commanded, as soldiers, to protect themselves by:

> *"...putting on the breastplate of faith and love; and for an helmet, the hope of salvation."*

Salvation basically means *deliverance.*

This phrase - *"the hope of salvation"* - is referring specifically to *deliverance* from the great latter-day judgments that will soon cause this earth to "reel to and fro like a drunkard." (Isaiah 24:20)

As we enter such a climactic era, we know that war will first erupt in the heavenlies. Michael, the archangel, and his militant host of subordinate angels, will apparently take over the first heaven (the atmospheric heaven just above this planet) forcing the prince of the power of the air to relinquish his long held position. Lucifer will then be cast down to the earth "having great wrath, because he knoweth that he hath but a short time." (Revelation 12:12)

> *"...but the Lord will be THE HOPE OF HIS PEOPLE and the strength of the children of Israel."*
>
> (Joel 3:16)

Through every trial, both then and now, believers can wear "for an helmet, *the hope of salvation*," expecting Jesus to ultimately return, deliver His own, and carry us forward into Kingdom Age glory.

All the pointed arrows of Satan's piercing lies and all the battle-axes of his crushing accusations can always be successfully deflected by this God-given *"hope-helmet."* Through it, we "gird up the loins of [our minds]...and *hope* to the end for the grace that is to be brought unto [us] at the revelation of Jesus Christ." (I Peter 1:13)

THE ANCHOR OF HOPE

● Not only do we have a *helmet of hope,* protecting us in these latter days; we have an *anchor of hope* that goes beyond the veil. The chain on this anchor extends from earth to heaven, from time to eternity, from the heart of each individual believer to the very heart of the Almighty God.

At a certain point in God's covenant dealings with Abraham, the Most High swore by Himself, promising with an oath that Abraham's seed would be as numerous as the sand and stars; that they would possess the gates of their enemies, and that they would inherit the earth. (See Genesis 22:16-18)

Hebrews 6:17-20 gives us a further unveiling of this truth:

> *"Wherein God, willing more abundantly to shew unto the heirs of promise the immutability of His counsel, confirmed it by an oath:*
> *That by two immutable things, in which it was impossible for God to lie, we might have a strong consolation, who have fled for refuge to lay hold upon the hope set before us:*
> *WHICH HOPE WE HAVE AS AN ANCHOR OF THE SOUL, BOTH SURE AND STEDFAST, AND WHICH ENTERETH INTO THAT WITHIN THE VEIL;*
> *Whither the forerunner is for us entered, even Jesus, made an high priest for ever after the order of Melchisedec."*

This unveiling of this *hope set before us* involves a revelation of the resurrection and the gift of eternal life.

Jesus was the forerunner, the firstborn from the dead.

He successfully conquered the greatest enemies of humanity.

The great deliverance He wrought as our Messiah was often referred to in the New Testament in *hopeful* terms. Paul called it "the *hope* of the promise made of God unto our fathers" and "the *hope* of Israel." These statements speak primarily of both His and our resurrection. (Acts 26:6; 28:20, See also 23:6)

● Peter also tied *hope* to the resurrection, saying - "Blessed be the God and Father of our Lord Jesus Christ, which according to His abundant mercy hath begotten us again unto a *lively hope* by the *resurrection* of Jesus Christ from the dead." (I Peter 1:3)

8

A lively hope is a living hope.

Something *living* is always something that has the ability to grow and reproduce itself. This speaks a dual message to our hearts.

First - that the *hope* of the resurrection is ever growing and taking over more territory in the world. With each new convert, this *glory-hope* reproduces itself in yet another soul.

And second - it also speaks that no matter how much *hope* we use up, still, *hope* is ever growing and always available. It is a rising, penetrating sun ever spreading its warm rays to embrace the uttermost parts of our lives.

It is a *living hope.*
It is *hope* that because He *lives,* we can *live* also.
Because He conquered death, we can conquer death also.
When we came to Jesus, we arrived - "dead in trespasses and sins." Our souls were dead already and our bodies swiftly progressing toward the same dreadful condition. (Ephesians 2:1)

But then, thank God, we discovered *"the hope of righteousness by faith"* and *"the hope of the Gospel."*

We came to the understanding that through the application of the blood of Jesus we could be quickened back to life and become "holy and unblameable and unreproveable in His sight." (Galatians 5:5, Colossians 1:22-23)

We were lost on the sea of time, tossed to and fro by one storm after another.
Waves of death continually crashed over our souls, soaking us with despair.
Winds of tribulation often ripped our sails, cracked our masts, and made our ships to list dangerously.

It seemed we would be swept away to crash on the dangerous reefs, never to recover again. But then we cried out to the Captain of our salvation.

In desperateness, we cast all of our *hope*, like an *anchor of the soul*, beyond the veil, into the very heart of God.
We were unsure if it would work.
We were full of doubts.
We were afraid.
But then we pulled hard from below.
The anchor held firm.
With great relief we realized it was lodged in the very "cleft of the Rock."

Since that time the storms have not ceased; at certain points, and in some ways, they may have even increased in size and fury.
But the anchor remains "sure and stedfast."
This anchor will hold.
It has held.
It is holding.
It will yet hold!
Because for those who trust, it can truthfully be said:

"As long as there is a God; there is hope."

Our anchor goes beyond the veil, because our *hope* goes beyond the veil.
We are not trusting in earthly, temporal things.
We are - **"HEIRS ACCORDING TO THE HOPE OF ETERNAL**

LIFE" - a *title* already mentioned in Volume One of **OUR GLORIOUS INHERITANCE.** (Titus 3:7)

Another translation calls us - **"HEIRS OF ETERNAL LIFE, to which we look forward in hope."** (Nor)

We can easily echo I Corinthians 15:19 - "If in this life only we have *hope in Christ,* we are of all men most miserable."

But praise be to God, this is not the case!

We have met *the King eternal, the true God and eternal life, and the Author of eternal life,* who has *"the words of eternal life."* (I Tim. 1:17, I Jn. 5:20, Heb. 5:9, Jn. 6:68, See I Jn. 1:2)

We dared to fulfill His requirements: eating His flesh (eating the Word) and drinking His blood (drinking in His life-giving Spirit). (See John 6:53-58)

By doing these things we came to know Him...and in knowing Him we possess *eternal* life. (See John 17:3)

When this took place we received *"eternal* redemption," an *"eternal* purpose," an *"eternal* inheritance" and an *"eternal* weight of glory." (Heb. 9:12, II Tim. 2:10, Eph. 3:1, II Cor 4:17, See also Jn. 6:54;17:3)

Now we have penetrated infinity itself and have become partakers of that Zoe-life of God which has no beginning and no end.

● **The most astounding Scripture passage we could quote, to bring this portion of the revelation to its peak, is Titus 1:2:**

In this verse we discover that God's greatest *hope*-promise - *the promise of eternal life* - was declared long before the Holy Ghost fell in the upper room, long before redemption took place on Calvary, long before the Messiah was born in Bethlehem, long before the law was given on Sinai, and long before the guilty pair trembled before God, clad with a mere fig leaf covering.

This passage declares that we live:

> *"In **hope** of eternal life, which God, that cannot lie, promised before the world began."*

If God promised it in the beginning, before we even asked, then certainly, we will possess it in the end, when every promise will be fulfilled.

We are **HEIRS ACCORDING TO THE HOPE OF ETERNAL LIFE...** and our *hope* is just as eternal as the life we have inherited.

Furthermore, if we can maintain *hope* in facing the terror of death (the worst thing encountered in this valley of the shadow) then certainly we can maintain *hope* in facing the lesser battles and problems encountered in this world.

So let us "fight the good fight of faith" and "lay hold on eternal life." Let us grip with our hearts this *hope* laid up for us heaven and refuse to let it go! (I Timothy 6:12)

BUILDING UP AN ETERNAL HOPE CHEST

● Sometimes when a young woman accumulates certain domestic furnishings or articles of clothing, she will, in anticipation of a future marriage, place them in something called *a hope chest.*

Often...especially in quiet, meditative moments...she will slowly empty the chest, item by item, and dream of the future.

In a similar, though spiritual sense, we who make up this "chaste virgin espoused to Christ" are in the process of stocking an everlasting *hope chest.*

Every revelation of who we are "in Christ" is stored away in the treasure chest of the "hidden man of the heart." (I Peter 3:4)

Often...especially in quiet, meditative moments...we "empty the chest" and dream of future possibilities.

- Our union with the Bridegroom.
- Being changed into His image.
- Inheriting all things.
- Reigning as kings and priests.
- The marriage supper of the Lamb.
- The splendor of eternity.
- And on and on and on!

In viewing this *"hope* set before us," we are not only able to endure the present hardship; we more clearly see its value, its purpose, its end result.

Trials, tribulations, temptations, persecutions are no longer just to be dreaded and despised.

Rather, they are choice opportunities for God to prove Himself **toward** us, reveal Himself **in** us, and manifest Himself **through** us.

● **No wonder Romans 8:20 declares:**

> *"For the creature was made subject to vanity, not willingly, but by reason of Him who hath subjected the same in hope."*

We never made the choice, of ourselves, to face the sore travail of this world with all its woes. From the beginning, God purposed that we be subjected to this realm...a place that appears so vain, so senseless, so useless.

But this was something God did *in hope.*

His *hope* - a *hope* that will never be thwarted - is that through all this adversity the nature and attributes of Jesus will be gloriously and permanently formed in us.

So God's original *hope* - "Let us make man in our image" - has remained the same throughout the passing ages. In every decade, century and millennium - yes, in every second, minute and hour - it resurfaces in the lives of those who yield. **This divine** *hope* **has also become the** "common denominator theme" **pervading every chapter of this volume.**

● Most of the *titles*, specifically chosen for this sixth volume of **OUR GLORIOUS INHERITANCE,** first point to a certain area of suffering, trial, adversity, or demand that all of God's chosen ones face.

But then...in each chapter and the revelation of each name...we see *the hidden hope.*

The hope of glory.

We view the glorious outcome that should result.

A few of the *titles* we are going to study even sound very unappealing, such as **HIS AFFLICTED, PRISONERS OF HOPE, STRANGERS** and **THOU WORM JACOB.** But just as rough-looking, weather-beaten, sun-darkened badger skins provided the outer covering of the tabernacle, secreting the

11

spectacular beauty of the ark and other items within, so these unappealing *titles*, though "rough" and unattractive in appearance, contain some of the most precious revelations of our sonship inheritance.

Other *titles* in this volume may sound very positive and appealing, but still, they reveal many of the difficult demands of sonship. For instance:

In the chapter entitled **HIS ABODE**, we especially discover the difficult and weighty responsibility of keeping God's Word. If we yield to God's demands, we are given a precious *hope of glory*. He promises to make us His dwelling place, the present abode of the spiritual ark of His covenant.

In **THE CLAY**, we find ourselves going through the difficult stages of wedging, throwing, firing and glazing, but we also have a *glorious hope*. The Master Potter is very skilled in producing vessels unto honor.

In the chapter on **CONTRITE ONES**, we view the inescapable inner pain of godly sorrow. But the conclusion is also reached that a certain *hope of glory* follows close behind. For a contrite attitude "worketh repentance to salvation not to be repented of." (II Corinthians 7:10)

In the chapter on **A FIRE**, we learn the inescapable destiny every human being has of facing the fire of God - some in damnation, others in transformation. Our God is a consuming fire and He intends to powerfully consume all that we are and draw us into Himself.

In the chapter on **HIDDEN ONES**, we find the godly surrounded with persecution and opposition. Our *glorious hope* is that God Himself will be our hiding place and that He will preserve us from all evil.

In **THE HUMBLE**, we are exposed to the divine mandate that we, like Jesus, must be willing to humble ourselves even unto death. Our *hope of glory* is that God will respond in highly exalting us, even as He did the firstborn Son of God.

In **THE PATIENT IN SPIRIT**, we are told to "count it all joy" when we fall into diverse temptations, knowing that the trying of our faith works patience (perseverance, steadfastness, constancy). Our *hope of glory* is that patience will have her perfect work that we may be "perfect and entire, wanting nothing." (James 1:2,4)

In the chapter regarding our call to be **THE PERFECT**, we first discover ourselves born into, and bound by, imperfection. Then, we read in Colossians 1:27 concerning "the riches of the glory of this mystery...Christ in you, the *hope of glory*." In the very next verse, this *hope* is defined - "that we may present every man *perfect* in Christ Jesus." This is our *ultimate hope*.

The final chapters carry us to a pinnacle of *glory*:
- The *glory* of being **HIS REST**, the conclusion and goal of His journey through time.
- The *glory* of forever being **THE TEMPLE OF THE LIVING GOD**, containers of the spiritual ark of His covenant, crowned and filled with the

glory of His Shekinah presence even in this present world.
- And the *glory* of being the bride, the Lamb's wife - **A WOMAN CLOTHED WITH THE SUN** - in the world which is yet to come.

Surely, by the time we reach the end of this volume, we will also reach the conclusion expressed by David unto Jehovah so many years ago:

"...I will HOPE CONTINUALLY, and will yet praise Thee more and more."
(Psalm 71:14)

"Now THE GOD OF HOPE fill you with all joy and peace in believing, that ye may abound in hope, through the power of the Holy Ghost."

(Romans 15:13)

"Let Israel hope in the Lord: for with the Lord there is mercy, and with Him is plenteous redemption."

(Psalm 130:7)

"Let Israel hope in the Lord from henceforth and for ever."

(Psalm 131:3)

"Unto Him be glory in the church by Christ Jesus throughout all ages, world without end. Amen."

(Ephesians 3:21)

> *Sense-knowledge cries - "It's hopeless! Why should we even try?"*
>
> *Revelation-knowledge shakes its head, saying - "Quit? I'd rather die!"*
>
> *For hopeless hearts find hope renewed in the resurrected King.*
> *If He conquered death and hell for us, we can conquer anything!!*

---

*1 It is suggested that the reader, if possible, review the chapter in Volume Two of **Our Glorious Inheritance** entitled *Partakers*. This chapter deals in depth with the subject of the glory of God and will help build an be even stronger foundation on which the remainder of this book's revelation can be erected.

THE TITLES

May "the God of our Lord Jesus Christ, the Father of glory . . . give unto you the spirit of wisdom and revelation in the knowledge of Him:

The eyes of your understanding being enlightened; that ye may know what is the hope of His calling, and what **THE RICHES OF THE GLORY OF HIS INHERITANCE IN THE SAINTS.**

And what is the exceeding greatness of His power to us-ward who believe, according to the working of His mighty power."

(Ephesians 1:17-19)

HIS ABODE

*"Jesus answered and said unto him, If a man love Me, he will keep My words: and My Father will love him, and We will come unto him, and make **OUR ABODE** with him."*

(John 14:23)

"...If anyone loves Me, he will obey My teaching. My Father will love him, and We will come to him and make [OUR DWELLING] OUR HOME with him."
(John 14:23 NEB, NIV)

"In whom ye also are builded together for [A DWELLING OF GOD] AN HABITATION OF GOD THROUGH THE SPIRIT."
(Ephesians 2:22 NAS, AV)

"In Salem also is His tabernacle, and HIS DWELLING PLACE in Zion."
(Psalm 76:2)

HIS DWELLING

HIS HOME

A DWELLING OF GOD

HIS DWELLING PLACE

THE HABITATION OF THE LORD

AN HABITATION OF GOD
THROUGH THE SPIRIT

A PLACE FOR THE LORD,
AN HABITATION FOR THE
MIGHTY GOD OF JACOB

A PLACE FOR HIS
DWELLING FOR EVER

HIS HABITATION

"I will not give sleep to mine eyes, or slumber to mine eyelids, Until I find out A PLACE FOR THE LORD, AN HABITA- TION FOR THE MIGHTY GOD OF JACOB."

(Psalm 132:4-5)

"For the Lord hath chosen Zion; He hath desired it for HIS HABITATION."

(Psalm 132:13)

HIS ABODE

*"Jesus answered and said unto him, If a
man love Me, he will keep My words: and My
Father will love him, and We will come unto
him, and make OUR ABODE with him."*

(John 14:23)

● Ever since Adam fell, and the gentle Holy Spirit rushed away in departure,
God has been searching for a suitable *abode* in this world...a place of dwelling,
a place of rest, a place of renewed habitation.

**Through the centuries of God's dealings with men, we read of certain
attempts that lasted only for a short season.**

When Jehovah visited the children of Israel in the wilderness and audibly
declared to them His ten commandments, Exodus 24:16 states that - *"the glory
of the Lord abode upon mount Sinai."*

Later on, when the tabernacle was finished and erected, Exodus 40:35
explains that - *"Moses was not able to enter into the tent of the congregation,
because the cloud abode thereon, and the glory of the Lord filled the tabernacle."* (See also Numbers 9:17)

And there were other objects and structures, besides mount Sinai and the
tabernacle of Moses, that God chose as a temporary residence:

The burning bush.
The pillar of fire by night.
The cloudy pillar by day.
The Rock in the wilderness.
The ark of the covenant.
The tabernacle of David.
And the temple of Solomon.

None of these proved to be permanent, though, for eventually God "moved
out" or else the place of habitation was forsaken, stolen, destroyed, lost in the
annals of history, or simply ceased to exist.

God evidently was not satisfied.

And justifiably so...

For a bush could not inherit His divine nature; a rock could not express the
depth of His love; a tabernacle or temple made with hands could not manifest
the gifts or the fruits of His Spirit.

**Only man is suitable to fulfill any of these precious privileges, for only
man has been created in the image of God.**

Under the Old Will, being in a fallen and sinful state, man could not legally
be indwelt by God.

The Holy Spirit, from time to time, would temporarily move upon certain
chosen and honored individuals, but would never abide within them on a
constant basis. (See Judges 3:10; 6:34;11:29;14:6)

A redemption, cleansing and restoration had to take place first.

Hallelujah! For this cause, and to accomplish this purpose, Jesus came!

THE FIRSTBORN ABODE
OF THE MOST HIGH GOD

God revealed Himself to men many times under the Old Will. But like the dove from Noah's ark who "found no rest for the sole of her foot," so He found no place of rest, no heart in which He could permanently reside. (Genesis 8:9)

Then Jesus, the spotless Lamb of God, was baptized in the river Jordan and John testified:

> *"I saw the Spirit descending from heaven*
> *like a dove, and it abode upon Him.*
> *And I knew Him not: but He that sent me to*
> *baptize with water, the same said unto me,*
> *Upon whom thou shalt see the Spirit descend-*
> *ing, and remaining on Him, the same is He*
> *which baptizeth with the Holy Ghost."*
> (John 1:32-33)

In other words, the One who would become the first permanent *abode* of the Holy Ghost in this world would then have the ability and the authority to pass such a supreme blessing along to others.

Having received the gift of the Spirit, the Son of God could then give this gift away...and all because of the cleansing, sin-blotting-out blood that He would yet shed forth on Calvary.

Later on, during His ministry years, Jesus stood in the temple area and cried:

> *"He that believeth on Me, as the Scripture*
> *hath said, out of his belly shall flow rivers of*
> *living water."*
> (John 7:38)

In the very next verse, John explained:

> *("But this spake He of the Spirit, which they*
> *that believe on Him should receive: for the*
> *Holy Ghost was not yet given; because that*
> *Jesus was not yet glorified.")*
> (John 7:39)

So we see, Jesus had to be crucified and buried, tasting death for every man, in order for us to be freed from the curse of death. Then the Son of God had to be resurrected and glorified in order for us to be raised to life in like manner. This was all necessary that we might become His spiritual temple, *His abode* on earth.

Certainly this is part of the reason the prophecy was given, centuries in advance, that Jesus' flesh would *"rest in hope."* (Psalm 16:9, Acts 2:26)

He willingly submitted to the cross, and was then laid to *rest* in the tomb. He could *rest in hope*...for He knew He would be resurrected. He also knew that by means of it all, He would be able to breathe His very essence and His constant presence into the lives of His disciples.

This is the restoration of what Adam lost in the garden and the main reason for the bringing in of a New Covenant.

Under the Old Covenant, God's dwelling places were always eventually forsaken. Under the New Covenant, He promises His own - "I WILL NEVER LEAVE THEE, NOR FORSAKE THEE." (Hebrews 13:5)

No wonder this is spoken of as a better covenant built upon better promises.

"For the law made nothing perfect, but the bringing in of a *better hope* did." (Hebrews 7:19)

ABIDING WITH HIS PEOPLE

● **The key word, other than *abode*, in this beginning chapter is the closely related word *abide*.**

To abide means *to remain stable or fixed in some condition or state.*

It can also mean *to remain constant, faithful and unchanging in some relationship.*

In order to maintain a *stable and unchanging relationship* with those He calls *His abode,* God has granted two main *abiding* gifts: the Word and the Spirit.

■ The Abiding Word ─────────────────────

I John 2:14 states - "I have written unto you, young men, because ye are strong, and *the Word of God abideth in you,* and ye have overcome the wicked one."

Notice that the above verse states, in the past tense, that we already "have overcome the wicked one."

This is not a mistake in wordage or an illogical, outlandish statement.

It is true and believable.

Before we even confront tomorrow's battles, we know that the *abiding* Word of God within us will ALWAYS be superior in strength.

No matter what we face, God's promises are sufficient and powerful enough, if we believe, to ALWAYS lift us to victory and to ALWAYS subdue the enemy.

■ The Abiding Spirit of God ─────────────────

In the same chapter that provides our main *title-scripture,* Jesus promised His disciples - "I will pray the Father, and He shall give you another Comforter, that He may *abide* with you for ever; even the Spirit of truth..." (John 14:16-17)

And again - "hereby we know that He *abideth* in us, by the Spirit which He hath given us." (I John 3:24)

The specific application of the Holy Spirit to a believer's life is referred to as his or her anointing. It is symbolized in Scripture as oil (which clings and penetrates) and is certainly intended to be a permanent inheritance gift.

John (the main gospel writer who used the words *abide* and *abode*) declared the following to those members of the church battling compromise and deception:

> *"But the anointing which ye have received*
> *of Him abideth in you, and ye need not that*

*any man teach you: but as the same anointing
teacheth you of all things, and is truth, and is
no lie, and even as it hath taught you, ye shall
abide in Him."*

(I John 2:27)

■ Abiding In Him

By this last scripture, it is apparent that the main reason the anointing *abides* in us is to train us how to *abide* in God.

The following Bible commands and promises reveal the blessed results of doing so:

- "Whosoever *abideth* in Him sinneth not." (I John 3:6)
- "He that *abideth* in Me...bringeth forth much fruit." (John 15:5)
- "If ye *abide* in Me, and My words *abide* in you, ye shall ask what ye will, and it shall be done unto you." (John 15:7)
- "If ye keep My commandments, ye shall *abide* in My love..." (John 15:10)
- "And now, little children, *abide* in Him; that, when He shall appear, we may have confidence, and not be ashamed before Him at His coming." (I John 2:28)

● So we see that *abiding* is a reciprocal act, a joint relationship, and a mutual responsibility. If we continue *abiding* in God, God continues *abiding* in us. If we keep seeking Him as *our abode*, we continue in the calling to be *His abode*.

And this is exactly what the Most High desires...not that we be a mere "office" or "storage shed" in which He can reside, but rather **HIS ABODE, HIS DWELLING, HIS HOME.** (See John 14:23, NEB, NIV)

This speaks of the warmth of companionship; a satisfying and fulfilling union of hearts; God meeting our need, as we meet His.

When Jehovah enters the heart and life of a yielded soul -

He becomes our *place of rest* and we become His. (See Heb. 4:3, Is. 66:1)

He becomes our *sanctuary* and we become His. (See Is. 8:14, Ps. 114:2)

He becomes our *tabernacle* and we become His. (See Is. 4:6, Ps. 76:2)

He becomes our *holy of holies* and we become His. (See Is. 57:15)

In a spiritual, New Testament sense, we become the *abode* of the ark of His covenant and the *dwelling place* of His glory.

THE MEANING OF "MONE"

Those who provide the Father, Son and Holy Ghost a suitable *abode* in this world are also promised a similar reward in the world to come.

The fourteenth chapter of John, our *title-chapter*, begins with the oft-claimed promise:

*"In My Father's house are many mansions
[many rooms, many dwelling places]: if it
were not so, I would have told you. I go to
prepare a place for you."*

(John 14:2 AV, Gspd, NAS)

24

The word translated *mansions* is *mone*, the same word translated *abode* in our *title-verse*, John 14:23. These are the only two places that the word *mone* appears in Scripture.

So the central truth is once again enhanced and established: if we provide God *a dwelling place* in time, He will create a *dwelling place* for us in eternity.

● The Father's house is as vast and infinite as He, so a "mansion" in that house could be a reference to something far more than just a large, luxurious building.

It could be speaking of a glorious place of inheritance in the kingdom to come, an entire realm in which we will dwell and over which we will rule.

Rooms or *dwelling places* in God's house (the translation of *mone* in two other versions of John 14:2) will certainly be far more spectacular than anything ever seen in this realm for "eye hath not seen, nor ear heard, neither have entered into the heart of man, the things which God hath prepared for them that love Him." (I Corinthians 2:9, John 14:2 Gspd, NAS)

It behooves us to remember that Adam's *abode* in the beginning was an entire paradise garden.

Only God knows the glorious fullness of what awaits us in the end.

Until that day comes, though, let us celebrate our *hope of glory* by refusing to let our hearts be troubled.

Individually and corporately, let us purpose to manifestly become "A DWELLING OF GOD" for all to see - "AN HABITATION OF GOD THROUGH THE SPIRIT." (Ephesians 2:22 NAS, AV)

In a New Covenant and eternal sense, let us become "THE HABITATION OF THE LORD", "HIS DWELLING PLACE"..."A PLACE FOR HIS DWELLING FOR EVER." (II Chr. 29:6, Ps. 76:2, II Chr. 6:2)

Let us make a covenant, not only to surrender our own members to God, but to zealously spread the gospel so that many others might be drawn into this, OUR GLORIOUS INHERITANCE.

Let us daily be as impassioned as David who claimed:

> *"I will not give sleep to mine eyes, or slumber to mine eyelids,*
> *Until I find out A PLACE FOR THE LORD, AN HABITATION FOR THE MIGHTY GOD OF JACOB."*
> (Psalm 132:4-5)

Of course, David was speaking more of a literal building, sanctified unto the worship of Jehovah; we are speaking of hearts that have been swept clean in anticipation of God's entrance.

Therefore, let those who are spiritually a part of Zion offer the King of Zion a holy life full of holy actions, holy attitudes and holy words that He might enthrone Himself in us...and that we might become "HIS HABITATION." (Psalm 132:5)

If we do so, His presence will overflow into even our thoughts, our emotions, and our praise (for Psalm 22:3 announces - "Thou art holy, O Thou that **inhabitest** the praises of Israel").

Attaining such a goal is undoubtedly one of the greatest expressions of *hope* that could ever be nurtured in the heart of man.

• HIS AFFLICTED •

HIS AFFLICTED ONES

THE AFFLICTED PEOPLE

AN AFFLICTED
AND HUMBLE PEOPLE

THE AFFLICTED CITY

"Sing, O heavens; and be joyful, O earth; and break forth into singing, O mountains; for the Lord hath comforted His people, and will have mercy upon HIS AFFLICTED [HIS AFFLICTED ONES].",
(Isaiah 49:13 AV, NIV)

*"For Thou wilt save THE AF-
FLICTED PEOPLE [AN AF-
FLICTED AND HUMBLE
PEOPLE]; but wilt bring down high
looks."*

(Psalm 18:27 AV, AMP)

*"O thou afflicted [O AFFLICTED
CITY] tossed with tempest, and not
comforted, behold, I will lay thy
stones with fair colours, and lay thy
foundations with sapphires."*

(Isaiah 54:11 AV, NIV)

*"For they be Thy people, and
THINE INHERITANCE, which
Thou broughtest forth out of Egypt,
from the midst of the furnace of iron."*

(I Kings 8:51)

HIS INHERITANCE

A PEOPLE OF INHERITANCE

THE INHERITANCE OF THE LORD

HIS ALLOTTED INHERITANCE

THE ALLOTMENT OF HIS INHERITANCE

A VESSEL FOR THE FINER

The following related *titles* are also found in this chapter:
**The People of His Inheritance, His Own Inherited People,
A People of His Own, A People For His Own Possession,
His Own Possession.**

"But the Lord hath taken you, and brought you forth out of the iron furnace, even out of Egypt, to be unto Him A PEOPLE OF INHERITANCE, as ye are this day."

(Deuteronomy 4:20)

"I am one of them that are peaceable and faithful in Israel; thou seekest to destroy a city and a mother in Israel: why wilt thou swallow up THE IN-HERITANCE OF THE LORD?"

(II Samuel 20:19)

"For the Lord's portion is His people; Jacob is THE LOT OF HIS INHERITANCE [HIS ALLOTTED INHERITANCE, THE ALLOT-MENT OF HIS INHERITANCE]."

(Deuteronomy 32:9 AV, NIV, NAS)

"Take away the dross from the silver, and there shall come forth A VES-SEL FOR THE FINER.

Take away the wicked from before the king, and his throne shall be established in righteousness."

(Proverbs 25:4-5)

HIS AFFLICTED

"Sing, O heavens; and be joyful, O earth;
and break forth into singing, O mountains; for
the Lord hath comforted His people, and will
have mercy upon HIS AFFLICTED [HIS
AFFLICTED ONES.]"
(Isaiah 49:13 AV, NIV)

● **N**eedless to say, this chapter's *titles* will be the most difficult to explain of this entire **OUR GLORIOUS INHERITANCE** series. And why is that?

Because dealing with the origin and purpose of human suffering is never easy...much less the suffering of God's chosen ones.

Certain ideas, if not worded very carefully, could easily be misinterpreted, misunderstood, or misapplied. Then, instead of this chapter being a means of edifying the body of Christ, it could well become a means of tearing down faith and promoting the acceptance of defeat.

To this I say - "God forbid!"

Yet with the same breath, I must admit that the opposite is also true.

If the subject of believers possibly facing severe afflictions is not dealt with realistically, if it is glossed over with a superficial, pleasing-to-the-ear approach, many could end up living in a spiritual dream world that disintegrates with the first disaster.

"Many are the *afflictions* of the righteous," declares the psalmist.

But don't stop quoting there!

The rest of the verse gladly heralds that - "THE LORD DELIVERETH HIM OUT OF THEM ALL." (Psalm 34:19)

One way or the other God will deliver His people and set them free.

One way or the other we will end up victorious.

So let us refuse to be as the ostrich: ignoring affliction, sticking our head in the sand, and hoping that all the problems and pressures will somehow just vanish away.

Rather, let us be as the eagle, who not only dares to fly into the stormy wind, but uses it as a means of rising higher.

Let us also carefully consider the next three statements which provide the tri-stone foundation of this chapter's revelation:

First - our theme and goal is not the defense of affliction, nor the acceptance of affliction, but rather, the value, purpose and conquering of affliction.

Second - we are not just ordinary, pitiful, afflicted persons (as are all the lost of this world). We are **HIS AFFLICTED.** We belong to God and we are convinced that He is overseeing every detail of our lives with the utmost care.

Third - We "know that all things work together for good to them that love God, to them who are **THE CALLED ACCORDING TO HIS PURPOSE"** - (a *title* yet to be unveiled in the fourth chapter of this book). (Romans 8:28)

These three statements sum up that "rejoicing of the *hope*" we are commanded to hold "firm unto the end." (Hebrews 3:6)

DEFINING THE BIBLICAL TERM

● Many of the passages in this chapter, using the word *afflicted,* employ the Hebrew word *aniy* which means *depressed in mind or circumstance.*

The main Greek word translated *affliction* is *thlipsis* meaning *pressure.*

Thlipsis comes from another word meaning *to crowd (as one who is pressed on every side).*

Our English word comes from the Latin *adflictus* which means *a striking (as one thing that strikes or smites another).* It speaks of being *stricken* or *smitten* with grief, pain, or distress of mind or body.

So *affliction* can mean any one of a number of things, including: tribulation, chastisement, persecution, adversity, temptation, humiliation, great suffering, severe distress, depression, grief, or anguish of heart.

When the word *affliction* is used it may embrace only one or two of the foregoing definitions or even mean something somewhat different. Each passage of Scripture must be closely inspected, in its context, in order to comprehend its true meaning.

THE FOUR MAIN SOURCES OF AFFLICTION

It is important to see that affliction comes from four main sources.

■ **Sometimes God afflicts us (with conviction or with chastisement).** In this ministry, He is referred to as **Jehovah-Makkeh,** which means *the Lord that smiteth.* (Ezekiel 7:9)

This divine name especially reveals how God uses even stern corrective measures to deliver His people from carnality and sanctify their lives.

Of course, restoration is always available to those who humble themselves, trust and believe. We should ever keep in mind that - "whom the Lord loveth He chasteneth" and we are brought under such judgment "that we should not be condemned with the world." (Hebrews 12:6, I Corinthians 11:32)

Moreover, chastisement is given "for our profit, that we might be partakers of His holiness." It yields "the peaceable fruit of righteousness unto them which are exercised thereby." No wonder the Bible declares that, especially in His chosen ones, God sends forth "judgment unto victory." And no wonder Hosea urged - "Come, and let us return unto the Lord: for He hath torn, and He will heal us; He hath *smitten* and He will bind us up." (Hebrews 12:10-11, Matthew 12:20, Hosea 6:1, See Isaiah 51:21-22)

It was such a condition that made the psalmist pen the following words:

> *"Before I was **afflicted** I went astray: but now have I kept Thy Word...*
> *It is good for me that I have been **afflicted**; that I might learn Thy statutes...*
> *I know, O Lord, that Thy judgments are right, and that Thou in faithfulness hast afflicted me...*
> *Let Thy tender mercies come unto me, that I may live...I am **afflicted** very much: quicken me, O Lord, according unto Thy Word."*
> (Psalm 119:67,71,75,77,107)

■ **Sometimes other persons or circumstances afflict us.** A good example of this is the suffering that the children of Israel went through as slaves in Egypt. God prophesied this to Abraham in advance, saying - "thy seed shall be a stranger in a land that is not their's, and shall serve them; and they shall *afflict* them four hundred years...and afterward shall they come out with great substance." (Genesis 15:13-14)

We are also "strangers" in this world, often *afflicted* or persecuted by unbelievers who do not understand. But we too will emerge from all our persecutions and *afflictions* "with great substance." Psalm 66:12 says - "Thou hast caused men to ride over our heads; we went through fire and through water: but Thou broughtest us out into a *wealthy place.*"

In the end, we will procure many valuable things as a direct result of all the negative treatment we have received in this world. The most significant is the development of the divine nature within: love, mercy, forgiveness and deep trust in God.

It is significant to see that according to Exodus 1:12, the more the Egyptians *"afflicted"* the Jews, "the more they multiplied and grew." It is just as true that the more children of darkness fight against the church, the more we grow and mature in Christ.

■ **Sometimes it is Satan who afflicts us.** We should consider the life of Job who, along with many of the prophets, became an "example of suffering *affliction*, and of patience." Having been assaulted by the devil on every side, this great patriarch declared - "the days of *affliction* have taken hold upon me." So it happens, from time to time, for all who are in a covenant relationship with God. Satan is out to "make war" with those who "keep the commandants of God, and have the testimony of Jesus Christ." Through his opposition, though, we learn the power of God, the authority we have as believers, and the confidence we should maintain in God's Word. (James 5:10-11, Job 30:16, Revelation 12:17)

■ **Sometimes we are called upon to afflict ourselves.** Under the Old Will, there was an essential, annual feast day called "the Day of Atonement." This was that choice time when the high priest would go beyond the veil into the holy of holies and sprinkle the mercy seat with blood to atone for the national sins of Israel. Specifically on that day, the children of Israel were given the mandate - "Ye shall *afflict* your souls, and offer an offering made by fire unto the Lord." Those who disobeyed were cut off from among the people of God. (The Hebrew word translated *afflict* in this passage is *anab* which means *to abase, chasten or humble self.*)

In a New Covenant sense, we who enjoy the benefits of Jesus' day of crucifixion - our "Day of Atonement" - must also *afflict* our souls. We must humble our souls in repentance and yield daily to the soul-smiting, convicting influence of His Word. This is absolutely necessary if we are to be included among His people and if we are to be that New Covenant holy of holies in which His blood-sprinkled ark abides.

Also, during the Passover feast, Jews were commanded to eat unleavened bread, otherwise known as *"the bread of affliction."* And, when they were chastised, they were spoken of as having drunk *"the water of affliction."* (See Leviticus 23:27-29, Deuteronomy 16:3, Isaiah 30:20)

Unleavened bread speaks primarily of a sinless life, being free from the corruption of this world. New Covenant believers are commanded to eat this *"bread of affliction"* in a spiritual sense, dying to sin and coming out of the world to be a separated people. (See I Corinthians 5:8)

Afflicting ourselves may also include fasting, acts of self-denial and any self-imposed, proper, religious discipline designed to bring the flesh under subjection. (See Psalms 35:13; 69:10)

● **All four of the aforementioned sources of** *affliction* **work together to present every believer "crucified with Christ."** (Galatians 2:20)

In this area Jesus Himself was, of course, our divine example.

As the sacrificial Lamb of God, He was carried forward toward the *affliction* of Calvary by the strong current of these four streams flowing together as one: the will of the Father, the rejection of the people, the plotting of Satan and His own submission to the plan of God. (See Jn. 18:11; 19:6, Lk. 22:3-4, Mt. 26:39)

Furthermore, it was love that constrained Jesus to make such a choice. Concerning His redeemed, the Scripture testifies:

> *"In all their affliction He was afflicted, and*
> *the angel of His presence saved them..."*
> (Isaiah 63:9)

Psalm 22:24 foretold the attitude the Father would have toward His suffering Son, saying:

> *"For He hath not despised nor abhorred*
> *the affliction of the afflicted; neither hath He*
> *hid His face from Him; but when He cried unto*
> *Him, He heard."*

Notice in this last verse Jesus is entitled *the afflicted* (*the afflicted One* in the NIV). He so identified with us in our *affliction* that He was actually named *the afflicted One*.

In like manner, we should so identify with Him in His *affliction* at Calvary that we, too, are named *the afflicted people*.

This is essential; for only those who are willing to suffer with Him, reign with Him. Only those who are willing to die with Him, live with Him.

In Psalm 18:27, David confessed to Jehovah - "For Thou wilt save **THE AFFLICTED PEOPLE [AN AFFLICTED AND HUMBLE PEOPLE];** but wilt bring down high looks." (AV, AMP, See NIV)

By this scripture we reaffirm that only those who humble themselves at the cross receive that grace unto salvation that it provides.

We are definitely partakers of victory, strength, power, prosperity and everlasting joy through the New Covenant; but only those who are "partakers of the *afflictions* of the gospel" know the blossoming of such glory. (II Timothy 1:8, See II Corinthians 6:4, I Peter 1:11)

Let it be emphasized that this does NOT mean we are called upon to accept sickness, mental pressure, emotional distress, spiritual bondage or demonic control of our lives. Quite the contrary, we are definitely commanded to rise up against all these things, fighting the good fight of faith.

What does it mean then?

The answer is fourfold.

34

1. When affliction comes from God (chastisement or conviction) we react with humility and true repentance...expecting the situation to change as a result.

2. When affliction comes from Satan, we react with authority, and faith-filled dominion...expecting the situation to change as a result.

3. When affliction comes from others, we react with wisdom, forgiveness, love and mercy...expecting the situation to change as a result.

4. And when affliction is something we impose on ourselves, it normally stems from a desire to bring the flesh under subjection in order to walk in sweet intimacy with God. **So even in this case, our expectation is for a change: a change in our attitudes, a change in the condition of our hearts, and a change in our relationship with God.**

So none of these things speak of cultivating a defeatist attitude: resigning ourselves over to failure and bondage. No, no - a thousands times no!

Rather, they speak of viewing life realistically and always reacting with confidence in God and faith in His promises and purpose.

As long as we are in this world, we are going to face *afflictions* from one source or another. This is undeniable and unavoidable! But the outcome will either be positive or negative according to our reaction.

● **As Jesus' representatives and ambassadors we, like Paul, are called to - "fill up that which is behind of** *the afflictions of Christ..."* (Col. 1:24)

In other words, we are called to yield to that heart-gripping compassion for the lost, humble submission to the Father, and intense denial of the flesh that yet overflows from that lonely, historic hill outside of Jerusalem.

How painful it can be, at times, to share the agony of Calvary! But to this cross-current we must all yield our members. Calvary must be impressed on our will, our mind, our thoughts, our emotions, our actions...yes, all that we are...if we are to fulfill our covenant responsiblity as sons and daughters of God. Moreover, our motive, like His, must be love...love for the Father and love for others. Thus, we die to self in order to become a living sacrifice to others.

This is the unchanging prerequisite, the unalterable demand, the immovable, memorial pillar of our high calling in Christ Jesus.

If this pillar is erected in our lives, Psalm 72 promises that the "royal son" (Jesus) will judge His *"afflicted ones* with justice" and "defend the *afflicted* among the people."* (Psalm 72:2,4 NIV)

Job 34:28 states that God "heareth the cry of *the afflicted,"* and Psalm 140:12, that "the Lord will maintain the cause of *the afflicted."*

We can definitely trust in these pledges that are a seal on this covenant established between the Most High God and His elect people.

So let us purpose never to rail at our enemies, charge God foolishly, or even whisper a murmur of complaint in the secret confines of our own heart, for Jesus was "oppressed, and...*afflicted,* yet He opened not His mouth." (Is. 53:7)

Rather, let us obey without question the Bible command to "endure *afflictions."* (II Timothy 4:5)

Even more so, let us "count it all joy." (James 1:2)

"For...the sufferings of this present time are not worthy to be compared with the glory which shall be revealed in us." (Romans 8:18)

This is *the hope of our calling...the blessed hope* of the dawning of a new day.

THE VALUE OF AFFLICTION

Not long ago, I was scheduled to preach for Bill Lowery and the "Christ is the Answer" team in a special meeting at the Washington Monument in Washington, D.C. Before it came my time to speak, a special singer was scheduled to share several songs.

Having suffered an attack of some kind of degenerative muscle disease several months prior, the singer rolled up onto the platform in a wheelchair. We all felt great compassion for the man, especially as Bro. Lowery spoke of how he had refused to be hindered by this "physical disability."

When the singer arrived at the microphone, his first statement grabbed our attention and our hearts, catching us a little by surprise. In a loving way, yet with a strong voice and a strong spirit, he readjusted his introduction, asserting:

> "I don't have a physical disability; I have a
> physical challenge!"

Immediately I thought to myself - "What a perfect way of wording it!" Then I began applying the statement to the broader spectrum of what all Christians face.

Negative mental, emotional, spiritual and even physical *afflictions* should never be labeled "disabilities," but rather "challenges." For through the same we are "challenged" to tap into our inner potential, stir up the hidden man of the heart, seek God diligently, humble ourselves before Him, appropriate His promises, and live in His victory.

So facing *afflictions* should never destroy faith; it should actually end up increasing our faith. The psalmist David said:

> "I believed, therefore have I spoken: I was
> greatly afflicted."
> > (Psalm 116:10)

Can we not see by this statement that our response to circumstance makes all the difference! For two people can suffer the very same problem in life: one can be made better off by it, and the other, destroyed.

So again, it is not what we face that determines what we are, BUT HOW WE REACT TO WHAT WE FACE!! This is an essentially important point...something of which we should constantly remind ourselves.

Bible commentator, Matthew Henry, offered the edifying idea that:

> "Extraordinary *afflictions* are not always the
> punishment of extraordinary sins, but sometimes
> the trial of extraordinary graces. Sanctified afflic-
> tions are often spiritual promotions."

Famed soul-winner and revivalist, Charles Finney, also declared:

> "The Lord gets His best soldiers out of the
> highlands of affliction."

We can see the truth of these two quotes excellently exemplified in many biblical characters: Moses, Joseph, Daniel and Paul, just to mention a few.

Concerning Joseph, the Bible stated that - "Until the time of his word came: the Word of the Lord tried him." (Psalm 105:19)

In other words, all of the *afflictions* he went through were a preparation for his day of spiritual *promotion*. Joseph even named one of his sons **Ephraim**, meaning *doubly fruitful*, for he said - *"God hath caused me to be fruitful in the land of my affliction."* (Genesis 41:52)

Our God is doing something very similar for all of us. As Joseph was enslaved and imprisoned in Egypt, so we have been enslaved and imprisoned in this world with its lusts. This is the *land of our affliction*, but it is here that God will cause us also to be *doubly fruitful*.

We will be *doubly* enriched for having sojourned in this place: enriched with the revelations we have received in time, and enriched with the treasure we have laid up in eternity.

God knows what He is doing. As Sir John Powell so aptly spoke - *"By afflictions God is spoiling us of what might have otherwise spoiled us."*

Knowing this, we can abide in confidence.

As we will yet learn in future chapters of this volume..."Better is the end of a thing than the beginning thereof." (Ecclesiastes 7:8)

Moreover, if God be for us, who and what can be against us?

No wonder Paul gave us the conclusion that:

> *"...our light affliction, which is but for a moment, worketh for us a far more exceeding and eternal weight of glory."*
> (II Corinthians 4:17)

Notice the epistle-writer did NOT say that *afflictions* work AGAINST God's chosen ones. He clearly revealed that they work FOR us.

This is all part of the *hope* that "maketh not ashamed." (Romans 5:5)

THE VALLEY SYMBOL

● **Often in Scripture, a valley is used as a symbol of a time of** *affliction*, **a time of being** *depressed in mind or circumstance*.

The most significant and symbolic valleys mentioned in the Bible are:
The valley of Baca - (*the valley of Weeping* - Psalm 84:6).
The valley of Berachah - (*the valley of Blessing* - II Chronicles 20:26).
The valley of decision - (*called the valley of Jehoshaphat* - Joel 3:12, 14).
The valley full of dry bones - (Ezekiel 37:1).
The valley of vision - (Isaiah 22:1).
The valley of Achor - (*the valley of trouble* - Hosea 2:15).
And the valley of the shadow of death - (Psalm 23:4).

I **will elaborate on the last two.** In Hosea's writings, God promised rebellious, adulterous Israel - a nation under judgment - that He would give her "**the valley of Achor** for a *door of hope*." Moreover, He foretold that "she shall sing there, as in the days of her youth, and as in the day when she came up out of the land of Egypt." (Hosea 2:15, See Isaiah 65:10)

The word **Achor** means *trouble*.

Originally, it was the name of the place where a rebellious Israelite named Achan was stoned. He had *troubled* Israel by taking the forbidden spoil of Jericho, so God *troubled* him.

Having been defeated before Ai, because of the "accursed thing" being in their midst, Israel was forced to search within their ranks for that person who had offended God. They found Achan, and he and his family were executed: stoned with rocks and burned with fire.

So also, when our lives do not measure up - and "accursed" things lodge in our hearts - *trouble* comes, chastisement comes, *affliction* comes. We go through a "valley experience": a time when our spirits get so low, and God seems so high, so distant, so far away, so difficult to reach.

In times like these, we are forced to search our hearts and purge out that which is sinful and offensive: by the rock of the Word and the fire of the Spirit.

Thus, **the valley of Achor, the valley of trouble,** becomes *a door of hope* for us as well - a place where we can sing of God's deliverance power.

All things work together for good, for God takes over more territory in our hearts and lives, and we progress, as the Jews did, in taking over more territory in our "Land of Promise" inheritance.

Moreover, we learn that our God is not only the God of the mountains; He is also the God of the valleys. (See I Kings 20:28)

He is the Lily of the valleys.

He makes a place of sorrow, a place of joy; a place of pain, a place of healing; a place of defeat, a place of victory. For this reason, when Jesus comes in our lives, every valley is exalted. (See Isaiah 40:4)

And though we pass through **the valley of the shadow of death** (the dark, foreboding, clouds of Satan's murderous intents toward us) we are to fear no evil. We know our God is with us.

His Shepherd's rod and staff will ever comfort us.

And we are sure...He will be our guide, even unto death. This is the *hope* that lies within us...every minute, of every hour, of every day.

THE FIERY FURNACE SYMBOL

● **Another primary biblical symbol for a time of *affliction* is a furnace.**

A furnace is a sealed installation containing fire. It can be an oven for baking bread, a kiln for hardening clay, or a smelter for liquifying and purifying metals. Because it is a place of intense heat, it represents those fiery trials, those times of intense *affliction* and adversity, that we all pass through in this world.

As in the case of bread, clay, iron, silver, and gold, the end result for God's people, of passing through "the fiery furnace" experience, should always be something very beneficial.

To the Jews, delivered out of bondage to Pharaoh, Moses proclaimed:

> *"But the Lord hath taken you, and brought you forth out of the iron furnace, even out of Egypt, to be unto Him A PEOPLE OF IN-HERITANCE, as ye are this day."*
>
> (Deuteronomy 4:20)

38

This inheritance procured by Abraham's natural offspring was primarily a natural "Land of Promise." In a similar way, we have also been brought out of bondage - out of an "iron furnace" of bondage to sin and Satan - and have been made, in an even greater way, **A PEOPLE OF INHERITANCE.**

We have inherited a spiritual "Land of Promise": exceeding great and precious promises making up a New Covenant "land" that flows with the milk of the Word and the honey of the Spirit.

● Other translations of Deuteronomy 4:20 call us:

The people of His inheritance. (NIV)
His own inherited people. (Rhm)
A people of His own. (Mof)
His own possession. (Amp)
People for His own possession. (NAS)

These *titles* make it apparent that we have not only received an inheritance from God, we have also become an inheritance to God.

We have inherited all that God is and all that God has. But He has inherited, in a positive sense, all that we are and all that we possess.

In II Samuel 20:19, it was a wise woman who referred to God's people as **the inheritance of the Lord.**

In Deuteronomy 32:9, we are named **the lot of His inheritance** and in Psalm 33:12 we are entitled **His own inheritance** (which have both been discussed already in Volume One of this series under *Heirs*). Other translations of Deuteronomy 32:9 call us **His allotted inheritance** and **the allotment of His inheritance.** (NIV, NAS)

All of these names clearly indicate that we belong to God now and are undoubtedly His most precious possession.

In the dedication of Solomon's temple, the King prayed to Jehovah and confessed concerning the Israelites:

> *"For they be Thy people, and THINE IN-*
> *HERITANCE, which Thou broughtest forth*
> *out of Egypt, from the midst of the furnace of*
> *iron...For Thou didst separate them from*
> *among all the people of the earth, to be*
> *THINE INHERITANCE..."*
>
> (I Kings 8:51,53)

As an expert smelter puts iron in his smelting furnace, then causes the fire to rage hot in order to liquify the metal and purge it of impurities, so has God done to His people.

He has allowed us all to be born into the "iron furnace" of this world with all of its woes, but He has done so with the intention of burning rebellion and carnality out of our earth-bound hearts. Having been saved and brought into the peace of God, the redeemed of the Lord should never even consider wandering back into the "Egyptian" trap.

● Too often, though, God's people forget how painful it was to be in bondage to sin. They wander away from the Master Smelter, purposing to follow after their own fleshly desires. They end up corrupted once again and God is forced to send them back into the furnace.

This happened with the Jews.

They rebelled against Jehovah, turned to idolatry and sin, and were swept away into Assyrian and Babylonian bondage.

But even then, the merciful God promised:

> *"For My name's sake will I defer Mine anger, and for My praise will I refrain for thee, that I cut thee not off.*
>
> *Behold, I have refined thee...I HAVE CHOSEN THEE IN THE FURNACE OF AFFLICTION."*
>
> (Isaiah 48:9-10)

And so God deals with all His offspring.

He brings us out of the *iron furnace*...but then, if we harden our hearts again in willful sin, He will place us in some *furnace of affliction*. In so doing, He reminds us of how painful it is to be separated from the assurance of His favor.

Sometimes we face this renewed *furnace* experience because of our backsliding and our stubbornness. At other times, we may be walking in righteousness, yet still face the intense heat of seemingly unbearable trials. Why?

In some cases, it may be an assault of the devil. Then again, it may be God purposefully maturing us, advancing us, and increasing our value in the kingdom.

One prophet declared that the coming Messiah would be as "a refiner's fire" (an intensely hot, smelting fire) and that He would "sit as a refiner and purifier of silver: and...purify the sons of Levi, and purge them as gold and silver, that they may offer unto the Lord an offering in righteousness." (Malachi 3:2-3)

And it was righteous Job who said of God - "When He hath tried me, I shall come forth as gold!" (Job 23:10)

So our Creator desires more for us than just the status of being purified iron. He wants us to be silver. He wants us to be gold.

Iron speaks of strength.

Silver speaks of redemption.

Gold speaks of the divine nature.

God gives His offspring the *strength* to rise above the grips of sin, *redeeming* us from all our battles, that we might emerge in the glory of *the divine nature*. In this we can see the progress, in a child of God, from iron to silver to gold.

It should be pointed out that, in Bible times especially, if the refiner did his job correctly, he would heat up his precious metal more than once. Each time he would scoop off the dross, allow the liquified metal to solidify, then heat it up again: in some cases, up to seven times.

Some say that silver was recognized as being pure when the refiner could gaze into the resplendent, steamy-hot, liquified metal and see his own image.

And is not the refiner's purpose, our Creator's goal as well?

Many trials, many battles, many *afflictions* come the way of a child of God, but through them all, the refining process is continuing. More and more carnal dross is being removed, and the image of Christ is increasingly manifesting in all who are yielded.

● It should also be mentioned that all the holy vessels of the Old Testament temple had to pass through the fire, and be anointed, in order to sanctify them unto holy use. So it is for us in an even higher sense.

Therefore we echo Peter's exhortation - "Beloved, think it not strange concerning the fiery trial which is to try you." This is transpiring "that the trial of your faith, being much more precious than of gold that perisheth, though it be tried with fire, might be found unto praise and honour and glory at the appearing of Jesus Christ." (I Peter 1:7; 4:12)

THE INTERVENTION OF THE GOD OF HOPE

It must be said that our God is not an insensitive and distant God, unable or unwilling to relate to us in our distresses and our difficulties. Charles Spurgeon once said:

> *"As sure as God puts His children in the furnace of affliction, He will be with them in it."*

● **The prime example of this truth is found in the third chapter of Daniel: the faith-building story of Meshach, Shadrach and Abednego.**

"Nebuchadnezzar the king made an image of gold, whose height was threescore [60] cubits, and the breadth thereof six cubits." (Dan. 3:1)

Nebuchadnezzar was the king of Babylon. His name means *Nebo defend the boundary.* Nebo was supposedly the god of wisdom and literature.

When Nebuchadnezzar lifted up the golden image in his day, it represented how men tend to exalt fleshly wisdom, deify the intellect, and worship their own carnal works. (How ironic it is that six - the number of man - is so associated with this idol!)

Meshach, Shadrach and Abednego (names given to these Jews by Nebuchadnezzar) refused to worship this image and, as a result, were thrown into a burning, fiery furnace, heated seven times hotter than normal.

Their original Hebrew names are very important to the understanding of this symbolic chapter.

Meshach was really **Mishael** which means *"Who is what God is?"*
Shadrach was **Hananiah** which means *"God is gracious."*
Abednego was **Azariah** which means *"God will help."*

Of course, all of us, at one time or another in our walk with God, must prove ourselves faithful by taking an unpopular stand against that which is of the world. Often we, too, end up being thrown in some *furnace of affliction*: hated by the devil and rejected by man.

In our weakness we cry - *"Who is what God is?"* - for we fall so far short of God's glory. But then we discover, to our delight, that *"God is gracious"* and *"God will help."*

When Nebuchadnezzar gazed into the furnace, he cried to his counsellors:

> *"Did not we cast three men bound into the*
> *midst of the fire?...Lo, I see four men loose,*
> *walking in the midst of the fire, and they have*
> *no hurt; and the form of the fourth is like the*
> *son of God."*
>
> (Daniel 3:24-25)

Nebuchadnezzar's observation was a little faulty. This celebrated fourth man was not just "like the Son of God"; He was the Son of God...in a preincarnate appearance.

Just as He gloriously invaded the fire to rescue these three young Hebrews, so will He visit us in our *furnace of affliction*. We will then be loosed and unhurt, walking with authority through the flames.

When we emerge from all our *afflictions* at the end of this life, as it was for Mishael, Hananiah and Azariah, so it will be for us.

No smell of smoke.

No singed hair.

There will be no haunting evidence; no lingering, negative effects, from having passed through this world.

Just as these three Hebrews were rewarded by Nebuchadnezzar with positions of authority in his earthly kingdom, so we will be exalted by God with positions of authority in His heavenly kingdom to come.

We will have passed the test.

We will have conquered *the furnace of affliction*.

We will come forth as gold.

But not only will we emerge with God's stamp of approval. God's infallible Word will be proven as well, for:

> *"The words of the Lord are pure words: as*
> *silver tried in a furnace of earth, purified*
> *seven times."*
>
> (Psalm 12:6)

● Approximately one hundred years before Mishael, Hananiah and Azariah went into the furnace, God gave the promise to His people through Isaiah:

> *"...when thou walkest through the fire, thou*
> *shalt not be burned: neither shall the flame*
> *kindle upon thee."*
>
> (Isaiah 43:2)

So when these three Hebrew men went into the *"furnace of affliction,"* God's promise went in as well.

It stood the fiery test and was fulfilled literally unto His great glory.

This passage has been, and will yet be, fulfilled figuratively for all of God's chosen ones...and it is still for His glory!

In *the fire of affliction*, we prove ourselves to God; but in *the fire of affliction*, *the God of hope* also proves Himself to us...for all time and eternity.

THE GLORIOUS OUTCOME

● Everything about this realm of time has been a hot, fiery furnace to us: the God we serve (Gen. 15:17), the world we are in (Dt. 4:10), the trials and chastisements we go through (Is. 48:10), and the transformation process to which we have been subjected.

The proverb writer gave us an exellent explanation:

> *"Take away the dross from the silver, and there shall come forth a vessel for the finer.*
> *Take away the wicked from before the king, and his throne shall be established in righteousness."*

(Proverbs 25:4-5)

In the highest level of interpretation, the whole body of Christ is becoming this **VESSEL FOR THE FINER**...containers of God's Word and God's Spirit.

God is presently involved in the process of refining us: removing us from among the wicked and removing wickedness from us. When this process is completed, by doing so, He will establish His throne in righteousness...forevermore.

● One thing we should always remember is that Jesus understands.

He knows what we are going through. With tender love, He feels our infirmities...for He, too, has suffered being tempted.

In the splendorous vision given to John the revelator, the resurrected Christ was depicted as having *"feet like unto fine brass, as if they burned in a furnace."*(Revelation 1:15, See also Daniel 10:6)

Oh, hallelujah! Jesus has walked through the fire too!
In all our *affliction*, He was *afflicted*!
At Calvary He bore our burdens as if they were His own!
So He will certainly come to our rescue now!

Though we have been nothing but a defiled woman, stained by the sin of this world, He will rejoice to bring us forth as **A WOMAN CLOTHED WITH THE SUN**. We will be married to Him forever in a covenant relationship and we will be that spiritual city through whom He will reign in regal authority for all eternity.

In us, the prophecy will be gloriously and finally fulfilled:

> *"O thou afflicted [O AFFLICTED CITY] tossed with tempest, and not comforted, behold, I will lay thy stones with fair colours, and thy foundations with sapphires.*
> *And I will make thy windows agates, and thy gates of carbuncles, and all thy borders of pleasant stones."*

(Isaiah 54:11-12 AV, NIV)

No wonder the same prophet exulted to proclaim:

> *"Sing, O heavens; and be joyful, O earth;*
> *and break forth into singing, O mountains: for*
> *the Lord hath comforted His people, and will*
> *have mercy upon HIS AFFLICTED."*
>
> (Isaiah 49:13)

In that day, **HIS AFFLICTED ONES** will never know the pain of affliction again. We will be **THE INHERITANCE OF THE LORD** and **A VESSEL FOR THE FINER,** filled to overflowing with the radiance of His glory.

We will be eternal proof that our God really is **the God of all grace, the God of patience,** and **the God of hope.**

Through **grace** and by **patiently** dealing with a fallen human race, millennium after millennium, God's original **hope** will be finally realized.

Dearly beloved, this is **OUR GLORIOUS INHERITANCE!!**

And this is:

> *"Christ in you, THE HOPE OF GLORY."*
> (Colossians 1:27)

• HIS CALLED •

HIS CALLED ONE

THE CALLED
ACCORDING TO HIS PURPOSE

THE CALLED OF JESUS CHRIST

---

*"Hearken unto Me, O Jacob
and Israel, MY CALLED [MY
CALLED ONE]; I am He; I am
the first, I also am the last."*
(Isaiah 48:12 AV, Rhm)

"And we know that all things work together for good to them that love God, to them who are THE CALLED ACCORDING TO HIS PUR-POSE."

(Romans 8:28)

"Among whom are ye also THE CALLED OF JESUS CHRIST."

(Romans 1:6)

HIS CALLED

"Hearken unto Me, O Jacob and Israel, MY
CALLED [MY CALLED ONE]; I am He; I
am the first, I also am the last."
(Isaiah 48:12 AV, Rhm)

● *A calling can be simply defined as an invitation. At times, though, it is more than just an invitation which can be easily scorned and rejected. It is rather a compelling demand, a divine summons to fill a God-ordained office.*

Therefore, a *called* person is either one who is *invited,* or one who is *appointed.*

God calls both ways and in various ways.

God called Old Testament Israel with a national calling. (See Ro. 11:25-29)

God has called the world to salvation with a universal call, an invitation - "Whosoever will, let him take the water of life freely" - and any and all can respond. (Rev. 22:17, See also Mt. 9:13, Lk. 5:32, Ps. 50:1)

But there is also an individual call of ordination sent out to certain persons to whom God chooses, of His own good pleasure, to profoundly reveal Himself. Whatever way this call goes forth, those who yield (at least, in this dispensation) become part of *the church* (an entitlement which appropriately means - *the called out ones*).

Though this company is depicted as a great multitude, which no man could number, still the Caller is extremely personal with each one included.

John 10:3 states that:

"...He calleth His own sheep by name, and
leadeth them out."
(See also Isaiah 43:1)

This scripture speaks of foreknowledge, guidance, and preservation. Its meaning is enhanced by our main *title-passage:*

"Hearken unto Me, O Jacob and Israel, MY
CALLED [MY CALLED ONE]; I am He; I
am the first, I also am the last."
(Isaiah 48:12 AV, Rhm)

This could be interpreted as if God was saying - *"Listen to Me, My people; I chose you from the start and called you from the foundation of the world. I am the author and finisher of your faith. I am the first; I also am the last. I have power to watch over you and to keep you to the very end. I have a goal for you and I intend, by My grace, to carry you all the way there."*

THE TRIUNE PURPOSE

We who are the rightful recipients of such a heaven-sent communication should abide in the utmost confidence...for we know that the King of creation is involved in the smallest details of our lives.

● Moreover, God has planted **a triune purpose** in the good ground of our regenerated, yielded, and believing hearts.

1. **An individual purpose** - the specific work or gift God has ordained each believer to fulfill here in the realm of time.
2. **A common purpose** - the common goal all believers have inherited of advancing the kingdom of God, reaching the lost and being presently conformed to the nature of Christ.
3. **An eternal purpose** - the destiny of being glorified, fully changed into the image of Jesus and reigning with Him as kings and priests in the kingdom of God to come.

The Most High is an expert at making all the events of life, both negative and positive, serve as steppingstones leading us to these God-ordained goals.

He is more than generous in supplying more than enough grace to get us all the way there. Those who understand this, also understand that:

> *"...all things work together for good to them that love God, to them who are **THE CALLED ACCORDING TO HIS PURPOSE.***
>
> *For whom He did foreknow, He also did predestinate to be conformed to the image of His Son, that He might be the firstborn among many brethren.*
>
> *Moreover whom He did predestinate, them He also **called**: and whom He **called**, them He also justified: and whom He justified, them He also glorified."*

(Romans 8:28-30)

Notice the last statement - *"them He also glorified."*

Even though this final stage in God's plan is yet to happen, being firmly grounded in God's eternal purpose, it is spoken in the past tense.

As far as God is concerned, the outcome for *His called* is sealed and sure (so much so that when John saw the vision of New Jerusalem descending out of heaven, he heard a voice proclaiming - "IT IS DONE." Revelation 21:6)

So God's plans concerning the resurrection of the dead, the translation of the living believers, and the coming kingdom are irreversible, unchangeable and unstoppable.

We are daily being "conformed to the image of His Son" - **molded like clay and refined like gold.** We will finally be presented "holy and unblameable and unreproveable in His sight" - glorified forevermore. (Col. 1:22) This is the *"hope of the gospel,"* a commonwealth inheritance shared by every believer, for:

> *"There is one body, and one Spirit, even as ye are called in **one hope** of your calling."*
> (Ephesians 4:4, See 1:18, Col. 1:23)

CERTAIN "CALLED" INDIVIDUALS

● There are certain individuals specifically described as being *"called"* in the Bible.

Moses - who was *"called"* by God to deliver Israel. (See Exodus 3:4)

Bezaleel - who was *"called"* to construct the tabernacle and its furnishings. (See Exodus 31:2)

Samuel - who was *"called"* to be a prophet/priest. (I Samuel 3:4)

Eliakim - who was *"called"* to be the royal treasurer during the reign of Hezekiah. (See Isaiah 22:20)

Cyrus - who was *"called"* to release the Jewish captives in order to rebuild Jerusalem. (Isaiah 44:28; 45:4)

Barnabas and Saul - who were *"called"* to minister to the Gentiles. (See Acts 13:2)

Paul (the same as Saul) - who was *called* "to be an apostle of Jesus Christ through the will of God." (I Corinthians 1:1)

And the Messiah, Jesus - who was *"called...in righteousness,"* *"called...from the womb,"* and *"called* of God an high priest after the order of Melchisedec."* (Isaiah 42:6; 49:1, Hebrews 5:10)

Furthermore, concerning the sons of Rebekah, Jacob and Esau, the prophecy was given even before they were born that -"The elder shall serve the younger." (Romans 9:12)

Paul explained this strange predetermination in the verse just prior:

> *"(For the children being not yet born, neither having done any good or evil, that the purpose of God according to election might stand, not of works, BUT OF HIM THAT CALLETH.)"*
>
> (Romans 9:11)

The main thing to be learned from the above list is the following:

All of these individuals - Moses, Bezaleel, Samuel, Eliakim, Cyrus, Barnabas, Saul, Jacob and, of course, Jesus - were not only *called* by God; they were equipped; they were qualified to do what God had *called* them to do.

Not one of them failed; for God always gave **HIS CALLED ONES** more than enough grace to fulfill His will and perform His purpose. For this cause, the purpose of God has stood, and will yet stand strong, throughout the ceaseless ages. (See I John 3:8, Ephesians 1:11;3:11)

That which God has elected will not be thwarted. That which God has ordained will not be stopped. As Gamaliel, a Pharisee of the Sanhedrin council, so aptly said - "If this counsel or this work be of men, it will come to nought: but if it be of God, ye cannot overthrow it; lest haply ye be found even to fight against God." (Acts 5:38-39)

TYPES OF CALLINGS

■ **A holy calling** - II Timothy 1:9 declares that God "hath saved us, and *called* us with *an holy calling,* not according to our works, but according to His own purpose and grace, which was given us in Christ Jesus before the world began."

This speaks especially of the soberness and seriousness with which we should embrace our callings. They are not to be taken lightly. They are sacred gifts, and we must live holy lives if these callings are to manifest in perfection. How convicting it is to realize that we are presently God's New Covenant "holy of holies" - the dwelling place of the ark of His covenant and the Shekinah glory of His presence! How it stirs the heart to realize that all of these *holy callings* were given to us "before the world began!" (See Ephesians 4:1, II Thessalonians 1:11)

■ **A heavenly calling** - Hebrews 3:1 commands that we, as "holy brethren, partakers of *the heavenly calling*, consider the Apostle and High Priest of our profession, Christ Jesus." The Old Covenant Jews knew primarily an earthly calling, a Spirit-led journey that brought them into a natural land of inheritance and promise. On the contrary, God's New Covenant people know they are looking for a "better country, that is, an *heavenly*." (Heb. 11:16) Our calling is an *heavenly* one because it originally came from *heaven* and will lead us back to the same spectacular realm. Jesus is the Apostle of our profession - the original God-sent leader, example and guide. He is also the High Priest of our profession - the perfect example of our eternal priesthood calling (which includes the calling to minister to God with sacrifices of praise forevermore).

■ **The high calling of God in Christ Jesus** - In Philippians 3:13-14 Paul explained - "Brethren, I count not myself to have apprehended: but this one thing I do, forgetting those things which are behind, and reaching forth unto those things which are before, I press toward the mark for the prize of *the high calling of God in Christ Jesus.*" This powerful statement could mean either of two things. First, reaching this *high calling* may be a reference to reaching the *highest* and most perfected manifestation of our *calling* here on earth. This would necessarily include perfection in all our thoughts, emotions, actions and reactions...perfection in all that we are, all that we say and all that we do. Second, it may be a reference to the future glorified state and the ultimate inheritance that awaits every believer.

Furthermore, we have all been:

- *"called* unto liberty." (Galatians 5:13)
- *"called*...to peace." (I Corinthians 7:15)
- *"called*...to glory and virtue." (II Peter 1:3)
- *"called* to be saints." (Romans 1:7, I Corinthians 1:2)
- *"called* unto the fellowship of [God's] Son." (I Corinthians 1:9)
- *"called*...into the grace of Christ." (Galatians 1:6)
- *"called*...out of darkness into His marvellous light." (I Peter 2:9)
- *"called"*...to patience when we do well and suffer for it. (See I Pt.2:20-21)
- *"called*...unto His kingdom and glory." (I Thessalonians 2:12)
- *"called*...unto His eternal glory." (I Peter 5:10)
- *"called"*...to return blessing for cursing. (See I Peter 3:9)
- *"called*...[to] receive the promise of eternal inheritance." (Hebrews 9:15)
- *"called* unto the marriage supper of the Lamb." (Revelation 19:9)

Those who receive these *callings* are, of all the people of this earth, most privileged and blessed. Those who respond and obey are, by far, the most wise.

THE FINAL ANALYSIS

● To bring this chapter to its conclusion, there are several scriptures that should yet be quoted and ideas that should yet be promoted.

First, it is important to see that we have not received this heaven-sent calling through any greatness, goodness, or effort on our part.
In Isaiah 41:9 God declares to His people - "I have taken thee from the ends of the earth, and *called* thee from the chief men thereof."
I Corinthians 1:26-29 is even more expressive in conveying this truth:

> *"For ye see your **calling**, brethren, how that*
> *not many wise men after the flesh, not many*
> *mighty, not many noble, are called:*
> *But God hath chosen the foolish things of*
> *the world to confound the wise; and God hath*
> *chosen the weak things of the world to con-*
> *found the things which are mighty;*
> *And base things of the world, and things*
> *which are despised, hath God chosen, yea,*
> *and things which are not, to bring to nought*
> *things that are:*
> *That no flesh should glory in His presence."*

Second, it is essential that we realize - God does not change His mind:

> *"For the gifts and **calling** of God are*
> *without repentance."*
> (Romans 11:29)

This scripture was given especially to underscore the fact that natural Israel is still special to God, though they have rebelled against the New Covenant that He has established. They are "beloved for the fathers' sakes" (a reference to Abraham, Isaac, Jacob and the other foreparents of the Jewish race who initially walked with God). (Romans 11:28)
Isaiah 54:6 and Zechariah 12:9-10 reveal that God will yet call to this nation again, in a very profound way, in these last days.
How comforting it is to know that God has not forgotten His natural chosen people! Even though they crucified their King, His arms are still open wide to them! His grace is still available!
And how this convinces our hearts that even when we err, God will not repent or change His mind concerning our position in His plan. If we sincerely humble ourselves and believe, He is always ready to restore.
We are "**THE CALLED OF JESUS CHRIST.**" (Romans 1:6)
We are not only called BY Him; we are OF Him. We are His. He claims us as His own.

Third, and finally, even though God normally will not change His mind concerning our calling, it is essential that we be in cooperation with Him.
We are commanded to add to our "faith" virtue (which is excellence: the perfection of moral, godly attributes). This is absolutely necessary if the

callings we have received are to manifest and bring forth fruit.

For this cause the Scripture exhorts all God's offspring:

> *"Give diligence to make your **calling** and election sure."*
>
> (II Peter 1:10)

> For *"they that are with Him are **CALLED**, and chosen, and faithful."*
>
> (Revelation 17:14)

Fulfilling such a challenge should ever be the *hope* that rises daily in our *hopeful* hearts!

A FINAL THOUGHT
CONCERNING GOD'S CALL

> *"The mighty God, even the Lord, hath spoken, and **called** the earth from the rising of the sun unto the going down thereof."*
>
> (Psalm 50:1)

If God renews His call to all humanity with the dawning of each new day, let us respond each day with fresh commitment, zeal and devotion to Him.

• THE CLAY •

THE WORK OF HIS HAND

EARTHEN PITCHERS

POTS OF CLAY

THE WORK OF THE HANDS OF THE POTTER

"But now, O Lord, Thou art our Father; we are THE CLAY, and Thou our potter; and we all are THE WORK OF THY HAND."
(Isaiah 64:8)

"The precious sons of Zion, comparable to fine gold, how are they esteemed as EARTHEN PITCHERS [POTS OF CLAY], THE WORK OF THE HANDS OF THE POTTER!"
(Lamentations 4:2 AV, NIV)

THE CLAY

"But now, O Lord, Thou art our Father; we
are THE CLAY, and Thou our potter; and we
all are THE WORK OF THY HAND."

(Isaiah 64:8)

● It was God's intention to express a prophecy in symbolic language and in a unique and unforgettable way.

So He commanded the prophet Jeremiah:

"Arise, and go down to the potter's house,
and there I will cause thee to hear My words."

(Jeremiah 18:2)

The young seer obeyed and walked to the potter's workshop. When he arrived, the craftsman was fashioning some kind of vessel out of a lump of clay on the stone wheel rotating before him.

The vessel, unfortunately, was marred in his hand.

So he picked up the clay, pressed it once again into a shapeless form, kneaded out any air pockets or lumps, removed unwanted gravel, threw it on the potter's wheel and "made it again another vessel, as it seemed good to the potter to make it." (Jeremiah 18:4)

The dreadful meaning was all too apparent.

Israel was marred.

Though she rested in the very hands of the Almighty God, she was full of unwanted "lumps" and "stones."

Her idolatry, her lustful connections with the world, her constant transgression of the law had reached such a critical state, it was impossible for the Master Potter to ignore the need any longer.

To create "a vessel unto honor," suitable for His indwelling, the God of all truth and justice must reduce the Jewish nation to a "formless lump" and begin afresh.

In declaring His power and willingness to administer such a judgment, the Most High protested:

"O house of Israel, cannot I do with you as
this potter? saith the Lord. Behold, as the clay
is in the potter's hand, so are ye in Mine hand,
O house of Israel."

(Jeremiah 18:6)

● **Such a prophetic analogy was fulfilled on two levels at two different points in history:**

First, it was fulfilled through the Babylonian captivity and subsequent restoration of the Jews. These restored ones returned to Jerusalem full of repentance and cleansed of rebellion: a fresh lump of *clay*, supple in the Potter's hands.

Second, this analogy was fulfilled when God discarded the Old Testament way of doing things to choose a new people through a New Covenant and a new way of dealing with men.

This analogy is also applicable on an individual instead of a national level.

When the attitudes or the lifestyles of certain children of God are unacceptable to Him, still, except in extreme cases, the faithful Creator will not cast away the dearly beloved of His soul.

Rather, He takes us in His hands, kneads out that which is offensive, then casts us again on the Potter's wheel to be reshaped.

This may involve tribulations, trials, chastisements, persecutions, or just the day-to-day pressure of living in this world.

But for those who are predestined to be "conformed to the image" of the firstborn Son - shaped into His exemplary form - ALL THESE THINGS WILL "WORK TOGETHER FOR GOOD." (Romans 8:28-29)

God's master design, in the end, will produce vessels of such eternal excellence that - "every pot in Jerusalem and in Judah shall be holiness unto the Lord of hosts." (Zechariah 14:21)

This is the reason believers can rejoice even in the worst of circumstances.

We have discovered the Potter's plan and *the hope of glory* that it contains for those who yield to His influence.

COMPREHENDING THE SYMBOL

In order for us to comprehend the precious truths contained in this clay-symbol *title-calling*, we should study the nine necessary steps that lead up to any potter's desired end result - a vessel of excellence.

These nine steps are: winning, aging, wedging, throwing, finishing, drying, firing, glazing and firing again.

Each one of these steps should be reviewed in more detail if we are to more fully understand the spiritual application.

■ **Winning**

The first step in the production of clay vessels or pottery is very simply mining the clay. This process is also called *winning*.

And how true it is that when we go forth to win souls we are, in a sense, digging for that kind of special clay that can produce vessels meet for the Master's use. Proverbs 11:30 says it beautifully and appropriately - "He that *winneth* souls is wise."

■ **Aging**

Sometimes, after *winning* the clay, it is *aged* for at least several weeks. This is usually accomplished by wrapping the clay in a moist cloth and storing it in a cool place. This is especially necessary when the clay begins in a dry, powdered state and is then mixed with water. *Aging* represents that blessed and relatively pressureless time, right after salvation, when we are protected, wrapped up in God's keeping power, soaking in the refreshing, cool moisture of His promises and affection toward us.

■ Wedging

Wedging is the preparation of a lump of clay: the kneading out of unwanted air pockets and lumps, the removal of gravel, the addition or subtraction of water - whatever is necessary for the lump to be pliable and perfect in the hands of the potter. This speaks of God's initial dealings with a newly saved person. There are still many "air pockets" or "lumps," especially in a new convert's soul: hidden areas of character where carnality is still trapped or the heart is yet hard in its self-will. If the lumps in clay are ignored, later on they could result in unsightly bulges. If the air pockets are left unattended, later on their presence could result in the cracking or exploding of a vessel during the firing process. So also, if character flaws are not dealt with immediately in a newly professing Christian, later on, unsightly problems could arise to the surface; or, in the heat of a trial, a person may "crack" under the pressure and totally backslide.

To avoid such a tragic end, God, from the start, begins a kneading process - flattening , twisting, rolling, folding, and compressing our clay-like human hearts with His nail-scarred hands - until we are purged, supple and submitted.

According to a potter friend who helped me wth the details of this chapter, *wedging* makes the clay "alive." It is more responsive. Daniel Rhodes, the author of *Clay and Glazes,* describes it as "a transmission of tone from potter to clay." How appropriate a description of what Jesus is doing in His church!*1

After kneading, the next associated step is to extricate the unwanted gravel. This gravel, or "grog" as potters call it, is allowable up to a certain degree in stoneware, but must be more meticulously removed for earthenware pottery. The smoother the texture being sought for, the more the gravel must be purged out (though all clay must have some in order to hold its shape). Grog-filled stoneware is stronger, heavier and hardier, and is fired at a much higher temperature. On the contrary, earthenware is made from an easier-to-work-with, softer, more elastic clay and is fired at a lower temperature. Both have their own unique purpose, beauty and worth - and it all hinges on the preference of the potter. So God has representatives and offspring that are more like stoneware - full of grit, toughness, soldier-like perseverance and stamina. These may be "fired" at a higher temperature by facing harder or harsher circumstances in life than other more normal Christians. In the end it proves to be beneficial, for it prepares such *"stoneware vessels"* for a more demanding work in the kingdom of God.

God's **earthenware vessels**, on the other hand, are those who may be more normal in their lifestyle, more at ease in their walk through this world, possibly even more refined, more gentle and more peaceful in some ways. These individuals may be less able to endure the demanding lifestyle in which stoneware vessels flourish, but in their place, they are just as important to God and to His work!

The wetness of clay is also a very important factor for us to consider.

A batch of clay, being prepared for the potter's use, must be neither sticky nor stiff. Too much water overly softens a lump of clay, making it sticky and giving it a tendency to sag. Too little water makes it stiff and unyielding. Just the right amount causes clay to hold any shape given to it.

This unique property is called plasticity.

No synthetic material can match clay with respect to this unique trait. Man cannot reproduce it. Scientists do not even fully understand it, but nature provides it - for the benefit and blessing of mankind.

Water represents a mixture of both the Word and the Spirit (See Eph. 5:26, Jn. 7:37-39). As two natural elements unite to make natural water (hydrogen and oxygen - H_2O), so two spiritual elements unite to make this spiritual living water. When God mixes His Word and His Spirit into our spirits, by yielding to this dual influence, we become shapeable and moldable...a joy to the Potter above.

Of course, if God, in a sense, poured too much of Himself into our lives, we could chance becoming too soft, too weak. God would be doing everything for us and we would never learn or grow! Without the presence of His life-giving Spirit and His living Word, though, we could become very rigid in carnality or brittle in mere religiosity, far from any real change into Christlikeness. So there must be the proper balance, the proper measure, the proper mixture...bringing us to a place of spiritual maturity.

When a batch is too watery, often the potter will throw the clay on a bat (which is a piece of absorbent material, usually plaster) until he sees that enough water has been drawn out of the lump for it to be used. This "bat" could represent the various "support groups" God places us in after salvation: prayer meetings, Bible study gatherings, churches, etc. When we are newborn in the Kingdom, God normally sets us amid other "absorbent" believers, both strong and weak, who proceed to draw forth the Word and the Spirit from our hearts. We learn to love. We learn to be patient. We learn to be servants. By this process, we experience both the positive and negative aspects of covenant living in the family of God.

Dealing with human relationships is often the main way we advance in God. Our emotions and our minds often come under pressure as we strive to maintain godly ties to one another. Sometimes this is a very "draining" experience. Of course, the Master Potter always knows when we have reached our limit, or when our supply of water needs to be replenished.

God's main purpose is developing character in us. Often, this can only happen by facing conflicts, problems or challenges. Sometimes we are tossed on the "bat" to dry; at other times, we are moistened, or "slaked" as potters put it. Through it all, as already stated, God is striving to develop in us this spiritual quality of **plasticity**: *the ability to hold whatever "shape" is given to us.* Having achieved this valuable trait, we are ready to proceed to the next step.

▪ Throwing (Centering, Raising and Shaping)

The next major step is *throwing*. This is a term used to describe the whole process of the formation of a piece of clay pottery on a potter's wheel.

First, the clay ball must be *centered* on the wheel. If this is not done correctly, the potter is bound to be unsuccessful in producing a good piece of pottery. One side will be thick and the other thin. This speaks of the great importance of new Christians being "balanced" in their doctrines, devotional life, relationships with others, etc.

Satan tends to drive us to extremes. He either influences us to become too dogmatic about non-essential doctrinal views, harassing and offending others, or he impresses us to remain wishy-washy and unsure. He seeks to render us unspiritual altogether or striving so hard for supposed spirituality that we live in a realm of self-created fantasy. The deceiver wants us numb and uncaring about the feelings and opinions of others or too easily affected and swayed by the same. He is always off-center, off-balance, and striving to make us fit his dreadful pattern.

God wants us *centered*. God wants us balanced; for it is then that we have the greatest potential to be shaped into something valuable for the kingdom.

Next, after *centering*, the bowl must be *opened* and *raised*. This is done by inserting the thumbs into the ball of clay and pressing downward. Once the cavity is created - and a significant amount of pressure must be applied - the walls can be *raised and shaped*. Hands must be kept moist at all times or the clay may peel off on the potter's fingers.

All of this speaks of the fact that once we become balanced, God then "digs down" into our spirits - through the pressure of His convicting Spirit, His challenging Word or the circumstances of life - to make room for greater depths of the anointing.

Once we learn how to stay full of the Spirit, God can *raise* up the walls of our vessel, giving us greater responsibilities and a greater strength to match those responsibilities. In His dealings with us, thankfully, the Master Potter always keeps His hands moist with mercy, tenderness, forgiveness and lovingkindness.

■ Finishing (Trimming, Smoothing, and Separating)

The third step of throwing a piece of pottery is the finishing stage. Bringing a piece to completion involves measuring, cutting, trimming, then smoothing the clay with an assortment of small tools or sponges. God similarly measures us by the strict standard of His Word and often trims us according to New Testament Scriptural specifications.

God never lets up. In fact, the closer we get to completion, the more meticulous He becomes in His demands.

In a final breath of artistic flare, the potter will go over his "creation" with a moist, spiritual sponge to make the surface, edges, ridges and dips as smooth as possible. This speaks of the Creator, in loving compassion, working on the finer details of our personalities - smoothing over the rough edges of any remaining pride, rebellion, hostility, lust, jealousy or unforgiveness. He wants nothing to mar our "appearance."

Next, the bowl or vessel must be separated from the bat. This cannot be done until the clay is 'leatherhard', not totally dry, but able to be touched and turned over without yielding or smashing. This speaks of a child of God becoming very firm, very set, very unchangeable in what they believe.

The *separation* is usually accomplished by pulling a wire, or even an old, toothless hacksaw blade through the rotating clay at its base. After removal, the foot rim is carved out so the pottery piece can stand securely on its own.

So God has to separate us from all our carnal dependencies - sometimes the very people, prayer groups or churches we have trusted in - that we might mature fully in the Lord and draw our strength only from Him. This does not mean that we must intentionally leave a ministry or cut off from certain Christian leaders, but that we no longer lean on that ministry or those leaders as our main support. We learn to lean on Jesus utterly and find our sole sufficiency in Him. We esteem the leadership in the body of Christ highly, showing due respect, loving support and proper submission, but our main devotion is to the Son of God alone.

When we arrive at this point, we can become givers instead of takers.

Rather than always requiring help, we are able to give it away, to support our leaders and other weak or needy persons in the body of Christ.

This is an extremely important step if we are to become leaders ourselves, capable vessels of the Lord, able to pour out the good things of God into the lives of others.

■ Drying

Next, pottery must be *dried* before it can be *fired*! Usually bowls and other objects are placed on a flat shelf in an upside-down position to dry. Handles and other extensions must be wrapped so *drying* will be uniform. If they dry first, they tend to crack off. Also, *drying* should be gradual. Too fast a *drying* process can damage pottery.

So God often takes His mature ones through a lengthy *"drying"* time when everything may even seem *upside-down* (opposite to what people normally go through).

John the Baptist, for many years, was "in the deserts till the day of his shewing unto Israel." And Jesus was even called "a root out of a *dry* ground" and was "led by the Spirit into the wilderness" in preparation for the day of His power. (Is. 53:2, Lk. 1:80;4:1)

This desert-experience should be the place where our longing for God increases. Psalm 63:1 states - "O, God...my soul thirsteth for Thee, my flesh longeth for Thee in a dry and thirsty land, where no water is."

If spiritual desire can be stirred up and intensified, walking through dry places should do it! How valuable the water of life becomes when our tongues are parched and the sun is beating down on us unmercifully.

The wilderness should also be the place where we become more hardened in our commitment to God's will. *Desert-dry* times may not be times of bubbly joy. There may be few apparent results, answers, victories or manifestations of the power of God; but, O, how we advance in endurance and steadfastness.

A lot of outpoured blessings and ecstatic spiritual sensations do not always promote such strength of character. *Drying* times do. No wonder, Paul (who knew some very trying, *drying* times) said - "In everything give thanks: for this is the will of God in Christ Jesus concerning you." (I Thessalonians 5:18)

■ Firing

For pottery to have permanence and usefulness it MUST go through the stage of *"firing."* This is normally done in a kiln and is a process requiring exceptional care (for a mistake during loading or firing could cause all previous efforts and time to be spent in vain).

Ancient kilns were heated by means of a wood fire, modern kilns by more modern means (gas or electricity). Even circulation of the resulting hot air is of the utmost importance. Usually pots are raised on some kind of structure so that the air will get underneath, equally affecting every surface area of the clay form.

This first *firing* is done at a relatively low temperature so that the pottery will come out firm enough to be handled without danger, yet not so dense that the glaze will not adhere correctly. Pots can burst in a kiln if the temperature rises too fast. This is called a "blowing." Also, if any cracks appear during the drying time, chances are, they will either be enlarged or totally split the clay vessel during the *firing* time. The great danger is that if one vessel "blows," other vessels in the kiln can be destroyed along with it.

All of these details reveal spiritual truths. This time of *firing* represents the intense *fiery* trials that believers face during this earthly sojourn (a subject already thoroughly covered in the previous chapter entitled *His Afflicted*).

I Peter 4:12-13 commands - "think it not strange concerning the fiery trial which is to try you, as though some strange thing happened unto you: but rejoice, inasmuch as ye are partakers of Christ's sufferings." Later in the same epistle, Peter wisely concluded that "the God of all grace, who hath called us unto His eternal glory by Christ Jesus, after that ye have suffered a while, make you perfect, stablish, strengthen, settle you." (I Peter 5:10)

Going through fiery trials is never meant to destroy God's own, but rather, to render them more stable in the end, more strong, more "permanent." Moreover, we know God will always test us for "cracks" during dry times before subjecting us to the "fire." He never demands of us more than we can bear.

He knows that if one child of God experiences a "blowing," chances are, other vessels will be destroyed in the process.

This stage of *firing* could also represent the overpowering influence of the divine nature working its way into our spirits ("for our God is a consuming *fire*" - Hebrews 12:29).

Both of the interpretations above are sensible and applicable, for both processes must take place if we are to become strong, enduring vessels.

We know that the revelation of God's Word and the impartation of His nature are a rich, heaven-sent treasure for God's own. Paul admitted, though, that "we have this treasure in earthen vessels" - nothing but common clay pots. (II Cor. 4:7) So if the treasure is to be secure, the clay container must be solid and sure as well.

Even distribution of the hot air in a kiln speaks of how God either orders or uses the events of our lives so that EVERY AREA of needful character growth can be dealt with. Through it all, though, God never heats the "kiln" up too quickly or makes it so hot that the results are not beneficial. If we are surrendered vessels, His grace is always sufficient...so there should never be any kind of spiritual "blowing." All that we experience in life, whether it be negative or positive, is intended to work "for us a far more exceeding and eternal weight of glory." (II Corinthians 4:17)

■ **Glazing and Firing Again**

Glazing **is the application of a liquid preparation to the surface of ceramic wares to form a moisture-impervious, and often lustrous, or-namental coating.** It is baked right into the clay. *Glazing* symbolizes the final stage of more perfectly "putting on Christ"; the *lustrous* excellence of His attributes and the *ornamental* glory of His abilities; baked by the heat of God's purpose into the depth of the inner man. It also speaks of the beautiful and protective seal of the Holy Spirit on God's vessels, making them sin-repellant and world-resistant.

Mature members of the body of Christ who radiate the divine nature, who are not "stained" by the world and its ways, are the finished, polished products that the Potter desires from the start. This is His *hope of glory* for us; the reason He lovingly subjects His clay-like image-bearers to all of the foregoing stages mentioned.

It must be included that in order for this *glaze* to be permanent and

reach its most glossy and lovely appearance, there MUST be a final *firing*. This is a considerably hotter fire than the first, for it brings the vessel to completion.

This beautifully represents the transformation that will take place in us when "the Lord Jesus shall be revealed from heaven...in *flaming fire*." (II Th. 1:7-8)

God has already consumed every believer with His divine fire in a hidden, spiritual way, but He will yet consume us all, both spiritually and physically, with a *resurrection-fire*, the likes of which we have never known. In that intense moment of creative expertise and ultimate craftsmanship, the Chief Potter will forever lift us from the "miry clay stage" and establish our goings. (See Psalm 40:2)

Clay vessels will then become glorious golden vessels - in the twinkling of an eye - ready to pour forth eternal, spiritual worship toward the One who miraculously made it all possible. Surely we will then marvel that:

> *"The precious sons of Zion, comparable to fine gold" - were ever - "esteemed as EAR-THEN PITCHERS [POTS OF CLAY], THE WORK OF THE HANDS OF THE POT-TER!"*
>
> (Lamentations 4:2 AV, NIV)

Too often, in the midst of this developmental process, we complain, we murmur, we feel God is somehow being unfair.

But Isaiah explicitly warned:

> *"Woe unto him that striveth with his Maker!...Shall THE CLAY say to Him that fashioneth it, What makest Thou?"*
>
> (Isaiah 45:9)

And Paul authoritatively declared:

> *"Hath not the potter power over the clay, of the same lump to make one vessel unto honour, and another unto dishonour...that He might make known the riches of His glory on the vessels of mercy, which He had afore prepared unto glory?"*
>
> (Romans 9:21, 23)

So let us yield to Him, abandoning our will to the gentle, loving touch of the Master Potter.

Let us no longer grumble over the circumstances of life or complain that we are nothing but mere *"houses of clay*, whose foundation is in the dust, which are crushed before the moth." (Job 4:19)

Rather, let us rejoice over the "mystery which hath been hid from ages and from generations, but now is made manifest to His saints...*Christ in you, the hope of glory.*" (Colossians 1:26-27)

And this is our *hope of glory*, that we who have been entitled *the clay* will eventually be termed *the clay* no longer!

We will emerge as vessels unto honor and vessels of mercy.

We will pass forever from that which is crumbling, decaying and temporal, to that which is God-like, irreversible and eternal.

The Potter will prevail in the end!

✿ THIS CLAY POT ✿

Out of the dark night - barren and stark,
The dug up clay resisted - was hard.

Found wanting, prosaic - unadorned,
This earthy substance must be formed.

So the potter kneads his chosen clay,
And the prideful airs are wedged away.

Mirrored in his eyes - the design shone,
He works for this one purpose alone.

Tenderly raises it on the wheel,
The rough edges moistened, smoothed
and sealed.

Set in a desert place to harden,
Fired - made perfect for his garden.

Wonderfully made
Never to fade.

JEANNE THOM OBEE

Note of Appreciation: Many thanks to potter Elaine Woodard for helping to supply the necessary information so that this chapter could be written.

*1   Daniel Rhodes, *Clay and Glazes for the Potter*, (Chilton Company, 1957) P. 71

THE CONTRITE ONES

"For thus saith the high and lofty One that inhabiteth eternity, whose name is Holy; I dwell in the high and holy place, with him also that is of a contrite and humble spirit, to revive the spirit of the humble, and to revive the heart of *THE CONTRITE ONES.*"

(Isaiah 57:15)

THE CONTRITE ONES

"For thus saith the high and lofty One that inhabiteth eternity, whose name is Holy; I dwell in the high and holy place, with him also that is of a contrite and humble spirit, to revive the spirit of the humble, and to revive the heart of THE CONTRITE ONES."

(Isaiah 57:15)

● The word **contrite** basically means *a grief-stricken or penitent attitude of heart over sins or shortcomings.*

This word appears only five times in Scripture, all in the old Testament, and is so translated from four very similar Hebrew words - *dakka, dakah, daka* and *nakeh*. It is illuminating to see that *dakka* can mean *to be crushed like powder or to be bruised*, while *dakah*, a primary root, can mean *to collapse*. *Daka*, also a primary root, basically means *to crumble* and has been translated *bruise, beat to pieces, break [in pieces], contrite, crush, destroy, humble, oppress and smite. Nakeh* means *smitten.*

All of these detailed definitions reveal that *contrite* persons are those submissive individuals who have been *smitten* and *humbled* by their own conscience, by the Word of God, or by the conviction of the Holy Spirit, insomuch that they feel almost *crushed like powder.*

They feel as though they could *collapse* under the heavy load of godly sorrow and the passionate desire to be right with God.

Emotionally *beaten to pieces* by the shocking realization of how detestable the flesh really is, they can only find relief in the Most High and in the *hope* that He can give.

True *contrition*, in its most potent form, rends, crushes, tears and bruises the heart...until the person so influenced feels as though he or she were almost bleeding inwardly.

So pained, so severely distressed over the ugliness of carnality, the hopelessness of our plight without God, and the damnation that should be our lot, *contrite ones* tend to cast themselves on the mercy of God, melting in remorse and utter surrender before His throne.

Some have said that such remorse is like - "beholding heaven and feeling hell." This is not only the anguish of a lost person seeking for salvation; this is the spiritual travail of saved ones who long to be free from every stain of sin, who long to bring to birth within the very kingdom of the Almighty God.

These spiritually sensitive persons tend to bleed inwardly at the thought of Jesus bleeding outwardly.

Such are not to be pitied, for to them the promise is extended:

*"A **bruised reed** shall He not break, and smoking flax shall He not quench, till He send forth **judgment unto victory**."*
(Matthew 12:20, See Isaiah 42:3)

We know that the "sorrow of the world worketh death" and this is certainly not God's will for His own. But "godly sorrow," though it bruises the soul, is "not to be repented of"...for it "worketh repentance to salvation." (II Cor. 7:10)

● **God's ultimate purpose for us is salvation and victory:** victory over sin, victory over the flesh, victory over Satan, victory over death, and victory over all the adverse circumstances of life. The testimony of David, the erring prophet/king, verifies this truth. Though he sank to the depths of sin, he repented and rejoiced to declare:

> *"The Lord is nigh unto them that are of a broken heart; and saveth such as be of a contrite spirit [those who are crushed in spirit]."*
>
> (Psalm 34:18 AV, NAS)

David also showed the superiority of this attitude, as compared to mere Jewish rituals of law, in Psalm 51 (a psalm of repentance):

> *"For Thou desirest not sacrifice; else would I give it: Thou delightest not in burnt offering.*
> *The sacrifices of God are a broken spirit: a broken and a contrite [penitent] heart, O God, Thou wilt not despise."*
>
> (Psalm 51:16-17 AV, Har)

God gives grace to *the humble* and to *the contrite*...grace to rise, grace to conquer, grace to win.

As Matthew 12:20 indicates, He sends forth *"judgment unto victory."*

God continually brings His own under *judgment*: He scrutinizes every attitude and action. When it is necessary, He chastens. If we react with sincere contrition, God then executes *judgment* on the sin and the satanic forces that fight against us. Thus, the whole process is *"unto victory"* - that we might emerge triumphant in all things.

This all transpires because we willfully fall on "the Rock" in remorse and brokenness. (See Matthew 21:44)

● **Jesus came to heal the brokenhearted,** so the logical assumption is that we must be broken before He can heal us. Yet it is also just as true that we cannot have this brokenness of heart without the help of the Creator.

The Scripture is clear on this issue.

Romans 2:4 teaches that "the goodness of God LEADETH thee to repentance." But not only does He guide us into this correct frame of mind, Acts 5:31 explains that the Saviour came to "GIVE repentance to Israel, and forgiveness of sins."

Acts 11:18 states that to the Gentiles, God has also "GRANTED repentance unto life."

Finally, II Timothy 2:25 reveals that we should be gentle and meek with argumentative persons in the hope that "God peradventure will GIVE THEM REPENTANCE to the acknowledging of the truth."

It is quite apparent, therefore, that a *contrite* spirit, a repentant heart, is another gift God gives to us in *hope*. We receive it in *hope* as well, knowing that it produces blessed, beneficial and fruitful results.

It leads us to the still waters of peace that passes understanding.

It cleanses the soul.

It renews the strength and vigor of spiritual life within us.

It soaks the ground of our earthen hearts - making it good ground - and causes the seed of the Word to more effectively germinate and spring forth.

It is not an end in itself, but a means of reaching a far better and far deeper place in God. So let us follow hard after the heart of God.

Let us be among those who "sigh and...cry for all the abominations that be done" in Israel. (Ezekiel 9:4)

As the Puritans of old, let us pray for "the gift of tears."

CONTRITION AND REPENTANCE

In order for us to understand **contrition** we must understand **repentance**, for the two are inseparable.

Though they are not totally synonymous, these two qualities of heart are definitely married together in oneness of meaning (so much so that in this chapter we will often use the terms interchangeably).

There is a slight difference, though, that should not be overlooked.

- **REPENTANCE is a change of mind that results from godly sorrow.**
- **CONTRITION is godly sorrow that causes a change of mind.**

It is also essential to understand that there are four main steps that lead a person to the goal of true repentance:
1. A genuine sorrow over sin.
2. An abhorrence of sin.
3. A forsaking of sin.
4. A sincere yielding to the will of God.

Unless all four of these steps are evident, repentance is only partial, and really less than effective.

● Such an experience of heart is not meant to be merely a one-time experience the day we are saved. Rather, true *contrition* and *repentance* should be a constant, gripping feeling in the inner man.

Charles Spurgeon once stated that:

> *"Repentance is not a thing of days and weeks...to be got over as fast as possible. No, it is the grace of a lifetime, like faith it- self...That is not true repentance which does not come to faith in Jesus and that is not true faith in Jesus which is not tinctured with repentance."*

Hebrews 6:1 adds to this thought with a very suitable analogy.

In this verse we find that the first two "foundation stones" of our Christian experience must be *"repentance from dead works"*...and then "faith toward

God." Without controversy, once a building is built, it must abide on the same foundation. So also, we must abide in *repentance* if we are to walk in the glory of faith.

We must abide in an attitude of introspection and self-judgment. We must abide in sincere remorse over failings and shortcomings. For then and only then will our faith have its full intended effect.

If we feel we have somehow progressed beyond the need for such a process, we are greatly deceived. The closer we get to God, the more pronounced, continual, and intense such an experience of heart should become.

Thomas Carlyle once said:

> *"Of all acts of man, **repentance** is the most divine. The greatest of all faults is to be conscious of none."*

Often those persons who think they are nearly faultless, who are comfortable in their Christianity and self-assured in their relationship with God are, in all actuality, far from Him and ever drifting further away.

Even righteous Daniel, when he came into the manifest presence of God, fell before the Most High as the fear of the Lord seized his soul. In recounting the experience, he later explained - "My comeliness was turned in me into corruption, and I retained no strength." (Daniel 10:8)

John the beloved, who lovingly laid his head on the Master's bosom in the upper room, later collapsed like a dead man at His feet...when he viewed the fiery-eyed Christ in His revelation splendor.

And God-fearing Job, upon hearing the voice of the Lord out of the whirlwind, cried - "I abhor myself, and *repent* in dust and ashes." (Job 42:6)

All of these are examples of that spirit-piercing brand of emotion that should ever be resident in the heart of any saint...Old Will or New.

● It is enlightening to see that at the dawn of the New Covenant, the predominant beginning theme of both John the Baptist and Jesus was:

> *"**Repent**: for the kingdom of heaven is at hand."*
>
> (Matthew 4:17, See also 3:1-2)

Why did this message precede the telling of all other New Covenant revelations? Because both the Son of God and His prophet/forerunner knew their followers would never be able to enjoy the full benefits of kingdom-living without such a proper preparation of the heart.

And as it was then, so it is now!

THE REWARD OF CONTRITION

● **The reward given to *contrite ones* is not only salvation and the privilege of entering God's kingdom; our main *title-scripture* promises that God will allow those who are *contrite* to dwell in *"the high and holy place."* (Isaiah 57:15)**

This must be that "secret place of the Most High" where yielded, righteous-ness-loving persons "abide under the shadow of the Almighty." (Psalm 91:1)

Once this place of fellowship and protection is discovered, even when powers of hell war against us, we can still be confident.

For in *the high and holy place*, not only do we stand in awe at the holiness of God, the glorious Father breathes His very nature and being into us.

We are made holy. We are given dominion.

We are lifted above the stain and the pain of our past, quickened in Christ.

We are renewed inwardly, restored to a position of blamelessness and righteousness, and made alive with an infusion of the very life of God.

● **This is all part of what God meant when He promised to** "*revive* **the spirit of the humble, and to** *revive* **the heart of** *the contrite ones.*" (Is . 57:15)

To revive means *to restore, renew or to quicken back to life.*

We know that in Adam we all died, but in Christ we are all *"made alive"*...or, as Isaiah put it, we are *revived.*

Though this *"reviving"* initially takes place the very moment we are saved, still, to grow in God and to advance in spirituality, it is necessary that we receive new outpourings of divine life often.

Through these visitations we receive fresh zeal, fresh joy, fresh righteous-ness, fresh power from on high.

And "though our outward man perish, yet the inward man is *renewed* day by day," hour by hour, and moment by moment. (II Corinthians 4:16)

If we do our part, God will do His.

If we maintain an attitude of humility and *contrition*, God will flow through us freely and deeply with the abundance of His grace.

The first verse after our *title-scripture* explains part of the reason God extends such mercy to His own:

> *"For I will not contend for ever, neither will
> I be always wroth: for the spirit should fail
> before Me, and the souls which I have made."*
> (Isaiah 57:16)

THE PLEA FOR REVIVAL

● In awareness of this pledge from Isaiah's writings, surely Habakkuk presented his classic petition:

> *"O Lord, revive Thy work in the midst of
> the years, in the midst of the years make
> known; in wrath remember mercy."*
> (Habakkuk 3:2)

And the psalmist voiced his plea:

> *"Wilt Thou not revive us again: that Thy
> people may rejoice in Thee?"*
> (Psalm 85:6)

● It is an established truth that if we repent, God will very likely repent of sending that judgment or chastisement we may deserve. (Of course, in God's case, *repentance* means *a change of mind* and certainly not a change of character and a turning away from sin, as it does in the case of man.)

A prime example of this truth is found in Jeremiah 18:8 - "If that nation, against whom I have pronounced, turn from their evil, *I will repent* of the evil that I thought to do unto them." (See Ex. 32:14; Jd. 2:18; I Sam. 15:11, Ps. 110:4)

By these passages and many others, it becomes apparent that *contrition* is the key to restoration and *revival:* in our own lives, in our nation, and in all the world.

In the words of W. Graham Scroggie:

> *"There never has been a spiritual revival which did not begin with an acute sense of sin."*

Mass media technics may bring crowds of people, but only deep-seated *repentance* and *contrition* can bring a sweeping move of God's power. There has never been any great spiritual awakening without this necessary ingredient.

A great portion of the professing church in our day has become so shallow, so superficial, with its ceremonies, its programs, its ecclesiastical order. Our stained-glass emphasis on materialism and ritualism has stolen greatly from the clarity of relationship we could have with God. As the light of the Word and the Spirit diffuses through Christianity's arched window, truth is being discolored and weakened.

Too often those who stand behind the pulpit are guilty of "tickling the ear" instead of "pricking the heart." They prophesy smooth things and have broken the blade off of God's plowshare of conviction with a rock-hard resistance to truth.

The "human soil" in their charge remains unturned, and thus, impervious to the seed of the true Word of God. There is little change in lifestyle and certainly not enough desire for intimacy with God among leaders and laity alike.

Having become minimally religious (enough to relieve guilt-ridden minds), too often they remain satisfied and smug in their tepid spiritual condition. The vast difference between the convenient hour-long Sunday morning service and the far-less-populated prayer meeting night is itself an accurate gauge of our present level of spirituality and fervency.

It seems a desire to be entertained has replaced the desire to worship in spirit and in truth. We are fast becoming a generation of expert onlookers and spectators instead of participants and partakers.

In this modern hour of glossed-over religiosity, sin is even being called by other more appealing terms, and deep sorrow over sin is looked upon as something that 'went out with the dark ages.' If so, then we are in a darker age than ever - for if "the light that is in thee be darkness, how great is that darkness!" (Matthew 6:23)

Even in many of our fundamental, pentecostal, and charismatic circles the pendulum has swung much too far to the left. We have become too liberal, too organized, too professional, and far too reluctant to preach or teach that which may sound negative lest the hearer's ever fragile self-image be injured.

O, how we desperately need prophetic voices to rise up, men and women impassioned for holiness, who will fearlessly "Cry aloud, spare not!" who will dare to say - "Woe to them that are at ease in Zion!" who will echo the once familiar call - "Come out from among them, and be ye separate, saith the Lord!" who will reprove, rebuke and exhort until we are smitten again with true *contrition*, until we are *bruised with sorrow* over our iniquities, and until we once again strive to follow hard after God. (Is. 58:1, Am. 6:1, II Cor. 6:17)

No longer can we allow ourselves to yawn in the face of the world's desperate need. No longer can we blindly become friends to the world and forget that by doing so we become the enemies of God. "For all that is in the world, the lust of the flesh, and the lust of the eyes, and the pride of life, is not of the Father, but is of the world." (I John 2:16)

As long as we ignore such stern biblical reproof, as long as we remain complacent and self-satisfied, chances are, we are still caught in the "world spirit." As long as we pet our sin, as long as we defend our weaknesses, as long as we are numb to our need, we cannot and will not change. And if there is no progress toward change, true revival cannot and will not come!

● **A doctor once explained to me that, contrary to popular belief, pain is a very beneficial thing.** It is the body's warning device. It shows us where we need to fix our attention, that necessary medical procedures might be implemented and healing might be effected.

So it is with *the pain of contrition.*

Contrary to popular, contemporary theology, it is a very beneficial thing.

It shows us the areas of our hearts and minds that need to be dealt with...lest any spiritual "sickness" or "injury" prove fatal.

By means of *contrition,* the Great Physician leads us to rest, recovery and perfect health (emotionally, mentally, spiritually, and even physically).

His indwelling presence is the *cause of contrition.*

His indwelling presence is the *cure of contrition.*

Therefore, even when we feel we are being *crushed like powder*, we can still shout aloud - IT IS CHRIST IN US, **THE HOPE OF GLORY**! THE HOPE OF HEALING! THE HOPE OF RESTORATION! SO LET US "REJOICE IN **HOPE** OF THE GLORY OF GOD"! (Romans 5:2)

BECOMING HIS TEMPLE

● Deeply related to all of this precious truth is the prophecy of Isaiah 66:1-2:

> *"Thus saith the Lord, The heaven is My throne, and the earth is My footstool: where is the house that ye build unto Me? and where is the place of My rest?*
> *For all those things hath Mine hand made, and all those things have been, saith the Lord: but to this man will I look, even to Him that is poor and of a contrite spirit, and trembleth at My Word."*

73

God was expressing His great dissatisfaction with mere physical structures of stone and wood being offered to Him as a dwelling place under the Old Will. His desire, both then and now, is to find poor-spirited individuals - those who *tremble with contrition* over the demands of God's Word - that He might make them *lively stones in a spiritual house,* filled with the glory of His presence!

Buildings cannot inherit the nature and attributes of deity, but we can! High-spired wonders of architectural achievement strike no wonder in the heart of God. They are not attractive to Him. They are not suitable to meet His great need.

But O, how attractive to God are those yielded ones who "rejoice with *trembling,*" whose faces often glisten with rivulets of tears as they strive to be holy unto the Lord! (Psalm 2:11)

How comfortable God feels in manifesting Himself to men and women of such spiritual caliber! To them, the promise is given - "I will dwell in them, and walk in them; and I will be their God, and they shall be My people." (II Corinthians 6:16)

So we see - a *contrite* attitude not only gives us the right to dwell in the holy of holies on high; it grants us the privilege of becoming God's holy of holies here below: the place where His covenant ark abides, the place where His glory dwells.

● At one point under the Old Will, because of rebellion, the name "Ichabod" was symbolically written over the temple (a word that means *"the glory is departed"*). That building, made by the hands of men, was only God's temporary abode. Because those associated with the temple became corrupt, it was finally burned to the ground.

Under the New Will, God has made a way for *the glory to remain.*

Because of the abiding presence of God in our hearts, there is an abiding source of *contrition.* This enables God to "sweep" and cleanse us daily as *His abode*...to preserve us now and to prepare us for that day when we will be drawn upward into the full splendor and majesty of heaven itself.

No wonder John Milton stated that **repentance** is...*"the golden key that opens the palace of eternity."*

THE ULTIMATE REVIVING - THE FINAL GLORY

● **Our main theme in this chapter is God's pledge to *"revive* the heart of the contrite ones."** (Isaiah 57:15)

On its highest level, this speaks of the restoration of redeemed men and women back to the perfection of paradise.

Hosea provides a choice prophecy concerning this ultimate *"reviving"*:

> *"Come, and let us return unto the Lord: for He hath torn, and He will heal us; He hath smitten, and He will bind us up.*
> *After two days will He revive us: in the third day He will raise us up, and we shall live in His sight."*
>
> (Hosea 6:1-2)

74

● This passage speaks, on one level, of God's people being *torn* and *smitten* under the Old Will: by the law that ministered death and by the judgment of God that fell on them because of their rebellion.

It also speaks of sensitive men and women being *torn* by conviction and *smitten* with grief over failing God.

But then Jesus came...

To heal us.

To bind us up.

This is happening now in a spiritual sense; it will transpire in an absolute sense at the resurrection.

● *"After two days will He revive us,"* the prophet foretold.

In this scripture *two days* speaks of two thousand years, two millenniums, between Jesus' first coming and His second (for "one day is with the Lord as a thousand years, and a thousand years as one day" - II Peter 3:8).

● *"In the third day He will raise us up, and we shall live in His sight."*

This speaks of the Kingdom Age, heaven on earth for a thousand years, the third divine day after Jesus' coming. The dead who died "in the Lord" will be *raised* into a glorious and glorified state at the onset of this era. Believers which are alive and remain unto the coming of the Lord will be *raised* out of this prison of dust, this form of clay, in a moment.

We will be changed in the twinkling of an eye: filled to overflowing with the essence of divine life, charged with the breath of immortality.

When the kingdom of God fully manifests in this earth-plane, the Lord of lords will actually walk in our midst. *"We shall live in His sight"* - in the conscious awareness of the nearness and watchfulness of the Holy One.

As the millions of red blood cells in a circulatory system all pulsate with the pulsation of the heart, so all the glorified saints in this world will be sensitive to the compassionate heart-throb of the King of kings who will sit on a throne in Jerusalem.

We will be in perfect unity with Him.

We will be His joint-heirs and co-rulers.

We will experience a heavenly ecstasy that knows no bounds.

And all because we were willing to submit ourselves to the temporary pain of godly sorrow, the rending of the heart that *contrition* effects.

● Surely it was with this in mind that Jesus promised - *"Blessed are they that mourn"* - over sin, over error, over this bondage of carnal flesh - *"for they shall be comforted."* (Matthew 5:4)

How fitting it is that the Hebrew word rendered *repent* forty times in the Old Testament is translated *comfort* about sixty-five times, so the two go hand in hand!

In Isaiah, 57:18, our *title-chapter*, God promised, concerning *repentant* Israel, to "restore *comforts* unto him and to his *mourners*." (See also Isaiah 66:10-13)

What a faithful and true statement we also find in Psalm 30:5:

> *"...Weeping may endure for a night, but joy
> cometh in the morning."*

Our God will yet turn our mourning into dancing.

He will yet remove our sackcloth - *of repentance, remorse and contrition -* and gird us with gladness!

Our time of spiritual travail will then be proven to have been quite worthwhile, birthing within us the fullness of Christ, and without, the glory of a New Creation.

Such is God's glorious *hope* toward us.

And such is our *hope of glory* toward Him.

Such a *desire* can be presently and fully married to *expectation* in God's offspring and bound with cords of love to every hopeful heart.

Though the fulfillment of this vision may tarry, we must wait for it!

It will surely come!

It will not tarry!!

REVIVE US AGAIN

Revive us again,
Fill each heart with Thy love.
May each soul be rekindled
With fire from above.
Hallelujah, Thine the glory!
Hallelujah, Amen!
Hallelujah, Thine the glory!
Revive us again!

ELIAKIM'S FATHER'S HOUSE

**THE OFFSPRING AND ISSUE
OF THE FATHER OF ELIAKIM**

**THE GLORY
OF HIS FATHER'S HOUSE**

**ALL VESSELS
OF SMALL QUANTITY,
VESSELS OF CUPS
TO VESSELS OF FLAGONS**

**THE INHABITANTS
OF JERUSALEM**

"And it shall come to pass in that day, that I will call my servant Eliakim the son of Hilkiah:

And I will clothe him with thy robe, and strengthen him with thy girdle, and I will commit thy government into his hand: and he shall be a father to **THE INHABITANTS OF JERUSALEM,** *and to the house of Judah.*

And the key of the house of David will I lay upon his shoulder; so he shall open, and none shall shut; and he shall shut, and none shall open.

And I will fasten him as a nail in a sure place; and he [ELIAKIM] shall be for a glorious throne to **HIS FATHER'S HOUSE.**

And they shall hang upon him all **THE GLORY OF HIS FATHER'S HOUSE, THE OFFSPRING AND THE ISSUE, ALL VESSELS OF SMALL QUANTITY,** *from the* **VESSELS OF CUPS,** *even* **TO** *all the* **VESSELS OF FLAGONS."**

(Isaiah 22:20-24)

THE OFFSPRING AND ISSUE
OF THE FATHER OF ELIAKIM

● In order to understand how the peculiar names and *titles* listed in this chapter can be applied to God's offspring, we must first review the entire five verses directly dealing with this revelation:

> *"And it shall come to pass in that day, that I will call my servant Eliakim the son of Hilkiah:*
>
> *And I will clothe him with thy robe, and strengthen him with thy girdle, and I will commit thy government into his hand: and he shall be a father to THE INHABITANTS OF JERUSALEM, and to the house of Judah.*
>
> *And the key of the house of David will I lay upon his shoulder; so he shall open, and none shall shut; and he shall shut, and none shall open.*
>
> *And I will fasten him as a nail in a sure place; and he [ELIAKIM] shall be for a glorious throne to HIS FATHER'S HOUSE.*
>
> *And they shall hang upon him all THE GLORY OF HIS FATHER'S HOUSE, THE OFFSPRING AND THE ISSUE, ALL VESSELS OF SMALL QUANTITY, from the VESSELS OF CUPS, even TO all the VESSELS OF FLAGONS. "*

(Isaiah 22:20-24)

● On the surface, this reading out of Isaiah is primarily dealing with the dismissal of unfaithful Shebna as treasurer in Hezekiah's court and the subsequent appointment of Eliakim, a righteous and God-fearing son of Hilkiah.

As often happens in Old Testament writings, prophetic and Messianic overtones fill every verse (for "in the volume of the book it is written" of the Christ to come - Psalm 40:7).

As we explore the hidden meaning of this passage of Scripture, let it first be established that:

1. **Eliakim** is a type of Christ.
2. **Hilkiah**, the father of Eliakim, is a type of the Everlasting Father.
3. **The offspring and issue of Hilkiah** represent the offspring and issue of God, who are joint-heirs with the firstborn Son.
4. **Shebna** is a symbol of Satan. (Note: For further background information read Isaiah 22:15-19)

These four comparisons provide the foundation for the revelation contained in this chapter. It is the basis for all that is yet to be said.

COMPREHENDING THE ANALOGY

■ When Isaiah prophesied to Shebna that he was going to lose his position and be carried away into captivity, this high-ranking official was in the process of preparing a sepulchre: a "place of death" for himself and his offspring.

In a parallel way, from the fall of Adam onward, Satan has busily occupied himself turning this world into a huge "sepulchre" of sorts: a place of mental, emotional, spiritual and physical death for all who are his "offspring" (the children of darkness). His purpose will be thwarted in the end, though, and like Shebna, he will also be led into captivity: the bottomless pit, then the lake of fire.

■ Isaiah prophesied that Shebna's robe and girdle, which represented his high position of governmental authority, would be taken from him and given to Eliakim. Then, as chief steward over all the king's treasures, Eliakim would become a father to *the inhabitants of Jerusalem* and the house of Judah.

In like manner, Lucifer was "stripped" of his position of authority in this world by the crucifixion and resurrection of the Messiah. In his place, Jesus has now been exalted as legal Lord over death and hell, and over all the earth. Similar to Eliakim's prophecy, Isaiah 9:6 announced that the coming Messiah would bear the government *upon his shoulder* and that He would be entitled *the Everlasting Father.* This will be true especially in the Kingdom Age and New Creation to come, when Jesus will manifestly walk among His glorified people and be a Father to *the inhabitants of Jerusalem* and the house of Judah. To get to King Hezekiah, all Jews had to go through Eliakim; so to get to God, all men must now go through Jesus. He is the mediator between God and men.

■ The name *Hilkiah* means *Jehovah is protection* or *portion of Jehovah.* His son's name, *Eliakim,* means *God will establish* or *whom God sets up.* In being exalted to Shebna's position, Eliakim was used of God to assist in "redeeming" Israel from a time of national and religious apostasy.

So also, the Everlasting Father instituted a plan *to protect* those who consider Jehovah-God their *portion* in this life. He *established* Jesus as the door to eternal life and *set Him up* as Lord and King in this world. On a much higher level, Jesus came to *redeem* us or *buy us back* from deception, sin, and religious apostasy.

■ Eliakim was given the "key of the house of David" so that he could open and no man could shut, and shut and no man could open.

Eliakim had authority over all the house of David and over all his riches. He bore the keys. He could gain entrance into any room and lock any door preventing the entrance of others. He was the chief steward. Quite possibly, he possessed the keys to the royal mausoleum as well, where former kings and members of the royal family were buried.

So Jesus has authority over the house of God - "all power...in heaven and in earth" - and is the Chief Steward over the treasures of heaven. In Him are "hid all the treasures of wisdom and knowledge" and through Him, those who are of the "royal family" obtain deliverance from the dark tomb of death. (Matthew 28:18, Colossians 2:3, See Hebrews 3:6)

It should be noted that Revelation 3:7 uses almost exactly the same language as Isaiah 22:22 and quotes Jesus telling the church in Philadelphia - "These things saith...He that hath the key of David, He that openeth, and no man shutteth; and shutteth, and no man openeth."

Jesus is spoken of as being the son of David and as inheriting the throne of David. (Luke 1:32; 18:38)

As a Son over the royal, spiritual house of David, Jesus too holds the keys...the keys of God's kingdom here on earth and the "keys of death and hell." He opens the door of eternal life to some and bars the entrance to others...and no one can reverse His decisions.

The NIV version renders John 14:2 - "In My Father's house are many rooms." Jesus, as Chief Steward, bears the keys to all of the rooms and chambers in the Father's house that any child of God would want to explore. This would include all the eternal promises, gifts, callings, and elections available to believers under the New Covenant.

■ **Eliakim was fastened as a nail in a sure place and all the glory of his father's house, the offspring and the issue, were hung upon him. These offspring, from the least to the greatest, were compared to "vessels of small quantities, from vessels of cups, even to all the vessels of flagons."**

In those days large nails were placed in the walls of homes in order to hang most of the valuable possessions of the homeowner. These pegs or nails were usually not driven in the walls as an afterthought; rather, during construction they were built into the wall, making them all the more strong and immoveable. In like manner, Jesus was not "driven" into the wall of time to gather the souls of men as an afterthought on God's part; rather, He was ordained from the foundation of the world to do so. He ever has been and ever will be "a nail in a sure place," the "nail in His holy place" and "the nail" out of the house of Judah. (Ez. 9:8, Zec. 10:4) All who are born again are His brethren, His joint-heirs and make up "the Father's house." (See Heb. 3:2,6; 10:21; I Pt. 4:17, Eph. 2:19)

In a symbolic, spiritual sense, therefore, we are **ELIAKIM'S FATHER'S HOUSE**, being sons and daughters of the Father above.

Of all of creation, we are His most glorious expression and achievement; so it is only right to boldly announce that we are also **THE GLORY OF THE FATHER'S HOUSE, HIS OFFSPRING AND ISSUE.**

This is our Scripture-based claim to a position of honor in God's great kingdom. We are the Father's glory, because of all created entities and beings, we supply Him with the most excellent proof of His greatness. (See chapter in this volume on *The Glory*)

● **In all of this spiritual boasting, though, we must often remind ourselves of two things:**

First - we are all hanging on that "nail in a sure place." Whether we are small or great in God's kingdom, whether we be **VESSELS OF CUPS** or **VESSELS OF FLAGONS,** still, we are totally dependent on Jesus.

Apart from Him, we have no glory. Without Him, we would all fall and be utterly dashed to pieces, then swept away into everlasting ruin.

Second - though we are the Father's glory and full of the wine of His Spirit, still, compared to the firstborn Son, that "nail in a sure place," we are only **VESSELS OF SMALL QUANTITY.**

He was from above.

We are from beneath.
He was God manifested in the flesh, flawless and holy.
We were only fallen sons of Adam, full of flaws and so prone to unholiness.

But then Jesus came into our lives and changed our status.
He made us "the head, and not the tail." (Deuteronomy 28:13)
So let all of God's vessels, *the cups* and *the flagons*, pour out the wine of adoration toward His secret place. By doing so we will quench the thirst of God, filling His heart up with the recognition He deserves and the fellowship He desires.

■ Finally, Eliakim was spoken of as being *a glorious throne* to his father's house. In other words, his family would share in his riches, influence, authority and dominion...just by virtue of being his relatives.

In like manner, Jesus has become for all of us *a glorious throne* - our place of inherited victory, rest and dominion.

In a spiritual sense, we are presently seated with Christ in heavenly places where we share in the riches of His grace and the bounty provided by all the promises in His Word. (See Ephesians 2:6)

In His name, we presently rule over principalities, powers and the very flesh in which we dwell. By His power, we presently take authority over sin, sickness and satanic forces that hold men bound.

In a literal and glorified sense, we will one day rule and reign with Him over all things in the absolute splendor of the celestial.

In Revelation 3:21 He gave the splendid promise:

> *"To him that overcometh will I grant to sit with Me in My throne, even as I also over-came, and am set down with My Father in His throne."*

Because Jesus, our heaven-sent **Eliakim**, has been *set up* as Lord over all and *established* on a glorious throne, we can expect to be *set up* as His subordinate lords and *established* as His royal priests, forever and ever.

In the New Creation to come we will be **THE INHABITANTS OF JERUSALEM** in a very profound sense: glorified saints ruling over all things from the holy city, New Jerusalem. Jesus will be a Father unto us and we will hail Him as our provider and protector. (See Isaiah 9:6, Revelation 21:7)

This is our *hope of glory*!
It is not an empty *hope*!
It is not a futile dream!
It is not a cunningly devised fable!

We will never be ashamed that we have expected such a phenomenal climax to our earthly sojourn. (For Word-based *hope* "maketh not ashamed.") (Ro. 5:5)

It has to happen. Because from the "alpha," the very dawn of creation, God has formed such a plan. He will carry it through to the "omega," the end of all things.

Reigning with Him as kings and priests has always been God's purpose for us - from the moment the Master Potter bent over in Eden and picked up that first handful of moldable, shapeable substance.

● Hannah, the mother of Samuel, said it so wonderfully:

> *"He raiseth up the poor out of the dust, and lifteth up the beggar from the dunghill, to set them among princes, and to make them IN-HERIT THE THRONE OF GLORY."*
>
> (I Samuel 2:8)

And Jeremiah said it so excellently!

> *"A glorious high throne from the beginning is the place of our sanctuary."*
>
> (Jeremiah 17:12)

Surely the Shekinah glory of God that will PERMANENTLY rest upon this heavenly throne will far exceed the glory cloud that TEMPORARILY hovered over the earthly mercy seat that foreshadowed it.

Moreover, instead of just two golden cherubim on the lid of the ark, there will be endless myriads of heavenly creatures, cherubim and seraphim, that surround the throne, ceaselessly proclaiming God's holiness, guarding His honor, and adoring His majesty.

And just to think...

We will share this celestial throne...

Ruling and reigning with Him forever!

O beloved, can we not see by the preceding throne-verses, and by the chapter we just absorbed, that God's greatest *hope* toward us and our greatest *hope* toward Him are one and the same?

Having reached such a profound realization, in great gratitude, let us offer ourselves to the Creator as vessels unto honor, sanctified and meet for the Master's use! And let us "hold fast the confidence and the *rejoicing of the hope* firm unto the end." (Hebrews 3:6)

• A FIRE •

A FLAME

A FLAMING FIRE

A FLAME OF FIRE

---

*"And the house of Jacob shall be **A FIRE**, and the house of Joseph **A FLAME**, and the house of Esau for stubble, and they shall kindle in them, and devour them; and there shall not be any remaining of the house of Esau; for the Lord hath spoken it."*
(Obadiah 18)

"Who maketh His angels spirits; His ministers A FLAMING FIRE."

(Psalm 104:4)

"And of the angels He saith, Who maketh His angels spirits, and His ministers A FLAME OF FIRE."

(Hebrews 1:7)

A FIRE

*"And the house of Jacob shall be A FIRE,
and the house of Joseph A FLAME, and the
house of Esau for stubble, and they shall
kindle in them, and devour them; and there
shall not be any remaining of the house of
Esau; for the Lord hath spoken it."*

(Obadiah 18)

● In most of the religions of the world - especially pagan religions - fire is considered sacred and is viewed with a mystical kind of reverence. Greek mythology attempts to explain the origin of fire by suggesting that a Titan, named Prometheus, stole it from Olympus, the mountain in Thessaly where the gods dwelt, and transported it in a hollow reed to the human race. This was supposedly against the orders of Zeus, chief of the gods, so Prometheus was punished by being chained on a rock in a wilderness area of Scythia.

Pyrolatry, or **fire worship**, is also a very common form of religious expression in many cultures from ancient times until this day. One prime example concerns the Mexican god of fire, Xiuhtecutli. On a certain set day each year, the people of that region would extinguish their house-fires. Then the representative priest would create new fire, by friction, at the base of a statue of Xiuhtecutli and distribute it to the people. This ritual suggested that the supernatural presence of the god was being transferred to every home, along with his provision and protection.

Of course, all of the traditions and superstitions mentioned above are gross perversions of the truth and an abomination to God. But in rejecting these false teachings, we must be careful, at the same time, not to overlook that which is true, positive and God-pleasing.

For in the holy Scripture, and in true and undefiled religion, fire is used as a significant and meaningful symbol of both God and His people.
We will first explore its use and meaning when representing the Creator.

GOD AS A FIRE

Ezekiel received a vision of God on the throne and claimed that he saw:

*"...the appearance of fire round
about...from the appearance of His loins even
upward, and from the appearance of His loins
even downward...the appearance of fire."*

(Ezekiel 1:27)

Daniel commented that on the throne of the Ancient of days were "wheels as *burning fire*" and "a *fiery stream* issued and came forth from before Him." (Daniel 7:9-10)

In recounting his apocalyptic vision, John the revelator said of the risen

Christ - "His eyes were as *a flame of fire*," and that "there were seven *lamps of fire* burning before the throne, which are the seven Spirits of God." (Revelation 1:14;4:5)

● **When employed to describe the Creator, fire speaks of the intensity of His emotions, the irresistibleness of His authority, the swiftness of His judgments, the invincibility of His power, the flawlessness of His holiness, the fearlessness of His actions, the fearfulness of His presence, the eternalness of His being, and the unapproachableness of His glory.** Being immaterial, fire is a far more perfect representation of God than some material substance. Theophanies (manifestations of God) under the Old Will include the burning bush, fiery Mount Sinai and, of course, the pillar of fire that often hovered over the holy of holies in the tabernacle and that guided the Israelites through the wilderness. (See Isaiah 4:5)

Specific Scripture references, comparing parts of God's character to fire, are as follows:

God's wrath - "Yea, I will gather you, and blow upon you in *the fire of My wrath...*" (Ezekiel 22:21)

God's jealousy - "Surely in *the fire of My jealousy* have I spoken..." (Ezekiel 36:5, See Song of Solomon 8:6)

God's judgment - "under His glory He shall kindle a burning like *the burning of a fire.*" (Isaiah 10:16, See Numbers 11:1)

God's protectiveness - "For I, saith the Lord, will be unto her *a wall of fire* round about..." (Zechariah 2:5)

God's guidance - "And the Lord went before them...by night in *a pillar of fire*, to give them light..." (Exodus 13:21)

God's discernment - "Every man's work shall be made manifest: for the day shall declare it, because it shall be revealed by *fire*; and the *fire* shall try every man's work of what sort it is." (I Corinthians 3:13)

God's power to sanctify - "He is like *a refiner's fire.*" (Mal. 3:2, See Is. 4:4)

God's power to destroy and recreate - "Looking for and hasting unto the coming of the day of God, wherein the heavens being on *fire* shall be dissolved, and the elements shall melt with fervent heat. Nevertheless we, according to His promise, look for new heavens and a new earth, wherein dwelleth righteousness." (II Peter 3:12-13)

It should also be noted that when divine fire fell on a sacrifice offered to God, it was a sign of His favor, His intervention, and the true consecration of the offerers. (See Leviticus 9:24, I Chronicles 21:26, II Chronicles 7:1)

At times, it was proof of God's presence and reality (Elijah said - "the God that answereth by *fire*, let Him be God." I Kings 18:24)

So when we present our bodies a living sacrifice on God's spiritual altar, we should expect the Most High to manifest His presence and reality by consuming us with His holy *fire*. Thus, in a New Covenant sense, we become an "offering made by *fire*" - the only kind of offering acceptable to God. (See Leviticus 7:5)

In viewing all these scriptural passages, it is plain to see that the fire of God can be something very negative or very positive.

It can be either dreadful or wonderful.

It can be either destructive or creative.

It can be either a sign of His disapproval or a token of His approval.

Our attitudes and actions determine the way that it manifests toward us, but either way the results are overwhelming and overpowering.

● **We will all undoubtedly face God's holy *fire* - in either damnation or transformation. For the Scripture testifies that "our God is a consuming *fire*" and that "every one shall be salted with *fire*."** (Heb. 12:29, Mk. 9:49)

For those who are rebellious, damnation will be the result (ultimately, in a lake of *fire* where the torment will be endless).

For those who are yielded, transformation will be the outcome (ultimately, on a sea of glass, mingled with *fire*, where the ecstasy will be never-ending).

And if we are privileged to face the fire of God in transformation - both now and eternally - we will be changed into the image of the God who transforms.

Being absorbed into *His fire*, we will become *a fire*.

In the process, we will take on some of the divine attributes compared to *fire* in God's holy Word. We will tend to show anger, jealousy or protectiveness over the things which solicit a similar reaction from God.

Jesus came "to send *fire* on the earth" and this is one way He does it: in the souls of those who dare to follow in His footsteps. (Luke 12:49)

Those whose hearts burn with anger over sin, wrath toward Satan, jealousy for the truth, and protectiveness toward the weak, are becoming very much like the God who burns within their regenerated spirits.

● **Speaking of the cooperative coexistence between the Father and the Son, and their joint way of manifesting, Isaiah prophesied:**

> *"And the light of Israel shall be for a fire,*
> *and His Holy One for a flame..."*
>
> (Isaiah 10:17)

If we are joint-heirs with Christ (and we are) then we share in the inheritance of our elder brother, Jesus.

If He is referred to in the above passage as *a flame*, then we, His many brethren, should also fill the role of being *flames:* a multitude of individuals consumed with the Father's presence, a multitude of individual *flames* blending together as one holy *fire* fulfilling the Father's will on earth.

Burning with devotion to God.

Burning with zeal for God.

Burning with revelation from God...that must be communicated to the lost and dying. Igniting this flame in fireless hearts is the only hope for a frigid, dark and trembling world.

OBADIAH'S FIRE-PROPHECY

● Obadiah, who gave us the shortest book of the Old Testament, built his single chapter toward its climax with the following prophecy:

> "And the house of Jacob shall be A FIRE,
> and the house of Joseph A FLAME, and the
> house of Esau for stubble..."
>
> (Obadiah 18a)

Jacob and **Esau** were twin brothers born to Isaac and Rebekah.

Esau, the eldest (whose name means *hairy*), was an impetuous, lustful, irresponsible man who thought nothing of selling his birthright for a morsel of meat. He represents all carnal minded men and women who willingly "sell" their inheritance in God, who sacrifice any potential birthright and blessing to satisfy the cravings of their fallen Adam flesh.

Jacob, the youngest (whose name means *deceiver* or *supplanter*), was a conniving opportunist who was willing, on the contrary, to use any means necessary to obtain the birthright and blessing from his father, Isaac. Though his methods were, at times, deceptive, underhanded and questionable, still, he had a sense of values that attracted God's favor.

Later on in life, wrestling with the angel of the Lord, Jacob's name was changed to **Israel** (which means *prince of God*). It seems that his nature was changed during that visitation as well.

This great patriarch personifies and represents all of God's covenant people who pursue an inheritance in God and who receive a nature-change from Him. (And God did say - "Jacob have I loved, but Esau have I hated." Romans 9:13)

Spiritually speaking, we are no longer of *the house of Esau*: children of irresponsibility and rebellion against God. We are of *the house of Jacob,* pursuing our birthright and yieldedness to the Most High.

● **In Obadiah 18, the house of Jacob is spoken of as a *fire*, the house of Joseph is represented as a *flame*, and the house of Esau is described as stubble. In the last half of this verse, the prophet foretold:**

> "...and they [the houses of Jacob and
> Joseph] shall kindle in them [the house of
> Esau], and devour them; and there shall not
> be any remaining of the house of Esau; for the
> Lord hath spoken it."
>
> (Obadiah 18b)

On its highest level of interpretation, this plainly reveals that, in the end, God's people will prevail. By the *fire* of the Word and the Spirit we will declare the truth to the "house of Esau" (the heathen and the unbelievers who fill this world). By doing so, we will kindle a *fire* in their midst.

If they receive the truth, *the fire of God* will burn the world and its lusts from their hearts and they will join a new family: the family of God. If they resist the truth, they will face irresistible judgment, like *flaming fire* devouring stubble, until there are none remaining (as the previous scripture states).

Stubble is a term used to describe *the broken and lifeless stalks in a field already harvested of its grain or corn.* It can also mean *that which is left over after threshing.*

Stubble speaks of those men and women who are without God, who have no "sap" of the Holy Spirit flowing in them and no fruit of the Spirit to indicate His indwelling.

They are no more than dead stalks: useless to God and useless to man. (The following scriptures show clearly that *stubble* has been used as a traditional, biblical symbol of evil men and their evil works - Ex. 15:7, Jb. 21:18, Ps. 83:13, Is. 5:24;47:14, I Cor. 3:12.)

According to Malachi 4:1, such persons will have no protection against the devastating judgments that will fall at the climax of this age:

> *"For, behold, the day cometh, that shall burn as an oven; and all the proud, yea, and all that do wickedly, shall be **stubble**: and the day that cometh shall **burn them up**, saith the Lord of hosts, that it shall leave them neither root nor branch."*

● Moreover, when the end comes, Jesus will be "revealed from heaven...IN FLAMING FIRE taking vengeance on them that know not God, and that obey not the gospel of our Lord Jesus Christ." (II Th. 1:7-8, See Ps. 50:3, Is. 66:15-16)

Malachi lamented concerning this day, saying:

> *"...who may abide the day of His coming? and who shall stand when He appeareth? for He is like a refiner's fire..."*
>
> (Malachi 3:2)

Only those who have yielded in advance to His intensely hot, heaven-sent fire will be ready for the grand and glorious appearance of the King of kings.

In that day - again, let it be emphasized - there "shall NOT BE ANY remaining of the house of Esau" and there will NOT BE ANY worldly attitudes remaining in us...for our God will remove every trace of opposition to His rule.

No wonder the Song of Solomon 8:6 discloses that the jealousy of God is as "severe as Sheol; its flashes are flashes of *fire*, the very *flame of the Lord*" - a *"most vehement flame."* (See NAS, AV)

COMPLETING THE FIRE/FLAME ANALOGY

Joseph was just one of twelve sons born to Jacob.

Even as a fire is made up of many individual flames, blending together as one, so the house of Jacob, under the Old Will, was comprised of twelve sub-houses. Each one of these sub-houses, including the house of Joseph, became an individual tribal *flame* making up the whole of that holy *fire* called Israel. (See Obadiah 18)

This pattern and analogy continues in the New Testament.

Every local body of believers should be a *flame* in their own communities, that united together, produces a raging conflagration called "the church" - burning to every corner of the earth.

● **The Word of God is represented in Scripture as a *fire*.** ("His Word was in mine heart as *a burning fire* shut up in my bones." Jeremiah 20:9, See also 5:14; 23:29)

The Spirit of God is also represented as fire. (Jesus came to baptize His own with "the Holy Ghost and with *fire*." Luke 3:16)

Because we have been begotten of the Word (which is *fire*) and born of the Spirit (which is *fire*) we have received a *fire-nature*.

It is interesting to see that when the *fire* of God's Spirit consumed the burning bush or mount Sinai, next you find the hot, *fiery*, anointed Word proceeding out of those objects so affected. So it should be with us.

The *fire* of the Spirit should activate the *fire* of the Word within us.

● Psalm 104:4 reveals that the Most High:

> *"...maketh His angels spirits; His ministers*
> *A FLAMING FIRE."*

Although this is definitely a reference to angelic ministering spirits, in a certain sense, it is applicable to every believer as well. (See Hebrews 1:7-14)

We are called to be *ministers* by the standard of the New Covenant: *ministering* to God in worship and *ministering* to others through the Word and through the Spirit. (See I Peter 4:10)

So we are all called to be *flaming fires*...a product of the fiery stream that issues forth from the very throne of God.

Those angels called **seraphim** (a word meaning *to burn*) are revealed as guardians of the glorious throne of God and His blazing holiness. (See Is.6:1-6)

One of them bore a live coal from off the altar in heaven and laid it on Isaiah's lips. From that moment on, God's Word was in his mouth as *fire*. So we see that these adoring seraphim, who burn with fervency toward God, at times share the gift of a fervent heart with lowly human beings. In the "holy of holies" on high, they "rest not day and night, saying Holy, holy, holy, Lord God Almighty, which was, and is, and is to come." (Revelation 4:8)

Neither should we rest in our adoration of the Great I Am, when we experience heaven's fire...and become His "holy of holies" on earth. His Shekinah glory now abides within us. Therefore, with every waking moment, praise should be the unquenchable passion of our inner man.

● **It behooves us to remember that the fire in Solomon's temple, which originally fell from heaven, was NEVER TO GO OUT!** By God's command, the priests kept combustible fuel on the altar so the flame and smoke would continue ascending before Jehovah.

The use of "strange fire" - fire of earthly origin - was a crime punishable by death. (See Leviticus 10:1-2, Numbers 3:4;26:61)

In a similar way, our spirits must be ignited with the true fire from above if our worship is to be acceptable to God. By the Word and by the Spirit we should daily *"stir up the gift of God"* within our hearts. (Note: This phrase - *stir up* - comes from an original Greek word *anazopureo* which means *to kindle afresh*, in essence, *to fan a flame*). (II Timothy 1:6)

All the cults, sects, societies and religions of this world - even some that claim to be "Christian" - produce and provide a "strange fire," of earthly and even hellish origin, that leads to deception, death and everlasting ruin.

We must not perish with them because of lack of knowledge. Rather, we must become versed in God's Word and sensitive to His Spirit that we might provide Him with a suitable "hearth" (or heart) in which He can place His burning presence. (See Zechariah 12:6)

Isaiah 31:9 reveals that God's *fire* is in Zion, and His furnace in Jerusalem."

Those who are eternally a part of this holy city will eternally burn with the ecstasy of His holy presence.

THE FIRE OF REVIVAL

● **The name and life of a unique Old Testament figure - King Josiah - provide a perfect illustration of the fulfillment of this *title* for all of us.**

Josiah began reigning over Judah around 634 B.C. He assumed the throne at the age of eight during a period in which the Jews were drowning in their own apostasy. Many decades of corrupt leadership, both political and religious, had taken its toll on the nation.

At the age of sixteen, Josiah began to "seek after the God of David his father." As a result, he initiated great reforms, purging the land of idolatry and repairing the temple of Solomon. (II Chronicles 34:3)

Josiah's name means *the fire of the Lord* or *Jehovah supports.*

How appropriate a name for the one whose heart burned with jealousy for God at such an early age! Jehovah undergirded and *supported* his soul with a *fiery* revelation of Himself, and through this righteous and fervent king, spread the *fire* of revival throughout the land.

Studying Josiah's life is of great importance to us, even more so, because he ruled in the "last days" of Judah and Jerusalem. It was just prior to the Babylonian invasion and the heartbreaking time of captivity that resulted.

Unfortunately, even though this surge of reformation and renewal was genuine, the sins of the people had mounted up to heaven for so long and to such degree that - "the Lord turned not from the fierceness of His great wrath." (II Kings 23:26)

In an even more profound way, we too are living in the "last days."

The fierceness of God's wrath is building up to an irreversible climax and will soon break forth, like a whipping, raging, wind-blown *fire*, on this untoward and adulterous generation.

But before *the fire of divine fury* comes, there will first be a great breaking forth of *the fire of revival* as God raises up a multitude of Josiah-like men and women to proclaim His name. The Word of God will be in our mouths as fire and the people wood "and it shall devour them." (Jeremiah 5:14)

Though the lust-filled children of darkness have their tongues "set on *fire* of hell," ours will be set on *fire* of heaven. (James 3:6)

Through us, God will fight *fire* with *fire*.

The "spirit of burning," that cleanses and sanctifies, will overpower the hearts and lives of multiplied thousands of repentant individuals as Jesus prepares this world for His return. (Isaiah 4:4)

● As fire is one of the most irresistible, uncontrollable and unpredictable things in nature, so should be this final "rising up" of God's army.

Joel said - "A *fire* devoureth before them; and behind them *a flame* burneth...like the noise of *a flame of fire* that devoureth the stubble, as a strong people set in battle array." (Joel 2:3,5)

As individual flames unite together as one, so we, the soldiers of Jesus Christ, must unite together with ardent enthusiasm and passionate zeal, to fulfill this final purpose and plan of God.

Many years ago John Wesley exclaimed:

> *"If I had three hundred men who feared nothing but God, hated nothing but sin, and were determined to know nothing among men but Jesus Christ and Him crucified, I WOULD SET THE WORLD ON FIRE!"*

This is still true today.

If God only had a few fearless men and women in every community, like Gideon's army, who would courageously sound out the trumpet blast of the Gospel message, break the clay vessel of their carnal nature, and reveal the fiery light burning within, the enemy would surely be set to flight.

What we need is another trip to the upper room, where we can receive a fresh baptism of the Holy Ghost! When this happens, the cloven tongues of fire (the outward evidence of a burning, inward experience of God) should be evident to all.

● So this is our *hope of glory*: that by abandoning ourselves to God's *fiery* influence, we will become one of His *flames*.

No longer self-willed.

No longer of the world.

No longer cold and indifferent to that which is spiritual and eternal.

No longer selfish and self-centered.

But ablaze with commitment to God.

A PRAYER OF JIM ELLIOT

In the light of these final statements, there is no better way to close this chapter than to quote a prayer of Jim Elliot, a notable missionary/martyr who gave his all to reach the unreached Auca Indian tribe of South America:

> *"God makes His ministers a flame of fire. Am I ignitable? God, deliver me from the dread asbestos of "other things." Saturate me with the oil of Thy Spirit that I may be a flame. Make my life Thy fuel, Flame of God."*

94

THE GLORY

---

*"And the Lord will create upon every dwelling place of mount Zion, and upon her assemblies, a cloud and smoke by day, and the shining of a flaming fire by night: for upon all **THE GLORY** shall be a defense."*

(Isaiah 4:5)

*"For as the girdle cleaveth to the loins of man, so have I caused to cleave unto Me the whole house of Israel and the whole house of Judah, saith the Lord; that they might be unto Me for A **PEOPLE**, and for A **NAME**, and for A **PRAISE**, and for A **GLORY [MY PEOPLE FOR MY RENOWN AND PRAISE AND HONOR]**: but they would not hear."*

(Jeremiah 13:11 AV, NIV)

*"At that time will I bring you again, even in the time that I gather you: for I will make you A **NAME AND A PRAISE AMONG ALL PEOPLE OF THE EARTH**, when I turn back your captivity before your eyes, saith the Lord."*

(Zephaniah 3:20)

*"...and under **HIS GLORY** He shall kindle a burning like the burning of a fire."*

(Isaiah 10:16)

A PEOPLE   A NAME
A PRAISE   A GLORY

HIS PEOPLE FOR HIS RENOWN
AND PRAISE AND HONOR

A NAME AND A PRAISE
AMONG ALL PEOPLE
OF THE EARTH

HIS GLORY

THE GLORY OF CHRIST

THE HOUSE OF HIS GLORY

"...they are the messengers of the churches, and THE GLORY OF CHRIST."

(II Corinthians 8:23)

"...they shall come up with acceptance on Mine altar, and I will glorify THE HOUSE OF MY GLORY."

(Isaiah 60:7)

THE GLORY

> *"And the Lord will create upon every dwelling place of mount Zion, and upon her assemblies, a cloud and smoke by day, and the shining of a flaming fire by night: for upon all THE GLORY shall be a defense."*
>
> (Isaiah 4:5)

● Of all the chapters in this sixth volume of **OUR GLORIOUS INHERITANCE**, this is probably the most fitting.

For our greatest *hope of glory* is to actually become *God's glory*: His greatest accomplishment in all of creation, the object of His devotion and His source of greatest praise.

In Isaiah 46:13 Jehovah-God refers to His covenant people as *"Israel My glory"* and in Isaiah 43:5-7 He encourages them, saying:

> *"Fear not: for I am with thee: I will bring thy seed from the east, and gather thee from the west;*
> *I will say to the north, Give up; and to the south, Keep not back: bring My sons from far, and My daughters from the ends of the earth;*
> *Even every one that is called by My name: FOR I HAVE CREATED HIM FOR MY GLORY..."*

By these two Scripture references we can deduce that God's people are primarily termed *His glory* for we, of all created beings, are uniquely able to supply Him with *the glory* He deserves.

● **We should consider the following partial glory-list:**

We are a source of glory to God because of the salvation He has wrought in our lives.
Romans 15:7 declares that because we believed the gospel "Christ also received us to *the glory of God.*"

We are a source of glory to God especially when we arise stronger than sin, sickness, satanic adversaries or adverse circumstances in our lives.
Isaiah 25:3 confesses to God that "the strong people *glorify* Thee."

We are a source of glory to God when He responds to our prayers in times of tribulation.
In Psalm 50:15 He promised - "Call upon Me in the day of trouble: I will deliver thee, and thou shalt *glorify* Me."

We are a source of glory to God when we live holy, sanctified lives.
In I Corinthians 6:15-20 and Ephesians 2:21 the Scripture reminds us that

we are the temple of God, called to be holy, and have been "bought with a price." So Paul urges believers to - *"glorify* God in your body, and in your spirit, which are God's."

We are a source of glory to God when we dedicate our actions and activities in life to Him and to the furtherance of His kingdom.
I Corinthians 10:31 commands - "whatsoever ye do, do all to *the glory of God."*

We are a source of glory to God when our hearts are full of praise.
In Psalm 50:23 God claimed - "Whoso offereth praise *glorifieth* Me..."

We are a source of glory to God when we are fruitful in works and in the development of the divine nature within (the fruit of the Spirit).
In John 15:8 Jesus said - "Herein is My Father *glorified,* that ye bear much fruit..."

And finally, we are a source of glory to God when we are persecuted for Jesus' sake or when we "suffer as a Christian." (I Peter 4:16)
I Peter 4:14 says - "If ye be reproached for the name of Christ, happy are ye; for *the spirit of glory* and of God resteth upon you: on their part He is evil spoken of, but on your part He is *glorified."*

● **We should consider that "glory" is associated with every part of the Godhead.**
Notice in the last verse quoted, the Holy Spirit is called *the spirit of glory.*
In Ephesians 1:17, the Father is entitled *the Father of glory.*
Then in James 2:1, Psalms 24:8, Isaiah 33:21 and Isaiah 49:5, respectively, the Son is referred to as *the Lord of glory, the King of glory* and *the glorious Lord* who is *"glorious* in the eyes" of the Father.
Furthermore, this triune *"God of glory,"* as He is called in Psalm 29:3, is totally involved in "bringing many sons unto *glory"*...and for this we are thankful. (Hebrews 2:10)

● It is interesting to see in I Corinthians 11:7 that man is spoken of as being "the image and *glory* of God: but the woman is the *glory* of the man."
In like manner, Jesus, the bridegroom, is spoken of as being "the brightness of [the Father's] *glory"* - but we, the bride of Christ, are the *glory* of the Son. (Hebrews 1:3)
In His great intercessory prayer for the church, Jesus even addressed the Father, saying - "All Mine are Thine, and Thine are Mine; and I am *glorified* in them." (John 17:10)
Our changed hearts and lives are a constant source of praise to Him and to the gospel that He preached.

● Ministers who preach this message of New Covenant reconciliation are called - "the messengers of the churches, and *the glory of Christ."* (II Corinthians 8:23)
Since all Christians are called, to one degree or another, to perpetuate Jesus' message, in a sense, we are all called to fill this *title-position* and be *the glory of Christ* in the midst of a dark and dreadful world.
How peculiar it is that God has chosen some of the very ones who have

"sinned and come short of *the glory of God*" to ultimately become *His glory*...in an exceptional and everlasting way.

But this is simply the merciful nature of our God and wonder of His plan:

> *"To the praise of the glory of His grace, wherein He hath made us accepted in the beloved."*
>
> (Ephesians 1:6)

CLEAVING TO GOD

● It must be reemphasized that the only way we can fill the position of being God's *glory* is to live separated, sanctified and consecrated lives.

We must be submissive to God's will and committed to His cause.

Otherwise, we are not a praise to Him, but rather, a source of disappointment and a shame to His name.

Jehovah's means of greatest *glory* was not in being the Jews' God while they were yet in the bondage of Egypt. On the contrary, His great *glory* was shown most by delivering them from that awful time of enslavement.

So also, God's source of *glory* in us is not in being our God while we are yet bound to our sins. His name is exalted most when we are delivered from this lustful world and give Him the credit for such strength. For *"God is the glory of [our] strength."* (Psalm 89:17)

● **One prime way of illustrating this point is found in Jeremiah 13.**

God told Jeremiah to put a linen girdle on his loins (probably a loincloth) as a symbol of the children of Israel.

To *"gird up the loins"* is a biblical expression that speaks of readying one's self for service.

For instance, I Peter 1:13 commands - *"gird up the loins* of your mind"* and Jesus said to His disciples - *"Let your loins be girded about,* and your lights burning; and ye yourselves like unto men that wait for their lord..."* (Luke 12:35-36, See also I Kings 20:11, Jeremiah 1:17, Isaiah 45:5)

At first, Jeremiah was not to let this article of clothing touch the water. Then God commanded that he hide it in the crevice of a rock in the Euphrates River until it was "marred" and "profitable for nothing." (Jeremiah 13:7)

This spoke of how, initially, the Jews were quite close to God and relatively untouched by the evil influence of the heathen. Unfortunately, later on, they too became "marred" and "profitable for nothing."

The Euphrates River was a body of water near Babylon, a heathen nation, full of idolatry, where the Jews would eventually be held captive. So the hole in the riverbed rock could have well represented the dungeons and prisons in which they would eventually be incarcerated.

Referring to the garment being marred and ruined, God said - "After this manner will I mar the pride of Judah, and the great pride of Jerusalem." (Jeremiah 13:9)

Judah was prideful partly because it contained the capital city of Jerusalem. Jerusalem was even more prideful because it hosted the temple and the king's palace, being the seat of the government, both in a secular and religious sense.

Instead of being sincere with God, though, they had become proud in their religiosity, glorying in an array of pompous ceremonies, and caught up in superficial, religious externalism. Moreover, they had drifted into idolatry and the corruptive practices associated with it.

But God had called them to something so much more meaningful, fulfilling and longlasting: real intimacy with the Creator Himself.

He expressed such a call in unique, symbolic terms:

> *"For as the girdle* **cleaveth** *to the loins of a man, so have I caused to* **cleave** *unto Me the whole house of Israel and the whole house of Judah, saith the Lord; that they might be unto Me for A PEOPLE, and for A NAME, and for A PRAISE, and for A GLORY: but they would not hear."*
>
> (Jeremiah 13:11)

The New International Version of the same passage says - "to be **MY PEOPLE FOR MY RENOWN AND PRAISE AND HONOR."**

The New English Bible explains - "to win a name for Me, and praise and glory."

This was the Creator's original purpose in choosing Israel, earlier expressed in such a touching way in Deuteronomy 26:18-19:

> *"And the Lord hath avouched thee this day to be His* **peculiar people,** *as He hath promised thee, and that thou shouldest keep all His commandments;*
>
> *And to make thee high above all nations which He hath made, in praise, and in name, and in honour; and that thou mayest be an holy people unto the Lord thy God, as He hath spoken."*

This entitlement - **a peculiar people** - means *a people who are separated, reserved exclusively unto God.*

This passage, and others previously quoted, prove undeniably that if we are to be a source of praise, renown and honor to God - if His name is to be exalted before the heathen through us - we must first obey His call to holiness, obedience and sanctity.

We must *cleave* to Him in covenant commitment, as a girdle *cleaves* to the loins of man.

● It is interesting to note that the word translated *cleaveth* in Jeremiah 13:11 is *dabaq,* also translated *followeth hard* in Psalm 63:8 - "My soul *followeth hard* after Thee."

Dabaq is the word used in Adam's prophecy concerning how a man would "leave his father and his mother, and ...*cleave* unto his wife: and they shall be *one flesh."* (Genesis 2:24)

102

It is also found in the Joshua 23:8 command that God's people should *"cleave unto the Lord."*

To do this we must walk in the conscious awareness that we are married to *the God of glory,* and "he that is joined unto the Lord is one spirit." (I Corinthians 6:17)

In *cleaving* unto the Lord or *following hard* after God, we enter the intimacy and spiritual passion of the "bride spirit." We realize we are His bones and flesh, and we yearn to walk in perfect submission to His will.

God has opened the door for such a relationship, but it is up to us to cultivate it and fulfill its requirements.

If we refuse, we will doubtless become polluted by the muddy waters of this world, "marred" and "profitable for nothing" like Jeremiah's loincloth.

But if we respond in obedience we will instead be for *"glory and beauty,"* like the curious girdle of the ephod worn by the high priest.

We will adorn our great High Priest in a *glorious* and *beautiful* way, by presenting an attractive and convincing witness to this lost world of what God can do for those who believe and yield.

Through us, His fame will be spread abroad, His name will be exalted, and the great glory of His true character will be vindicated.

In a New Covenant sense, we will fulfill the Jeremiah 13:11 promise excellently and become...**HIS PEOPLE FOR HIS RENOWN AND PRAISE AND HONOR.**

We will be, for God Almighty, **A PEOPLE, A NAME, A PRAISE** and **A GLORY.**

God, let it be so, in Jesus name!

THE PROMISE OF DIVINE DEFENSE

● **Our main *title-passage,* Isaiah 4:5, is one of the most interesting and edifying promises contained in this revelation.**

In it we are referred to as **THE GLORY** - so translated from the Hebrew *kabod,* which speaks of *something weighty, as being laden with honor.*

To pinpoint the full meaning of this verse, though, and to grasp its importance, we must first review its context.

Verse two of the same chapter is a Messianic prophecy that refers to Jesus as "the branch of the Lord" who will be "beautiful and glorious." Then, in an apparent reference to New Covenant offspring, it states that the "the fruit of the earth" [that which grows on the branch] "shall be excellent and comely for them that are escaped of Israel." (See Zec. 3:8; 6:12, Jer. 23:5)

Verse three, on its highest level, unveils the sanctifying effect of the New Covenant. It promises that "he that is left in Zion...shall be called holy, even every one that is written among the living in Jerusalem." The "living" are those who are alive in Christ, quickened and made holy by His life-giving Spirit.

Verse four then foretells that God will wash away "the filth of the daughters of Zion" and purge "the blood of Jerusalem" (our guiltiness in the sight of God)

103

by *"the spirit of judgment, and by the spirit of burning."*

Surely this is a reference to the experience of salvation when Jesus brings the sin of a repentant person under *judgment* and cleanses them by the burning, sanctifying *fire* of the Holy Ghost.

It should be remembered that Satan was brought under *judgment* at Calvary and Jesus became our substitute in *judgment* there. *The spirit of judgment* reveals and activates these truths in our lives.

Moreover, Hebrews 12:29 testifies that "our God is a consuming *fire.*" When He comes into our lives, by *the spirit of burning,* He proceeds to purge out of us all that is unlike the nature of deity. (See also Ro. 8:3, Jn. 16:11)

● **Now let us read verse five, our main *title-verse,* and verse six in entirety:**

> *"And the Lord will create upon every dwelling place of mount Zion, and upon her assemblies, a cloud and smoke by day, and the shining of a flaming fire by night: FOR UPON ALL THE GLORY SHALL BE A DEFENSE.*
>
> *And there shall be a tabernacle for a shadow in the daytime from the heat, and for a place of refuge, and for a covert from storm and from rain."*

Mount Zion is now a place of spiritual gathering, the united and worshipful response of God's people worldwide. (See Heb. 12:22 for scriptural proof)

Every dwelling place of mount Zion could mean every individual, family or home consecrated to the Lord.

The assemblies of mount Zion is a phrase describing meetings that are much larger - church meetings, Bible study groups, open-air crusades and so on - all truly anointed worship gatherings in the New Covenant Age.

Over both of these - *the dwelling places and assemblies of mount Zion* - God promises *" a cloud and smoke by day, and the shining of a flaming fire by night."*

The *cloud by day* is protection from the intense light and heat of a desert day. *The fire by night* is protection from the gripping cold and the hidden dangers that lurk in every desert night.

The spiritual application of this dual-promise is very apparent.

This world is nothing but a desert and a wilderness to those who love God.

But our God is still a pillar of fire leading us through this "wilderness of Sin" into the joy of a "Promised Land" inheritance.

He is always there, burning toward us with fervent love, guiding us with His eye, delivering us from our enemies and giving us light in the night.

For the Jews of old, the pillar of a cloud was literal and visible. It was the **angel of the Lord** that went before them (an Old Testament term for the preincarnate Christ). In this pillar dwelt the name of God and out of it He spoke.

For us, this pillar is figurative, spiritual and invisible, but real just the same.

It is the "secret of His presence" that hovers over us constantly...the angel of the Lord that camps round about them that fear Him.

He will never leave us nor forsake us.

He will ever be our covering and our shield for He pledged - "upon all *the glory* shall be a *defense."* (Isaiah 4:5)

During the Jews' trek through the wilderness the pillar of a cloud by day and the pillar of a fire by night usually hovered over the tabernacle...for in the holy of holies the *glory* rested upon the mercy seat between the cherubim...insomuch that the ark was even called *"His glory."* (Psalm 78:61)

BUT NOW, WE HAVE BECOME GOD'S TABERNACLE; OUR REGENERATED SPIRITS HAVE BECOME HIS NEW HOLY OF HOLIES WHERE THE ARK OF THE COVENANT AND *THE GLORY OF GOD* ABIDE. How much more, therefore, should we now be termed *His glory!* The host of heaven must watch over us constantly, for the promise is established - "upon all *the glory* shall be a defense." (Isaiah 4:5)

● It is valuable to see that the word translated *defense* in this verse is *chuppah* (a word rendered *defense* only once).

Chuppah is translated *chamber* in Psalm 19:4-5 ("...the sun, which is as a bridegroom coming out of his *chamber...").*

It is translated *closet* in Joel 2:16 ("Let the bridegroom go forth of his chamber, and the bride out of her *closet").*

In both cases the reference is to *a marriage canopy* where a Jewish bride and bridegroom would traditionally reside during that first week of their intimacy, their time of "coming together."

So in this initial stage of the heavenly Bridegroom *cleaving* to His earthly bride, we abide under His cloud by day and fire by night: a celestial kind of *marriage canopy,* a covering of God's everlasting love. (See Is. 4:5 NAS)

As the bride is *the glory* of the bridegroom, so we are *His glory* now.

We are His *hidden ones,* His *protected ones,* His *bride....*laden with that lasting honor that comes from God above.

In time of trouble, we can always go to Jesus. We know that He is - "a tabernacle for a shadow in the daytime from the heat, and for a place of refuge, and for a covert from storm and from rain." (Isaiah 4:6)

This is also our *hope* in the midst of a hopeless world.

THE GLORIOUS CULMINATION

● In an epistle to the church he had birthed in Thessalonica, the apostle Paul asked a thought-provoking question:

> *"For what is our hope, or joy, or crown of rejoicing?"*

Then he answered:

> *"Are not even ye in the presence of our Lord Jesus Christ at His coming?*
> *For ye are OUR GLORY and joy."*
> (I Thessalonians 2:19-20)

At another time, he addressed the dearly beloved brethren of the Philippian church as his *"joy and crown."* (Philippians 4:1)

If Paul, under inspiration, could refer to small portions of the church in this way, is it not to be expected that God, on a much grander scale, would declare to all His offspring:

"You are My hope, My glory, My joy and
My crown of rejoicing."

The Thessalonian church was proof that Paul's ministry in that city was not in vain. So the church as a whole is proof that Jesus' ministry on this earth and His death on Calvary were not in vain.

We are *His hope* and *His glory.*

As Paul confessed, this will become all the more apparent "in the presence of our Lord Jesus Christ at His coming." (I Thessalonians 2:19)

The words *glory, glorified* and *glorious* are very much associated with this wonderful future event.

In that day, He who "hath triumphed *gloriously*" will reign "before His ancients *gloriously*"..."when He shall come to be *glorified* in His saints, and to be admired in all them that believe." (Ex. 15:1, Is. 24:23, II Th. 1:10)

Upon Him shall hang "all *the glory of His Father's house, the offspring and the issue....*" (Isaiah 22:24)

We are those offspring and our *blessed hope* is the promise that Jesus will return in "power and *great glory.*" (Matthew 24:30)

● On its highest level of interpretation, the following prophetic passage refers to this blessed and rapturous day of the resurrection and translation of God's people:

"At that time will I bring you again, even in
the time that I gather you: for I will make you
A NAME AND A PRAISE AMONG ALL
PEOPLE OF THE EARTH, when I turn back
your captivity before your eyes, saith the
Lord."

(Zephaniah 3:20)

● Another translation of this verse claims that God will give us **"A NAME OF DISTINCTION AMONG ALL THE PEOPLES OF THE EARTH."**

At the *"glorious appearing* of the great God and our Saviour Jesus Christ," He will make "His *glorious voice* to be heard" and gather us with "His *glorious arm.*" (Titus 2:13, Isaiah 30:30; 63:12)

We will then emerge as the *"glorious church"* with *"glorious power,"* possessing bodies "fashioned like unto His *glorious body.*" (Ephesians 5:27, Colossians 1:11, Philippians 3:21)

All creation will experience the *"glorious liberty* of the children of God," for the *"glorious gospel"* will have its full effect. (Ro. 8:21, II Cor. 4:4)

As **THE HOUSE OF HIS GLORY,** His true and everlasting temple, we will dwell in the *"glorious land"* and worship in the *"glorious holy mountain."* (Isaiah 60:7, Daniel 11:41, 45)

There the *"glorious Lord"* - who is *"glorious in power"* and *"glorious in holiness"* - "will be unto us a place of broad rivers and streams." And "His rest shall be *glorious."* (Isaiah 11:10; 33:21, Exodus 15:6,11)

As the King's daughter, we will be *"all glorious within,"* adorned with the wrought gold of the divine nature. (Psalm 45:13)

We will inherit *"the throne of glory"* and a *"crown of glory"*: ruling in God-given honor and majesty over a restored paradise-creation. (I Samuel 2:8, I Peter 5:4)

The difficult days of being captivated in the bonds of fallen human flesh will be over. "For our light affliction, which is but for a moment, worketh for us a far more exceeding and eternal *weight of glory"*. (II Corinthians 4:17)

Having been sown in corruption and dishonor we will then be *"raised in glory."* (I Corinthians 15:43)

Having beheld "as in a glass *the glory of the Lord"* we will then be "changed into the same image *from glory to glory."* (II Corinthians 3:18)

In that day, the world will no longer "provoke *the eyes of His glory"* but will capture His affectionate and appreciative gaze. (Isaiah 3:8)

Habakkuk foretold that this earth will be "filled with the knowledge of *the glory of the Lord,* as the waters cover the sea." (Habakkuk 2:14, See also Psalm 72:19, Isaiah 6:3)

God will "set *glory* in the land of the living" and make "the place of [His] feet *glorious."* (Ezekiel 26:20, Isaiah 60:13)

"The wise shall inherit *glory,"* be received into *glory* and "be joyful in *glory"* (*glory* being another name for the eternal state). (Pro. 3:35, Ps. 73:24; 149:5)

Concerning Jerusalem in the Kingdom Age and the New Creation to come, Psalm 87:3 says - *"Glorious* things are spoken of thee, O city of God."

Isaiah 60:19 prophesied of this holy city saying - "the Lord shall be unto thee an everlasting light, and thy God thy *glory."*

In that day, all sin and error will be gone from God's own. We will be established and rooted forever - "trees of righteousness, the planting of the Lord, THAT HE MIGHT BE GLORIFIED." (Isaiah 61:3, See also 60:21)

As we consider all these wonderful details of **OUR GLORIOUS IN-HERITANCE,** we can understand why Isaiah declared with such intensity:

> *"Sing, O ye heavens; for the Lord hath done it: shout, ye lower parts of the earth: break forth into singing, ye mountains, O forest, and every tree therein: for the Lord hath redeemed Jacob, and GLORIFIED HIMSELF IN IS-RAEL."*

> (Isaiah 44:23)

● So it is clear to see by now that all of the *glorious* things God will do will one day *gloriously* return to Him as praise.

At the start Jesus prayed - "Father...*the glory* which Thou gavest Me I have given them." (John 17:1,22)

In the end, all the combined *glory* of all His redeemed people will be heaped together, melted down, and forged into a splendorous *"crown of glory* in the hand of the Lord." (Isaiah 62:3)

By crowning the New Creation with the bride of Christ (His most glorious achievement of all) He will simultaneously be crowning Himself with all the acclaim that will accompany such a spectacular, redemptive act.

As Isaiah 63:14 states - HE WILL MAKE UNTO HIMSELF "A GLORIOUS NAME."

By choosing us to be for **A PEOPLE, A NAME, A PRAISE** and **A GLORY,** He will provide for Himself a source of honor that will never end.

Such enlightening truth is an integral part of *the cord of hope* that binds our hearts to the very heart of God; *the helmet of hope* that protects our minds from the oppression of this world; and *the anchor of hope* that firmly holds our souls to that which is beyond the veil.

So let us "make His praise *glorious*." (Psalm 66:2)
And let us ever be careful that:

> *"Unto Him be glory in the church by Christ Jesus throughout all ages, world without end. Amen."*
>
> (Ephesians 3:21)

108

• HIDDEN ONES •

PROTECTED ONES

TREASURED ONES

PRECIOUS ONES

"They have taken crafty counsel against Thy people, and consulted against Thy HIDDEN ONES [Thy TREASURED ONES, Thy PROTECTED ONES, Thy PRECIOUS ONES]."
(Psalms 83:3 AV, RSV, NAS, RBV)

HIDDEN ONES

*"They have taken crafty counsel against
Thy people, and consulted against Thy HID-
DEN ONES."*

(Psalm 83:3)

● This comforting *title - hidden ones -* is itself *hidden* amid the bulk of Scripture, appearing only one time in the entire Holy Writ.

It is so translated from the Hebrew *tsaphan,* a primary root which basically means *to hide (by covering over).*

Though this is an Old Covenant reference, it seems even more appropriate in a New Covenant setting.

Born again believers are *"hid with Christ in God,"* so that their sins, their very souls, are *covered over* by His love, His Spirit, His atoning blood. (Col. 3:3, See Ps. 32:1, Is. 30:1, I Pt. 4:8)

Tsaphan can also mean *to protect or reserve...*as a man who *protects* precious treasure, *reserving* it unto himself.

These word-associations become all the more applicable when we see that three other translations have rendered this *title* - His **PROTECTED ONES,** His **TREASURED ONES** and His **PRECIOUS ONES.** (Ps. 83:3 RSV, NAS, RBV)

O, what a supreme blessing it is to know these things: that in all of our trials, tribulations and temptations, we have this blessed and glorious *hope!* Our God will *protect* us, for we are His *treasure;* we are more *precious* to Him than His own blood. **In the time of trouble - as we will yet discover - He will** *hide* **us in His pavilion, under His wings, in His hand and in His quiver.**

HIDDEN IN HIS PAVILION

● Psalm 27:5 brings out this portion of **OUR GLORIOUS INHERITANCE** in an excellent way:

*"For in the time of trouble He shall hide
(tsaphan) me in His pavilion: in the secret of
His tabernacle shall He hide me: He shall set
me up upon a rock."*

In Psalm 31:20, David also confessed to the Most High concerning His saints:

*"Thou shalt hide them in the secret of Thy
presence from the pride of man: Thou shalt
keep them secretly (tsaphan) in a pavilion
from the strife of tongues."*

111

● Both of these verses speak of believers being hid in *God's pavilion.*
This is a unique analogy and worthy of our attention.

A pavilion is an enclosed place, quite often a temporary moveable tent or habitation. (Note: Two of the words translated *pavilion - cok* and *cukkah -* have also been translated *tabernacle* and *covert*; *cukkah* has been rendered *tent* and *booth* as well.)

When David spoke of being *hid in God's pavilion,* he must have been referring first to a literal tent; either the tabernacle of Moses or the tabernacle that David had erected on mount Zion for the worship of Jehovah.

In both of these, at different times, the ark resided, that golden box which contained the tablets of stone engraved with the fiery finger of the Almighty God. Crowning the ark was the mercy seat where yearly atonement was made by the sprinkling of blood. Between the cherubim, upon the ark, the Shekinah glory of God would appear.

In both of these tents, the priests ceaselessly ministered to God: in the tabernacle of Moses with blood sacrifices, and in the tabernacle of David with praise.

Because the presence of God manifested, at select times, in both of these sacred structures, surely the Jews considered them to be places of comfort, redemption, refreshing, visitation and spiritual renewal. Troubled Israelites would hurry to the tabernacle to be forgiven of their sins and restored to God. God's tabernacle, *God's pavilion,* was to them a place of refuge from the storms, pressures and burdens of life.

● **On a much higher level, David must have been referring to a spiritual *pavilion*: that place of communion with God to which covenant believers can always resort.**

Psalm 18:11 describes a time when God made "darkness His *secret place*; His *pavilion* round about Him were dark waters and thick clouds of the skies."

As we "move" through life, from one setting to another, from one experience to another, this spiritual *pavilion* - the overshadowing presence of God - "moves" along with us. Beyond the veil of darkness, beyond the thick clouds, He is always there: our place of refuge, our place of protection, our place of rest.

Within this transcendent *pavilion* (as it was with the earthly tabernacle) we find a "holy place" where we come to know Jehovah-God in the "lampstand light" of His Word. We discover, as well, an even deeper "holy of holies" where we experience sweet communion with Him through the manifestation of His Spirit, His *glory*.

This is our *hope of glory.*

If we become *His abode*, He becomes *our abode.*

If we become *His tabernacle*, He becomes *our tabernacle.*

If we become *His holy of holies,* where the ark of His covenant and the glory of God abides, then He becomes our *holy of holies* as well.

In coming to Him, we enter into a covenant relationship and discover "in Him" the symbolic fulfillment of everything that was in the literal ark of the covenant.

The tablets of stone relate to God's law being engraved in our hearts.

Aaron's rod that budded speaks of the priesthood calling given to believers, authority, enlightenment, a spiritual awakening, and resurrection life (to be explained in greater detail later in this volume).

The golden bowl full of manna represents the "hidden manna" of the deeper, soul-sustaining, soul-preserving, soul-satisfying revelation of God's Word. Both the written Word and the living Word are bread to the believer, sent down with the "dew of heaven" as the manna of old.

Furthermore, as the glory of God hovered over the ark in God's literal pavilion, so when we run into this spiritual "holy of holies," the glory of God hovers over us and even becomes our rereward (our rear guard). (See Isaiah 52:12)

The angels of the Lord camp round about us and watch over us constantly. The prideful and the unbelieving may speak against us; strife and contention may stir all around us; but we can still abide securely in *the secret of His presence.* (See Job 5:17-22)

"There is a *place* by Me," the Creator told Moses, who later responded by writing - "Lord, Thou hast been our *dwelling place* in all generations." (Exodus 33:21, Psalm 90:1, See Isaiah 40:22)

God's people have always been like nomadic desert dwellers, strangers passing through a barren wasteland of sin on a pilgrimage to another world.

We are full of victory and praise, though, for we have found that permanent spiritual *tent* - that *"tabernacle* that shall not be taken down; not one of the stakes thereof shall ever be removed, neither shall any of the cords thereof be broken." It is our God, who has always been - "an *hiding place* from the wind." For those who trust, He is now and will always be "a *tabernacle* for a shadow in the daytime from the heat, and for a place of refuge, and for a covert from storm and from rain." (Isaiah 4:6; 33:20, See also 32:2, Revelation 21:3)

HIDDEN UNDER HIS WINGS

● In a time of great persecution and distress, David also requested of the Lord:

> *"Keep me as the apple of the eye, hide me*
> *under the shadow of Thy wings."*
> (Psalm 17:8)

Another time, when fleeing from Saul, he and his men hid in a cave.

Knowing he needed yet a greater protection, he confessed to the Most High - "in *the shadow of Thy wings* will I make my refuge, until these calamities be overpast." (Psalm 57:1)

What a tender analogy this is! How it touches the heart to imagine God as a gentle, devoted and protective mother-bird, wrapping *wings* of compassion around weak, defenseless, trembling offspring.

Jesus even addressed rebellious Jerusalem saying - "how often would I have gathered thy children together, as a hen doth gather her brood under her wings, and ye would not." (Luke 13:34)

Now if such a promise was given to those who were stubbornly pitting themselves against Him, how much more does God give pledges, like the following, to those who are yielded:

> *"He that dwelleth in **the secret place** of the*
> *most High shall abide **under the shadow** of*
> *the Almighty.*
> *He shall cover thee with His feathers, and*
> ***under His wings** shalt thou trust..."*
>
> (Psalm 91:1, 4)

In this place of security and comfort, so near the very heart of God - "There shall no evil befall thee, neither shall any plague come nigh thy dwelling. For He shall give His angels charge over thee, to keep thee in all thy ways." No wonder the psalmist also asserted that *under His wings* - "Thou shalt not be afraid." (Psalm 91:5, 10-11)

● In completing this thought, it should be mentioned that being *hid under the shadow of God's wings* speaks of more than just security, comfort and loving protection. Such a blessed spiritual position also speaks of being reserved unto a certain calling or election and being nurtured by God until such an ordination is matured and perfected in us.

A prime example of this is found in the book of Exodus.

The Bible character is **Bezaleel.**

His name means *under the shadow of God.*

When God gave Moses the commission of making the tabernacle with all its luxurious and intricately designed furnishings, the Most High also explained:

> *"See I have called by name **Bezaleel**...*
> *And I have filled him with the Spirit of God,*
> *in wisdom, and in understanding, and in*
> *knowledge, and in all manner of workman-*
> *ship,*
> *To devise cunning works, to work in gold,*
> *and in silver, and in brass."*
>
> (Exodus 31:2-4)

● **This scripture-passage, in its application to this chapter on *Hidden Ones*, reveals an essential and edifying truth.**

From the time of His birth, Bezaleel was reserved *under the shadow of God's wings*. In other words, he was set aside unto a particular calling and election, and trained by God to fulfill the same.

No ordinary person could have performed such an important task. It had to be one chosen and anointed with God-given abilities.

Neither Moses, the great prophet, nor Aaron, the high priest, could have accomplished this work, for their abilities were in other key areas.

God had a man who was neither a prophet nor a priest, ordained to meet such a need.

In like manner, God has multitudes of men and women set aside - *hidden under the shadow of His wings* - appointed for specific and essentially important works in the body of Christ.

Similar to Bezaleel, many of these do not fill key leadership positions that are quite visible and awe-inspiring. Their abilities may be primarily natural rather than spiritual; and their callings may be subordinate and supportive; but they are chosen of God nonetheless.

From the moment of their spiritual conception, they are *hidden in God*, nurtured by Him unto a certain predetermined purpose...as are all of God's own. Their primary purpose, like unto Bezaleel's, is to provide, "A PLACE FOR THE LORD, AN HABITATION FOR THE MIGHTY GOD OF JACOB" - a "holy of holies" where the ark of His covenant can abide. (Psalm 132:5)

HIDDEN IN HIS HAND AND IN HIS QUIVER

● Isaiah spoke the following prophetic words concerning the Messiah who was, at that time, yet to come:

> *"And He hath made My mouth like a sharp sword; in the shadow of His hand hath He hid Me, and made Me a polished shaft; in His quiver hath He hid Me."*
>
> (Isaiah 49:2)

In this passage Jesus is spoken of as being *a choice arrow*, gripped in the Father's hand and *hidden* away in His *quiver* (a container for arrows).

As a polished shaft, with unhindered swiftness and inerring accuracy, He was shot out of God's bow toward a certain multifaceted target: the spoiling of Satan, the conquering of death, the destruction of sin's dominion, and the fulfillment of all that the Father sent the Son to accomplish.

● **But Jesus certainly was not, and is not, the only arrow in the Father's possession.** As the Father sent the firstborn Son, so has He sent us. We have inherited a similar calling and purpose.

Psalm 127 explains how "children are an heritage of the Lord" and are "as *arrows* in the hand of a mighty man."

It then explains - "Happy is the man that hath His *quiver* full of them."

So our God is a mighty man of war.

With a *quiver* full of *arrow-like* offspring, He goes forth to conquer the powers and principalities that rule this dark, fallen world. Psalm 45:5 protests that His *"arrows* are sharp in the heart of the king's enemies."

In a very real sense, we are those *arrows*.

We have been *hid in the shadow of His hand* - redeemed, protected and reserved unto a certain predetermined purpose - and nothing can pluck us out of His hand.

Moreover, we have also been stored safely in His *quiver* (the family of God), strengthened by the fellowship of other like-minded arrow-sons and arrow-daughters. At certain appointed times, He will load us in His bow and shoot *His polished shafts* toward that which opposes the progress of His kingdom in this world.

We need not be weak nor feeble in accomplishing such a purpose, for we are convinced of two things: the Captain of our salvation is an expert marksman and the strength of God has drawn the bow!

THE ONLY PLACE OF SAFETY AND DEFENSE

● Originally, Psalm 83 (the psalm that contains our *title-scripture*) was written by Asaph as a plea that Jehovah would protect Israel from their natural enemies: the Edomites, Ammonites, Jebusites and so on.

He prayed concerning those oppressive nations and their armies - "O my God, make them like a wheel; as the stubble before the wind. As the fire burneth a wood, and as the flame setteth the mountains on fire; so persecute them with Thy tempest, and make them afraid..." (Psalm 83:13-15)

Now our enemies are primarily spiritual, but we still need God's intervention and we still need a *hiding place*.

In these last days especially, just an outward show of religion will never suffice in bringing us into this portion of **OUR GLORIOUS IN-HERITANCE.** Multitudes join churches, adhere to Christian doctrines and participate in rituals, yet so many never find the true place of refuge.

They may even claim - "we have made a covenant with death, and with hell are we at agreement." But the Scripture goes on to say - "when the overflowing scourge [the judgment of the last days] shall pass through, then ye shall be trodden down by it." (Isaiah 28:15,18)

Because such individuals try to *hide* themselves "under falsehood," in the end, "the waters shall overflow *the hiding place*." (Isaiah 28:15, 17)

So there is both a false and a true *hiding place*.

Mere religion is the false.

A personal relationship with the living God is the true.

● In the beginning Adam tried to *hide* himself from the presence of the Lord in the garden. In the last days they will call to the rocks and mountains saying - "Fall on us, and *hide* us from the face of Him that sitteth on the throne." (Revelation 6:16)

But we seek not to hide ourselves FROM God; rather we desire deeply to be hidden IN God...for there is no place of greater safety.

And again, if we *hide* ourselves in God, God will *hide* himself in us (for "Verily, Thou art a God that *hidest* Thyself" - Isaiah 45:15).

In the *"hidden* part" He will make us to know wisdom - something Paul called "the *hidden* wisdom." (Psalm 51:6, I Corinthians 2:7)

He will feed us with *"hidden* manna" that the *"hidden* man of the heart" might grow in understanding and might. (Revelation 2:17, I Peter 3:4)

This *"hidden* man" is the born again, new creation part of every child of God, the *hidden* part in each of God's *hidden* ones.

In this inward, secret sanctuary we commune with the King of all creation - "in whom are *hid* all the treasures of wisdom and knowledge." (Col. 2:3)

If we mortify our members on this earth, shun that which is carnal, and set our affection on that which is heavenly, then we can enjoy all the benefits of such a spiritual position and heritage.

If we meekly submit to God's authority in our lives, He has promised that we can be *"hid* in the day of the Lord's anger." (Zephaniah 2:3)

Furthermore, we can look forward to that spectacular day when the sons of God shall no longer be *hidden,* but fully manifested in the splendor of eternal life:

116

*"For ye are dead, and your life is **hid with
Christ in God.***
*When Christ, who is our life, shall **appear,***
then shall ye also appear with Him in glory."
(Colossians 3:3-4)

This is the joy of our hearts, our *hope of glory* and our ultimate crown.

In that day we will no longer want to be *hidden,* nor will we need a place to *hide*...for all our enemies will be subdued and all our trials will be over.

But until that day...while we are still sojourning in this vale of tears...let us daily celebrate our confidence in Jehovah by singing and shouting the following words:

*"I will abide in Thy **tabernacle** for ever: I
will trust in the **covert** of Thy wings. **Selah.**"*
(Psalm 61:4)

*"Thou art my **HIDING PLACE**; Thou shalt
preserve me from trouble; Thou shalt compass
me about with songs of deliverance. **Selah**"*
(Psalm 32:7)

Both of the above verses end with the word **Selah.**

This term is most likely a musical notation meaning *Pause and reflect.*

It could not have been placed in any more appropriate verses.

For having discovered the everlasting *hiding place:* the spiritual tabernacle, the covert of His wings, and the family of God quiver...

And having discovered that we are His **HIDDEN ONES,** His **PROTECTED ONES,** His **TREASURED ONES** and His **PRECIOUS ONES...**

We should all *pause and reflect.*

We should *reflect* on the unfathomable goodness of our God, the exceeding greatness of our destiny, and the irrevocable security of our position.

Not only is *the glory* hidden in us...

We are hidden in *the glory.*

We are seated together in heavenly places in Jesus Christ.

This is our day-to-day source of strength...

This is "the true tabernacle, which the Lord pitched, and not man." (Heb.8:2)

And this is our *hope of glory*...

Both now and forevermore.

117

****

> *While I draw this fleeting breath,*
> *When my eyes shall close in death,*
> *When I rise to worlds unknown,*
> *And behold Thee on Thy throne,*
> *Rock of Ages, cleft for me,*
> *Let me hide myself in Thee.*

From *Rock of Ages*

by Augustus M. Toplady

****

• THE HUMBLE •

THE HUMBLE IN SPIRIT

A HUMBLE
AND LOWLY PEOPLE

• THE LOWLY •

"For thus saith the high and lofty One that inhabiteth eternity, whose name is Holy; I dwell in the high and holy place, with him also that is of a contrite and humble spirit, to revive the spirit of THE HUMBLE, and to revive the heart of the contrite ones."
(Isaiah 57:15)

"A man's pride shall bring him low: but honour shall uphold **THE HUMBLE IN SPIRIT.*"
(Proverbs 29:23)

"But I will leave among you ***A HUMBLE AND LOWLY PEOPLE.*** *And they will take refuge in the name of the Lord."*
(Zephaniah 3:12 NAS)

"Better it is to be of an humble spirit with ***THE LOWLY,*** *than to divide the spoil with the proud."*
(Proverbs 16:19)

THE HUMBLE

"For thus saith the high and lofty One that inhabiteth eternity, whose name is Holy; I dwell in the high and holy place, with him also that is of a contrite and humble spirit, to revive the spirit of THE HUMBLE, and to revive the heart of the contrite ones."

(Isaiah 57:15)

● **There are two spiritual kingdoms in this world that are continually clashing against one another, vying for the control of men's hearts.** One kingdom - the kingdom of darkness - is ruled by pride. The other - the kingdom of light - is ruled by *humility*. In the end, we know this kingdom of light will prevail, as will all who yield to its demands and its character.

Much of the Bible provides a striking contrast between the lofty and *the lowly*, the proud and *the poor*, the haughty and *the humble* and these two opposite kingdoms to which they belong.

It provides keen insight into the present status of both of these groups, and a sure word concerning their future destiny.

Those who are smug in their own conceits will never prosper in God now, nor will they ever inherit the glory of the kingdom which is yet to come.

On the contrary, those who are *humble* before God may live in the lowest, most despicable surroundings naturally, yet if their hearts are right with God, the promise has been given that they can dwell in the highest of all places spiritually - "the high and holy place" - with the lofty One who inhabits eternity.

This is the hidden place where God's *hidden ones* can always find sweet refuge. This is the spiritual realm, the heavenly tabernacle, where God "revives the spirit of **THE HUMBLE**" by His Word and His Spirit. (Isaiah 57:15)

And this is the reason that *hopeful* and *humble* ones can always look beyond their problems and courageously declare that - "I shall yet praise Him." (Psalm 42:11)

THE DEFINITION AND THE PRIME EXAMPLE

Our present day word *humble* comes from the word *humus* meaning *earth.*

Certain Hebrew and Greek words translated *humble* in Scripture have also been rendered *base, lowly, afflicted, needy, poor, abase* and *low estate.*

The Hebrew word rendered *humility - anavah -* is also translated as *gentleness* and *meekness.* The Greek word for *humility - tapeinophrosune -* is also rendered *lowliness.*

By these varied definitions, we obtain a full, round view of the meaning of this simple term. Blending them together, we come up with the following: to be persons of *humility* we must first be willing to admit that we are of the *earth* - mere *earthen* vessels - and therefore in great need of God's help.

We must acknowledge our humanity, how *poor* and *needy* we are in the sight of heaven, and be willing to *"afflict"* our own souls with repentance in order to receive His grace.

121

In our relationships with others, we must strive for *gentleness, meekness, and all lowliness.* In our lifestyle, we are commanded to "mind not high things, but condescend to men of *low estate."* (Romans 12:16)

Men and women of such character are not haughty, arrogant, or overly aggressive and self-assertive. They are not vain, overbearing, insolent or showy.

Very simply put, they are Christlike.

For it was the glorious Lord of all, veiled in human flesh, who walked in the midst of a prideful, self-sufficient world and gave the gentle invitation:

> *"Come unto Me, all ye that labour and are*
> *heavy laden, and I will give you rest.*
> *Take My yoke upon you, and learn of Me;*
> *for I am meek and lowly in heart: and ye shall*
> *find rest unto your souls.*
>
> (Matthew 11:28-29)

● It is somewhat startling, yet pleasant and heartwarming, to hear the King of all creation describe His own heart in such terms. It penetrates even deeper when we hear the challenge He gave each one of us to be His "yoke-fellow."

When animals share a yoke, they must be very cooperative: always willing to move at the same speed and go the same direction. Part of sharing Jesus' yoke is to cooperate with the influence of His indwelling character and move through life with the same kind of "lowliness of heart" that He manifested...toward God and toward man.

This is a healthy, soul-strengthening attitude, far removed from that false brand of humility which is self-condemning, self-defeating, negative, depressed and injurious to faith. On the contrary, this quality of character is positive, God-pleasing, faith-building, and kingdom promoting.

It is part of being crucified with Christ, a necessary step we must all take before we can share in His great success, His spectacular victory, His exalted status, His resurrection glory!

Philippians 2:5-9 presents the challenge:

> *"Let this same mind be in you, which was*
> *also in Christ Jesus:*
> *Who, being in the form of God, thought it*
> *not robbery to be equal with God:*
> *But made Himself of no reputation, and*
> *took upon Him the form of a servant, and was*
> *made in the likeness of men:*
> *And being found in fashion as a man, HE*
> *HUMBLED HIMSELF, and became*
> *obedient unto death, even the death of the*
> *cross.*
> *Wherefore God also hath highly exalted*
> *Him, and given Him a name which is above*
> *every name."*

Jesus was the firstborn Son, our divine example in all things.

Though higher than all, He thought it not "beneath His dignity" to become the servant of all. Though holy beyond description, He thought it not an insult to dwell among the defiled. Though strong in the absolute, He thought it not compromise to minister freely to the weak and unstable. Though existing from everlasting to everlasting, He thought it not waste to sacrifice His life for the helpless captives of time.

Now all God asks is that we follow suit...*humbling ourselves and becoming obedient unto death*...in order to serve others and fulfill a perpetuation of this purpose.

If we yield to this charge, the resulting rewards are clear:

● "God...giveth grace to the *humble*." (I Peter 5:5)
● "By *humility* and the fear of the Lord are riches, and honour, and life." (Proverbs 22:4)
● "He that *humbleth* himself shall be exalted." (Luke 14:11, See 18:14)
● "Honour shall uphold *THE HUMBLE IN SPIRIT*." (Proverbs 29:23)

THE DESTRUCTIVE AND DEADLY SIN

● **Before searching any further into the soothing subject of** *humility*, **let us first explore its opposite: the destructive and deadly sin of pride.**
Pridefulness was the first evil and disturbing influence in an otherwise placid and perfect, virgin creation. Lucifer (whose name means *Shining one* or *Light-bearer*) was the anointed cherub that covered the throne of God - "full of wisdom, and perfect in beauty." (Ezekiel 28:12)
But his heart was lifted up because of his radiant appearance and his exalted position. He ended up corrupting his own wisdom by reason of his brightness and was thrust out of heaven as a result. (And so will we be thrust out of a heavenly place of deep fellowship with God if we begin to glory in our own spiritual maturity and achievements.)
Lucifer's visage was grossly changed, marred by the ugliness of sin, and an angel of spectacular and unsurpassed splendor became nothing more than a hideous and repulsive, serpentine creature.
He is symbolically referred to as "a great red dragon" in the book of the Revelation and as the monstrous "Leviathan" in the Psalms, Job and Isaiah. He is also described as being *"king over all the children of pride."* (Job 41:1, 34, Psalms 74:14, Isaiah 27:1)
Job 41:15 further reveals that *"his scales are his pride."*
In other words, pridefulness has worked its way so deep into Satan's character that instead of grieving over his depraved and cursed state, he even glories over how haughty, hard and unrepentant his heart has become (*scaled-over*, impenetrable and resistant to any kind of conviction or godly sorrow).
How ironic it is that through pride, Lucifer lost the very things that initially birthed pride within him: his beauty and wisdom! And so it is, quite often, with those who are his offspring...who are among *"the house of the proud."* (Proverbs 15:25)

Having fallen by this deadly sin, it is no wonder that Lucifer then wielded it as a primary weapon of destruction against our foreparents in delightful Eden. "Ye shall be as gods," the wicked one whispered...and in believing this self-exalting lie, Adam and Eve's trouble began. (Genesis 3:5)

So if man's depravity, his shattered spiritual condition, began with a prideful lunge toward the dissolving mirage of greatness, it is only to be expected that his restoration into wholeness must necessarily begin with the uprooting of this weed and the cultivation of its opposite.

Andrew Murray said it powerfully and bluntly:

> *"Pride must die in you, or nothing of heaven*
> *can live in you."*

And Jesus penetrated to the very core of the issue when He reproved His disciples for their carnal competitiveness, saying:

> *"Verily I say unto you, Except ye be con-*
> *verted, and become as little children, ye shall*
> *not enter into the kingdom of heaven.*
> *Whosoever therefore shall **humble** himself*
> *as this little child, the same is greatest in the*
> *kingdom of heaven."*
>
> (Matthew 18:3-4)

By these two verses we see clearly that the kingdom cannot even enter into us and we cannot enter the kingdom, if this debilitating, crippling attitude - *pride* - resides within.

"A proud look" is first on the list of seven abominable things that God hates (So a "look of *humility*" must be first on the list of things He loves.)

"The pride of life" is listed along with "the lust of the flesh and the lust of the eyes" as being the main corruptive influences dominating the world system. (I John 2:16)

Surprisingly, the root evil of the city of Sodom, bringing the severe judgments of God, was not so much their perverted sexual sins. According to Ezekiel, it was their *"pride,* fulness of bread, and abundance of idleness."* (Ezekiel 16:49)

We find that the "wicked, through the *pride* of his countenance will not seek after God: God is not in all his thoughts." (So again it follows that *the humble* are those who follow hard after God and focus their thoughts, day and night, on His greatness and His glory.) (Psalm 10:4)

"Pride compasseth [the wicked] about as a chain." It is a self-imposed bondage and imprisonment to those who yield to its influence. (Psalm 73:6)

It is a sure means of self-deception. Galatians 6:3 states - "If a man think himself to be something, when he is nothing, he deceiveth himself." And to Edom, the prophet Obadiah declared - "the *pride* of thine heart hath deceived thee." (Obadiah 3)

It is the source of all dissension between individuals and nations for - "Only by *pride* cometh contention" - "He that is of a *proud* heart stirreth up strife" - and also - "In the mouth of the foolish is a rod of *pride.*" (Proverbs 13:10;28:25;14:3)

Sowing such haughtiness, boastfulness, and cold-hearted self-sufficiency definitely means reaping misery and tragedy in return.

God has already warned us in His Word:

- "When *pride* cometh , then cometh shame." (Proverbs 11:2)
- "*Pride* goeth before destruction." (Proverbs 16:18)
- "The Lord will destroy *the house of the proud.*" (Proverbs 15:25)

For this cause the proverb writer urged:

> *"Better it is to be of an humble spirit with*
> *THE LOWLY, than to divide the spoil with*
> *the proud."*
>
> (Proverbs 16:19)

In other words, it is better to have only minimal accomplishments and to have very little materially, yet maintain meekness and gentleness before God and man, as to have all the success and prosperity in this world and be steeped in arrogance and vanity.

WOE TO THE CROWN OF PRIDE

● **A person's dominant characteristic is what "crowns" him - affecting and influencing everything else that he says or does.**

"Woe to the crown of pride," God says. For when this attitude prevails in a person, it repels all the blessings and benefits God could potentially pour out. (Isaiah 28:1)

Like the silicone coating that makes certain normally absorbent materials become water-repellent, so pride makes our hearts Spirit-repellent and blessing-resistant. Like a spiritual dam, it cuts us off from the generous flow of mercy and favor that descends like a river from His throne.

Men and women can err in numerous ways, yet *humble* themselves under the mighty hand of God, and He will lift them up in due time.

For "though the Lord be high, yet hath He respect unto *the lowly*" - "He giveth grace unto *the lowly*" - so it is understandable why He said - "with *the lowly* is wisdom." (Psalm 138:6, Proverbs 3:34; 11:2)

(Note: this word *lowly* describes a person free from self-assertive pride and self-centered conceit. It is found six times in the KJV: four times it is a challenge to us; twice it is used in reference to Jesus - See Zec. 9:9, Mt. 11:29.)

Those who foolishly lift up themselves on a pedestal, though, God will lift no higher. Quite the contrary, He will cause them to be brought low until they learn well the lesson of His sovereignty, holiness and omnipotence.

A heart lifted up and a mind "hardened in pride" is sure to be melted by the fire of God's judgment (and to this Nebuchadnezzar of old can surely attest). (Daniel 5:20)

● **It must be emphasized that pride is not only a trap set for the wicked; it is a subtle, deceitful net set by the fowler to snare the saintly as well.**

For if the wicked one cannot succeed in wooing us into the depths of sin, he will lure us beyond the borders of true righteousness into that hard-hearted, judgmental, Pharisaical, holier-than-thou religiosity that renders a person useless, and even destructive, to the kingdom of God.

Jonathan Edwards, that famed revivalist of "the Great Awakening," gave this much needed, and often unheeded warning:

> *"Spiritual pride is the main door by which the devil comes into the hearts of those who are zealous for the advancement of truth. It is the chief inlet of smoke from the bottomless pit to darken the mind and mislead the judgment."*

C.S. Lewis also wisely observed:

> *"The devil is perfectly content to see you becoming chaste, brave and self-controlled, provided all the time he is setting you up in the Dictatorship of Pride."*

It is too easy to forget that, were it not for the grace of God, our plight on earth would be miserable and our hearts irreversibly corrupt. It is too easy to forget that we are totally dependent on Jesus.

So let us set fervent self-analysis and prayerful diligence as two watchmen over our souls lest this be the case in any of our lives.

And let us be wise as serpents: always mindful that the enemy's strategy is to build a man up so he can tear him down; but God's strategy is to tear a man down so He can build him up.

AN UNAVOIDABLE DEMAND

● Developing the quality of *humility* is not an option; it is not some "workshop elective" that can be ignored or overlooked. It is God's demand: a required part of our spiritual "curriculum"...if we are to receive our degree and graduate *cum laude* (with the honor and distinction that heaven alone can grant).

Such is only to be expected.

For if the faultless One on high "*humbleth* Himself to behold the things that are...in the earth," it is only logical that we fault-filled humans must *humble* ourselves to behold the things that are in heaven. (Psalm 113:6)

This does not necessarily mean groveling in the dust before God, or passively drawing back from making any attempts at manifesting our calling with authority.

As Abbe de Saint-Cyran explained:

> *There is no greater pride than in seeking to humiliate ourselves beyond measure and sometimes there is no truer humility than to attempt great works for God.*

In this area, just as every other area of Christian character development, we must strive for balance: not going to one extreme or the other.

● **The acquisition of humility will normally be accomplished one of three ways: either we take the initiative ourselves, negative circumstances push** us this direction, or God enforces His desire and firmly impresses our hearts with this trait. Without controversy, the former is the preferred course of action.

James 4:10 presents the mandate and promise - *"Humble yourselves* in the sight of the Lord, and He shall lift you up."

Moreover, in II Chronicles 7:14 God announces - "If My people, which are called by My name, shall *humble themselves, and pray...* then will I hear from heaven, and will forgive their sin, and will HEAL THEIR LAND."

O, the overflow of divine favor that descends when we take charge of our hearts this way; when we do not wait for circumstances or for God to do it, but when we out of sincere, mature devotion *humble ourselves* before the Creator. Of course, if we refuse, or neglect our spiritual duty, God knows exactly how to use every negative situation to produce the end result that He desires.

The Israelites, newly delivered from Pharaoh's bondage provide a perfect example. The Master Potter had to wedge out the pride of the Egyptian culture from the clay-like hearts of His people, that they might become vessels of excellence unto Him. So the trip from Egypt to the Land of Promise, that should have taken two weeks, INSTEAD TOOK FORTY YEARS.

Deuteronomy 8:2 explains that all the events during that difficult period transpired to *humble* the Israelites, to prove them, and to see what was in their hearts.

They were under "the mighty hand of God" - whether they liked it or not - and every day was an experience in being molded into submissiveness and obedience by the inescapable "pressure" of God's Word and Spirit.

God will surely work in a similar way with us. If we refuse to willfully *humble* ourselves in "the sight of the Lord" (taking the initiative) we may will end up HAVING to *humble* ourselves under the hand of God (as the Potter wedges out the carnal "grog" that is so offensive to Him).

We may even find ourselves wandering through some spiritual wilderness, taking years to achieve goals that could have, and should have, been attained in a much shorter span.

If this seems to be the handwriting on the wall against us, still, if we repent before the Master, He "giveth more grace." (James 4:6)

This gracious and generous God will grant us sufficient grace to show forth a *humble* attitude of heart, and then, in His amazing way, He will give us even more grace because of the *humility* we display.

Furthermore, if *humbling* ourselves before God can bring healing to our land - as II Chronicles 7:14 promises - how much more should it bring healing to our homes, our families, our minds, our emotions, our hearts, and even our bodies.

In the absolute end result, we will be healed and made every whit whole because of *humbling* ourselves before God - changed from corruption to incorruption, from mortality to immortality, from degeneration to regeneration.

THE HUMBLING EFFECT OF HUMAN RELATIONSHIPS

● **Human relationships serve God's purpose excellently in this particular area of sonship development...two primary ways.** They are often God's means of developing *humility* in us, as well as His means of testing or proving our commitment to this godly character trait.

This is true in all of our relationships, but especially in those relationships in which an arrogant attitude could go unchecked. **The following words of Benjamin Franklin are especially appropriate here:**

> *To show humility to superiors is duty; To*
> *show humility to equals is courtesy; But to*
> *show humility to inferiors - this is nobility!*

Furthermore, the *"humility* lesson" is not only something we learn in times of strife, conflict or confrontation. In the words of Bernard of Clairvaux:

> *"It is no great thing to be humble when you*
> *are brought low; but to be humble when you*
> *are praised is a great and rare attainment."*

So whether we are exhorting, rebuking, training, challenging or applauding one another, as we come together in covenant relationships, we quite often succeed in "knocking the rough edges off."

Let us therefore, consider the following two scriptures our daily goal:

> *"Let nothing be done through strife and*
> *vainglory; but in **lowliness of mind** let each*
> *esteem other better than themselves."*
>
> (Philippians 2:3)

> *"Yea, all of you be subject one to another,*
> *and be clothed with **humility**..."*
>
> (I Peter 5:5)

BOASTING IN THE LORD

● How true it is that when worship becomes too exuberant,too sincere and too Christ-centered, the proud almost always get uneasy! (Consider the Pharisees' reaction at Jesus' triumphant entry into Jerusalem for proof.)

The flesh delights to glory in its own achievements, to rejoice in outward religious trappings, to parade men's accomplishments before the eyes of all, to boast in natural things that will ultimately pass away. The psalmist cut against the grain of this carnal tendency when he declared:

> *"My soul shall make her boast in the Lord:*
> ***THE HUMBLE** shall hear thereof and be*
> *glad."*
>
> (Psalm 34:2)

The humble boast, not in their eloquent and intellectual pulpiteers, but in the Saviour who sends His grace to the most unworthy sinners who repent.

The humble boast, not in their successful promotional campaigns, but in the God who draws by the power of the Holy Spirit. *The humble* boast, not in those who pray for miracles, but in the God who supplies them from on high.

And as we have already discovered, just as *the humble* rejoice to exalt the Lord, so the Lord rejoices to exalt *the humble*. So - "Let not the wise man glory in his wisdom, neither let the mighty man glory in his might, let not the rich man glory in his riches." "But he that glorieth let him glory in the Lord." (Jeremiah 9:23, II Corinthians 10:17)

Isaiah described the last days as a dreadful time when:

> *"The lofty looks of man shall be **humbled**,*
> *and the haughtiness of men shall be bowed*
> *down, and the Lord alone shall be exalted in*
> *that day.*
> *For the day of the Lord of hosts shall be*
> *upon every one that is proud and lofty...and he*
> *shall be brought low."*
>
> (Isaiah 2:11-12)

Malachi also commented:

> *"For behold, the day cometh, that shall*
> *burn as an oven; and all **the proud**...shall be*
> *stubble: and the day that cometh shall burn*
> *them up.."*
>
> (Malachi 4:1)

● But Zechariah insisted that in the culmination a remnant would inhabit Jerusalem who would no longer be full of religious pride - "**A HUMBLE AND LOWLY PEOPLE**. And they will take refuge in the name of the Lord." (Zephaniah 3:12 NAS)

On its highest level of interpretation this could well be a reference to the glorified saints who will reign from the holy city during the Kingdom Age and the New Creation beyond.

All of the above scriptures prove that, in the end, a just, holy God will vindicate His own and deal out to the wicked a final recompense which is meet.

The lofty will finally be brought low.

The lowly will finally be lifted up on high.

In that day it will be proven of the Most High that - "He forgetteth not the cry of *the humble*." (Psalm 9:12)

Pride and self-will will end up debasing the once-exalted Lucifer and his confederate angels to the torment of the bottomless pit.

On the contrary, *humility* and repentance will end up lifting debased, fallen human beings to the measureless, incomparable height of heaven's throne.

We will dwell forever in "the high and the holy place"- revived, quickened by the quickening life of God, into the fulness of His image.

This is the secret of Jehovah's plan and our *hope of glory*.

● **In that day we will realize all the more that the Most High never has desired to dwell in buildings made with hands, but rather:**

*"This is the one I esteem: he who is **humble**
and contrite in spirit, and trembles at My
Word."*

(Isaiah 66:2 NIV)

Such a God-pleasing attitude, so overlooked by the world, will finally procure for God's own the unspeakable honor of being *His abode, His habitation, His rest, His temple* and *the place where His honour dwells*. In a spiritual sense, we will not only dwell in "the high and the holy place"; we will actually become His holy of holies for all eternity: the dwelling place of the ark of His Covenant, the permanent residence of His Shekinah splendor.

In the light of such anticipated glory, let us rejoice to yield every chamber of our hearts even now.

Many centuries ago, God refused to allow the ark of His covenant to share a temple with Dagon: a false Philistine deity, depicted as being half-fish and half-man. The God of the Jews actually cast this idolatrous statue face-first to the ground. When the priests of Dagon erected it a second time, not only did God topple the idol again, He cut off its head and arms. We who are God's present-day temple should seriously consider this story and take the necessary steps to purge every idol out of our lives...knowing that Jesus will not share the inner sanctuary of our hearts with any other worshipped person or thing.

May we gladly implement this attitude...until nothing reigns in us but devotion to the King of kings and utter submission to His will.

This is *true humility*, the path that leads to eternity and the fertile ground in which *hope* can grow to perfection.

> *Do not look at pride as only an unbecoming temper, or at humility as only a decent virtue. The one is death, and the other is life; the one is all hell, the other is all heaven.*
>
> *If you could see what a sweet, divine, transforming power there is in humility, how it expels the poison of your nature, and makes room for the Spirit of God to live in you, you would rather wish to be the footstool of all the world than lack the smallest degree of it.*
> Andrew Murray

THE PATIENT IN SPIRIT

*"Better is the end of a thing than the beginning thereof: and **THE PATIENT IN SPIRIT** is better than the proud in spirit."*
(Ecclesiastes 7:8)

THE PATIENT IN SPIRIT

"Better is the end of a thing than the beginning thereof: and THE PATIENT IN SPIRIT is better than the proud in spirit."

(Ecclesiastes 7:8)

● *A patient person is -*
...*one who bears pains or trials calmly or without complaint.*
...*one who shows longsuffering, gentleness or forbearance when under provocation or strain.*
...*one who is not hasty, anxious or impetuous.*
...*one who is steadfast despite opposition, difficulty or adversity.*
...*one who is able or willing to bear with problems or hardships.*

The original Hebrew of the word *patient* in the above *title-scripture* is *arek*, translated this way only once in the Old Testament. It is from the root word *arak* which means *long* (as one who suffers *long*, endures *long*, or perseveres *long*).

Sometimes we tend to think of a *patient person* as being one who has given up, resigned himself over to failure, and purposed to endure life in a joyless kind of way.

This definition is quickly exposed as being false under the scrutinizing light of the Word of God and the spirit of revelation.

When viewed from a biblical perspective, *patience* becomes something not dreary, but intense; not passive, but forceful.

Having a *patient spirit* does not mean we unresistingly submit to living in the doldrums; rather, it means we persistently keep paddling until we get out.

It does not mean being without motivation, fervency, zeal or commitment to a cause.

On the contrary, it means soldier-like dedication - in season and out of season - to all of the above.

The possessor of *patience* continues fighting the good fight of faith when others would put their swords in their sheaths and hang their shields on the wall.

The possessor of *patience* perseveres even when there are no apparent victories, no evident results, and no manifest successes.

Such a quality of character is truly admirable in the sight of men and in the sight of God.

Those who possess it are not tepid individuals.

Irregardless of the winds and waters of adversity,

The heat in their spirit refuses to diminish;

The fire in their soul refuses to burn low.

As the original Hebrew implies, it continues *long*...persistently shining forth when by all natural standards it should have been fatally snuffed out.

Such persons have a certain *hope of glory* - a God-given goal in life - and they intend to reach it, no matter what!

THE END OF A THING

● The next verse after our *title-verse* exhorts:

> *"Be not hasty in thy spirit to be angry: for*
> *anger resteth in the bosom of fools."*
>
> (Ecclesiastes 7:9)

Those who are "proud in spirit" are quick to release their temper, striking out angrily at any and all who oppose them.

The patient in spirit are those who have learned to walk in love.

They are calm, smiling in the face of rejection and opposition, knowing that God is in control.

They are peacemakers: full of forgiveness, longsuffering and faithfulness.

In a Christlike manner, they have tapped into such a deep well of compassion that even their enemies are given of its waters to drink.

Vessels of such quality tend to see things from an eternal perspective, so the pressure of the moment has far less of a debilitating effect.

They tend to look beyond fleshly, carnal, surface attitudes and see instead, the souls of men. They have learned to wait on God and let time perform its all-important task...in their own lives and the lives of others.

In hopeless situations they have learned to keep on hoping, knowing that:

> *"...we are saved by hope: but hope that is*
> *seen is not hope: for what a man seeth, why*
> *doth he yet hope for?*
> *But if we hope for that we see not, then do*
> *we with patience wait for it."*
>
> (Romans 8:24-25)

So **patience** could also be labeled *confidence in God, confidence in His promises, confidence that He holds the future in His hands, confidence that He will finally bring us forth to success and victory.*

Again, our *title-passage* claims that - *"the patient in spirit* is better than the proud in spirit."

A "proud in spirit" individual is usually a confident person as well, but his confidence is in the flesh, in his own will power, or in his own abilities.

A *patient in spirit* person is one whose confidence rests in the Most High alone - "whose *hope* the Lord is." (Jeremiah 17:7)

● Such *hope* - such *desire married to expectation* - should often compel true believers to confess the very beginning of our *title-passage:*

> *"Better is the end of a thing than the begin-*
> *ning thereof..."*
>
> (Ecclesiastes 7:8)

This is true with respect to the individual trials we go through (if we put our trust in the Most High God).

This is true with respect to our lives in entirety (if we surrender ourselves as clay in the Potter's hands and gold in the hands of the Refiner).

And this is true with respect to all of creation (for the New Creation will far surpass the original glory of Eden in splendor and depth).

In the beginning, Adam was of the dust.

In the end, those who are redeemed from the Adamic race will rise far above a dust-bound state. The promise has been given that we will shine like the sun in the kingdom of God.

The plan of God leading us to such a glorious goal is not hasty, but very gradual. It is not sporadic, but very steady in unfolding...

Like a blossoming flower,

Like a crystal in formation,

Like the development of a child within the womb.

Such things can never be rushed for they reach maturity at an appointed time. And as it is naturally, so it is spiritually...for those who are called the children of the Most High God. In any situation we can dare to say - "I shall yet praise Him!" (Psalm 42:11)

TWO WORDS AND SIX ARENAS

There are two Greek nouns translated into the word *patience* in the Scripture: *hupomone* and *makrothumia*.

Hupomone means *to abide under,* stemming from two other words, *hupo* which means *under,* and *meno,* which means *abide.*

Makrothumia also comes from two other words, *makros* which means *long* or *far* and *thumes* which means *hot, anger* or *wrath.*

It conveys the idea of one who is the opposite of a short-tempered person. Rather, they are *"long-tempered"* - long in being aroused to wrath, resentment, or a desire to retaliate. It also means *to bear long.*

The first word *hupomone* speaks of endurance, perseverance, and steadfastness. The second word *makrothumia* speaks more of longsuffering.

Both are translated *patience,* and along with the words *patient* and *patiently,* they form an arched gateway leading us into six arenas of life in which we are commanded to display this virtue.

Let us research them all, one at a time.

■ Patience with the unbeliever

II Timothy 2:24-25 commands that - "the servant of the Lord must not strive; but be gentle unto all men, apt to teach, *patient,* in meekness instructing those that oppose themselves; if God peradventure will give them repentance to the acknowledging of the truth."

How easy it is to get impatient, on-edge and angry with those who are blind to the gospel - especially family members. But let us consider our ways. Would we rail at some blind person who stumbles over a chair in their path, or would we rebuke a deaf person who does not respond to our call? Of course not. Yet those who are blind and deaf spiritually are just as prone to stumbling and just as incapable of responding to the proclamation of the gospel without the aid of God. They are captives of the devil at his own will.

So let us be *patient* - especially with our loved ones - knowing that no man can come to Jesus except the Holy Spirit draw Him. Our responsibility is to pray, live an exemplary life, and speak the truth in love.

Then with all *patience,* gentleness and mercifulness, we must wait for God to do the rest.

I Thessalonians 5:14-15 says it well:

> *"Now we exhort you, brethren, warn them that are unruly, comfort the feebleminded, support the weak, BE PATIENT TOWARD ALL MEN.*
>
> *See that none render evil for evil unto any man; but ever follow that which is good, both among yourselves, and to all men."*

■ Patience with other believers

In Romans 15:5, Paul prayed that - *"the God of patience and consolation grant you to be likeminded one toward another according to Christ Jesus."* Dwell on this truth. God has been so *patient* with His own, *consoling* us so often in times of weakness, disappointment and grief, that He has earned for Himself this unique *title - the God of patience and consolation.*

In this verse He also urges that we be of the same mind: ever ready to *console* others in their suffering, rather than reminding them of their failures, and to *patiently* walk them through their trials, rather than criticizing them for stumbling. To the same degree that God has been *patient* with us, so we should be *patient* with others.

This challenging statement is especially illustrated in **The Parable of the Unmerciful Servant - Matthew 18:23-35.** Peter had just asked the Master if he should forgive a brother that sinned against him up to seven times. How Jesus must have astounded His apostle when instead He declared - "Until seventy times seven!" (Incidentally, this would be four hundred and ninety times a day, one time every three minutes.)

Jesus then explained, in parabolic fashion, how a certain servant owed a king ten thousand talents (which equals about one hundred and fifty million dollars). Since he was unable to pay, the king decreed that all he had, including his family, be sold. But the servant pled - "Lord, have *patience* with me, and I will pay thee all." The king fully and frankly forgave the debt. But then that same servant found a fellow-servant who owed him a hundred pence (which equals about four dollars). He, too, could not pay it and pled for *patience.* Instead of following the king's example, though, the unmerciful servant threw his co-worker in prison until he should pay the debt. The king was wroth over such unfair treatment, and in retribution, delivered the unmerciful servant "to the tormentors, till he should pay all that was due unto him." Jesus summarized the parable by saying - "So likewise shall My heavenly Father do also unto you, if ye from your hearts forgive not every one his brother their trespasses."

There are several major points in this symbolic story that need to be emphasized. **The vast difference in indebtedness.** There is no comparison between a massive one hundred and fifty million dollar debt as opposed to a meager and measly four dollar debt. In like manner, our indebtedness to God, our sin-debt, is so great that the little ways others offend and hurt us are really nothing in comparison. We should always keep this in mind. **The miracle of** forgiveness. The first servant's debt was so large, he never could have paid it off. Similarly, we never could have paid off our sin-debt or earned our salvation by works. In great compassion, though, *the God of patience* blotted out all our iniquities, just as if we never sinned. Such love is nothing short of miraculous. **The demand to forgive others.** One of the main things that God demands of His forgiven ones is that we forgive others. If we refuse, in essence, we are throwing those persons, who are indebted to us, into a prison of their own past failures. We are withholding grace from them, assuming they will not change and that God cannot transform their hearts supernaturally. If we make this grave attitude-error, it will definitely return to us. With the same measure we meet, it will be measured to us again. We will also end up in a prison - a prison of our own past - tormented by guilt and unable to be free in our relationship with God. The promise is clear: if we are *patient* with others, God will be *patient* with us.

■ Patience in tribulation

In the beginning of the book of the Revelation the author introduced himself saying - "I John, who also am your brother, and companion in tribulation, and in the kingdom and *patience of Jesus Christ.*" (Revelation 1:9)

By this statement, John was encouraging the saints not to be troubled by any present tribulation they were being subjected to, or by the ensuing prophecies that would speak of dark, foreboding storm clouds awaiting in the future. In other words, he was communicating - "We are in this together and we are co-heirs, not only of a glorious kingdom, but of *the patience of Christ.*" This is undoubtedly a reference to the spirit of perseverance and forgiveness that our elder brother so consistently displayed. Jesus could endure all of the cruel and senseless persecution He faced because He knew the Father was with Him and He knew that He was part of a plan. We can have just as much confidence, for we are His joint-heirs.

II Thessalonians 3:5 even presents the prayer for each member of the church - "The Lord direct your hearts into the love of God, and into *[the patience of Christ].*" (AV, RV) We should claim the answer to this prayer being evidenced in our lives daily...lest we be weary and faint in our minds. Another version says "the *steadfastness* of Christ" and still another "Christ's *perseverance.*" (RSV, NIV)

There are many other scriptures that deal with this all-important area of our sonship character calling.

In Romans 5:3-5 Paul boasted - "We glory in tribulations also: knowing that *tribulation worketh patience;* and *patience,* experience; and experience, *hope*: and *hope* maketh not ashamed; because the love of God is shed abroad in our hearts by the Holy Ghost." Later on, in the same epistle, he exhorted that believers ever be - "Rejoicing in *hope; patient in tribulation*; continuing instant in prayer." (Romans 12:12)

Both of these passages tie *tribulation, patience* and *hope* together." *Tribulation worketh patience*" because the more adversity a child of God faces, usually the more they develop steadfastness and firmness in commitment to the truth. The more *patient continuance* we display, the more we "experience" the never-failing promises of our God. This works *hope* into our spirits, for no matter what changing situations we encounter in life, we know our God has declared - "I am the Lord, I change not." (Malachi 3:6)

In this vein, James also wrote:

> *"My brethren, count it all joy when ye fall into divers temptations;*
>
> *Knowing this, that the trying of your faith worketh patience.*
>
> *But let patience have her perfect work, that ye may be perfect and entire, wanting nothing."*
>
> (James 1:2-4)

What is this *perfect work of patience*? It is the fulfillment and completion of God's purpose in allowing us to face the trials of life. Adverse circumstances are never meant to destroy; rather, they are meant to develop a true child of God. This is not to say that God authors the tribulations of life, but that He uses them all to both His and our greatest advantage.

It is through the dark nights, the low valleys, the dry deserts, that we discover the true revelation of the nature of our God. We find Him to be the bright and morning star, the lily of the valleys, and a fountain of living waters. These are also the times when the divine nature is most formed in our hearts. We see the Lord and then become like Him...if we patiently persevere. **This is the dual outcome and the perfect work of patience**...and how exceedingly valuable this end result really is! At the resurrection, we will be permanently sealed into the completion and perfection of this process forevermore! Realizing these truths should make us each boldly reaffirm - "I can do all things through Christ which strengtheneth me." (Philippians 4:13)

■ Patience in receiving promises

Hebrews 6:12 commands that we "be not slothful, but followers of them who through faith and *patience* inherit the promises." Then Abraham was given as a prime example. Not only did Abraham hear from God that he would have a promised son; God swore unto him that this promise would definitely come to pass. Two things - the impossibility of God lying and the oath He gave - became Abraham's *hope, "an anchor of the soul, both sure and stedfast. "* (Heb. 6:19) Surely, whenever a storm of unbelief would hit Abraham, the *anchor of hope* still held firm. But not only did it take hope and faith for this great patriarch to receive his miracle; it took a great deal of *patient perseverance.*

Approximately twenty-five years elapsed between God's original pledge and the final fulfillment. Meanwhile outward circumstances did not get better, they got worse. Sarah's barren womb became dead and Abraham's body eventually became impotent. This exemplary man of faith held on still and became an exemplary man of *patience* in the process.

And there are others in the Word who have become role-models and examples of *patience* to us: Joseph, who persevered thirteen years until his dreams from God came to pass; David, who endured such senseless persecution before assuming the throne; Noah, who waited one hundred and twenty years until the arrival of the prophesied flood; and Job, who faced insurmountable problems, yet claimed - "He knoweth the way that I take: when He hath tried me, I shall come forth as gold." (Job 23:10)

Later on, the epistle-writer, James, encouraged believers, saying - "Take, my brethren, the prophets, who have spoken in the name of the Lord, for an example of suffering affliction, and of *patience*. Behold, we count them happy which endure. Ye have heard of *the patience of Job,* and have seen the end of the Lord; that the Lord is very pitiful, and of tender mercy." (James 5:10-11)

We also read that the latter end of Job was greater than his beginning. God is no respecter of persons. If He was a God of restoration to Job, He will be a God of restoration to us. Moreover, the victory that God has wrought for all His covenant people in times past testifies to us daily that God can do it again.

Hebrews 12:1-2 boldly announces - "Wherefore seeing we also are compassed about with so great a cloud of witnesses, let us lay aside every weight, and the sin which doth so easily beset us, and LET US RUN WITH PATIENCE THE RACE THAT IS SET BEFORE US, looking unto Jesus the author and finisher of our faith."

We know He will carry us through to triumph. He will always come through with His grace. So beloved - "Cast not away therefore your confidence, which hath great recompense of reward. For ye have need of *patience* [you need *to persevere*], that, after ye have done the will of God, ye might *receive the promise."* (Hebrews 10:35-36 AV, NIV)

It is God's will that we claim His promises, praise Him in advance for the desired answer, and strive to obey both the written and living Word. After having done these things, if the breakthrough has not yet come, we should still maintain confidence. In a spirit of determination we must keep praying, keep trusting, keep believing. After doing all that we can do, we "Rest in the Lord, and wait *patiently* for Him." (Psalm 37:7)

We *persevere* in confessing the Word and claiming strength, healing, deliverance, prosperity or whatever we may need from God.

A believer must never give up and never concede defeat...for we are *heirs according to the hope of eternal life*. And we know: as long as there is a God, there is *hope*.

■ Patient continuance in well doing

Romans 2:6-7 states that God "will render to every man according to his deeds: to them who by *patient continuance in well doing* seek for glory and honour and immortality, eternal life." A child of God who seeks to please God, and who desires to earn the most excellent, eternal reward possible, must learn to serve both God and men consistently and faithfully. We must be instant in season and out of season. Eternal life is the prize. And God definitely did say - "Behold, I come quickly; and My reward is with Me, to give every man according as his work shall be." (Revelation 22:12)

This reward may not match the greatness or size of an accomplishment as much as the spirit with which it is done: quality, not quantity. Paul confessed - "If I do this thing willingly, I have a reward: but if against my will, a dispensation of the gospel is committed unto me. What is my reward then?" (I Corinthians 9:17-18)

Maintaining the correct attitude makes all the difference. Even though results seem small in our eyes, they may be great in God's eyes. And if our motives are misread, or the sincerity of our actions is questioned by others, God takes everything into account. Matthew 6:6 promises - "thy Father which seeth in secret shall reward thee openly." Moreover, I Peter 2:19-20 reveals - "For this is thankworthy, if a man for conscience toward God endure grief, suffering wrongfully. For what glory is it, if when ye be buffeted for your faults, ye shall take it *patiently*? but if, when ye *do well*, and suffer for it, ye take it *patiently*, this is acceptable with God."

■ Patience unto the coming of the Lord ────────────

James again provides us with the main scripture reference for this subheading. Challenging us to have the foresight of a farmer, he says - "Be *patient* therefore, brethren, unto the coming of the Lord. Behold, the husbandman waiteth for the precious fruit of the earth, and hath long *patience* for it, until he receive the early and latter rain. Be ye also *patient;* stablish your hearts: for the coming of the Lord draweth nigh." (James 5:7-8)

The sons and daughters of God are "the precious fruit of the earth" - a crop that has been growing for nearly two thousand years. To begin with, Jesus, the Sower, planted the seed of the Word in the hearts of men during His sojourn on this earth. Then, starting with Pentecost, the "early rain" began to fall as the Holy Spirit began watering the seed.

Speaking both naturally and spiritually, the "early rain" is a very gentle rain that causes the seed to germinate and the first tender shoots to spring upward. Then, according to the normal Middle East weather pattern, there is a long dry spell. This happened spiritually to the professing church when it became institutionalized and ritualized for so many centuries. But now we are living in the days of the "latter rain" - a final deluge that will bring the crop to full maturity. Only God knows when the final ingathering will take place...but surely, it can not be far away. Therefore, let us refuse to grow discouraged or disbelieving. "The Lord is not slack concerning His promise, as some men count slackness; but is longsuffering to us-ward, not willing that any should perish, but that all should come to repentance." (II Pt. 3:9, See also Ho. 6:3)

At the Father's appointed time - and we must *patiently* wait for it - Jesus will descend from heaven and the angel will cry aloud - "Thrust in Thy sickle, and reap: for the time is come for Thee to reap; for the harvest of the earth is ripe." (Revelation 14:15)

POSSESSING OUR SOULS

● Jesus described this final age as a time of "great distress" and "great tribulation," a time when men's hearts will fail them for fear, "and for looking after those things which are coming on the earth." (Mt. 24:21, Lk. 21:23,26)

To God's chosen, though, He commands - "Lift up your heads; for your redemption draweth nigh," and also - "IN YOUR **PATIENCE** POSSESS YE YOUR SOULS." (Luke 21:19,28)

The soul is the realm of the mind, will and emotions, and all of these must be brought under control. Our hearts could easily be carried away into worry, fear, anxiety and a host of other negative emotions. Especially as we dwell on the disastrous events soon to transpire in this world, our souls could swiftly and easily gallop out of control...that is, unless we keep the reins tight. With determination and perseverance (synonyms to the word *patience*) we must stabilize our hearts. We must will to win every trial, bring "into captivity every thought to the obedience of Christ," cultivate every positive, faith-building emotion, and ever look for our *"blessed hope*...the glorious appearing of the great God and our Saviour Jesus Christ." (II Corinthians 10:5, Titus 2:13)

This is how we *possess our souls,* a process that must be executed diligently and consistently...or, as Jesus said, *"in patience."*

THE PATIENCE AND THE FAITH
OF THE SAINTS

● In the book of the Revelation, chapters twelve and thirteen, we read how the dragon (the devil) will make war against those who have the testimony of Jesus, and how the beast (the Antichrist) will also make war against the saints. Although these prophecies will definitely rise to a peak of fulfillment in the last days, satanic powers and the spirit of Antichrist have always warred against God's church from the very beginning.(See I John 4:3)

This seemingly endless barrage could weary God's people greatly, and even give cause for despair, were it not for the following irreversible promise from God's Word:

> *"He that leadeth into captivity shall go into captivity: he that killeth with the sword must be killed with the sword. Here is the patience and the faith of the saints."*
> (Revelation 13:10)

● *"He that leadeth into captivity"* is a reference to the devil, the one who cruelly takes men and women "captive...at his will." Jesus came, though, to "proclaim liberty to the captives" and to lead "captivity captive." This will happen in perfection when Satan shall *"go into captivity"*...cast into a bottomless pit for a thousand years and then imprisoned in the lake of fire forever.

In the light of such truth, saints of God should be able to *patiently* endure any battle...for we already know: IN THE END, WE WIN! (See II Timothy 2:26, Isaiah 61:1, Psalm 68:18)

● *"He that killeth with the sword"* is a sure reference to the Antichrist. This satanically inspired, political leader may very well pervert the Word of God, which is *the sword of the Spirit,* to falsely prove that He is the Messiah. In this manner, he will *kill with the sword,* for his false doctrine will lead many to spiritual death. Of course, this prophecy will also be fulfilled physically and literally, for there will be many martyrs under his rule.

True believers will have a wonderful hope, though, for John depicted the returning Christ as having a sharp *sword* proceeding out of His mouth and that with this *sword* He would smite the nations, bringing them under His rule. By *the sword of the Word,* Jesus will bring final judgment on the Antichrist and the world. This man of perdition will then be cast into the lake of fire, along with the dragon who empowered and inspired him. All those who worshipped the beast and his image on the earth will also receive this final retribution.

The foretelling of their damnation is also called *"the patience of the saints"*...and for a similar reason. If we know the ultimate destiny of all those who choose to serve the spirit of Antichrist in this world, it should give us all the more *patience,* all the more steadfastness, perseverance, and determination to keep walking in the truth. Though at times, children of God may not always appear triumphant in this life, we certainly will be eternally. Though we may be persecuted and ostracized now, in the end we will be received into the loving arms of the Almighty God and reign with Him forevermore.

Again - *"Here is the patience and the faith of the saints."*

THE "FULL OF HOPE" CONCLUSION

● In I Thessalonians 1:3 Paul praised that church for their *"patience of hope in our Lord Jesus Christ, in the sight of God and our Father."*

By this statement, we see that the very character of *hope* includes *patience,* for the two are inseparably joined together. (See also Romans 15:4)

Moreover, both are born of love, for "love is *patient"* and love "always *hopes."* (I Corinthians 13:4,7 NIV)

● **The Spirit and the Word are also both characterized by *patience.***

According to the New International Version, *patience* is one of the fruits of the Spirit (in the place of *longsuffering* in the King James). (Gal. 5:22)

Also, in **The Parable of the Sower,** Jesus explained that "good ground" signifies those persons who receive the seed of the Word in "an honest and good heart...and bring forth fruit with *patience. "* (Luke 8:15)

So if we are begotten of the Word and born of the Spirit, there is a dual inner influence that should bring forth the fruit of *patience.*

One of the qualities that wins God's stamp of approval on a minister is *patience.* (See II Corinthians 6:4)

Moreover, *patience* is listed as one of the seven attributes added to faith that cause believers to "neither be barren nor unfruitful in the knowledge of our Lord Jesus Christ." (II Peter 1:8)

Some things, like youthful lust and greed, we are commanded to flee from in Scripture; others, like *patience,* we are commanded to "follow after." (I Tim. 6:11, See I Cor. 6:18; 10:14, II Tim. 2:22)

Once we have apprehended a spirit of *patience,* we can then "run with *patience* [resolution and determination] the race that is set before us." Jesus was able to do this - enduring the cross and making it all the way to the throne of God - by looking to "the joy that was set before Him." (Hebrews 12:1-2)

If the joyous thought of God's coming kingdom gave such steadfastness, endurance, and final victory to the firstborn Son, then we should also focus our gaze toward this future, restored, paradise state.

Moreover, it behooves every member of the church to remember the promise Jesus gave to the church of Philadelphia:

> *"Because thou hast kept the word of My patience [obeyed My call to patient endurance] I also will keep thee from the hour of temptation, which shall come upon all the world, to try them that dwell on the earth."*
> (Revelation 3:10 AV, PME)

So let us rejoice in *hope* of the glory of God.

If the lesson in this chapter has truly been inscribed on our hearts, there should be a positive and blessed effect.

By now we should be able to trust wholeheartedly that our God will keep us during this earthly sojourn. We should be able to believe unreservedly that our Saviour will take us all the way to heaven.

As the Master Refiner, we know He expects to purify us of dross in order to bring us forth as gold. As the Heavenly Husbandman, He plans to carefully plow, plant, trim and nurture each one of us that we might produce much fruit. As the Chief Potter, He intends to shape us all into vessels of spectacular excellence.

In knowing and considering these things, we should be able to joyfully endure the difficult road that leads to the glorious goal. Once achieved, surely eternity itself will ring with the time-proven truth:

> *"Better is the end of a thing than the beginning thereof."*
>
> (Ecclesiastes 7:8)

Thank God, we have an anchor of the soul, both sure and steadfast, that goes beyond the veil.

The Grace of Vital Perseverance

"The grace of vital perseverance is that quality of patience which is always equal to the pressure of the passing moment, because it is rooted in that eternal order over which the passing moment has no power."

Albert M. Wells

THE END OF A THING
(Ecclesiastes 7:8)

The Creator urges patience
  In tribulation sore,
To quietly wait with hopeful hearts
  Toward the God whom we implore,

To bring to pass His promise,
  To pour out on us His grace,
To give us strength to take each step,
  'Till we see His lovely face.

Now the only way to accomplish this
  Is to look beyond the veil;
And see that God who started the work,
  In the end, will yet prevail.

For "the end of a thing" is better
  Than the beginning (for there is gain).
So why be crushed in the midst of it all,
  Distraught over temporal pain.

Our affliction is but for a moment,
  And as vapor, it will vanish away.
Time will yet bow to the glorious throne
  And eternity will have full sway.

So have **patient hearts,** O struggling ones!
  Be enthroned with Christ on high!
And rule over life's adversities,
  ASSURED...the coming of the Lord is nigh!!

• THE PERFECT •

HIS PERFECT ONE

• A PERFECT MAN •

A MATURE MAN

THE PERFECTION OF BEAUTY

---

*"For the upright shall dwell in the land, and **THE PERFECT** shall remain in it."*

(Proverbs 2:21)

*"But My dove, **MY PERFECT ONE** is unique: She is her mother's only daughter..."*
(Song of Solomon 6:9 NAS)

*"Till we all come in the unity of the faith, and of the knowledge of the Son of God, unto **A PERFECT MAN [A MATURE MAN]**, unto the measure of the stature of the fulness of Christ."*
(Ephesians 4:13 AV, NAS)

*"Out of Zion, **THE PERFECTION OF BEAUTY**, God hath shined."*
(Psalm 50:2)

THE PERFECT

"For the upright shall dwell in the land, and
THE PERFECT shall remain in it."

(Proverbs 2:21)

● The adjective **perfect** has multiple meanings, such as: *being entirely without fault or defect: FLAWLESS...satisfying all requirements: AC-CURATE...corresponding to an ideal standard...faithfully reproducing the original...or that which is pure, total, complete and lacking in no essential detail.*

It means *soundness and excellence in every part.*

It can also mean *fullness* or *maturity.*

This last definition is especially conveyed by one of our main *title-passages,* Ephesians 4:11-13:

> *"And He gave some, apostles; and some, prophets; and some, evangelists; and some, pastors and teachers;*
> *For the perfecting of the saints, for the work of the ministry, for the edifying of the body of Christ:*
> *Till we all come in the unity of the faith, and of the knowledge of the Son of God, unto A PERFECT MAN, unto the measure of the stature of the fulness of Christ."*

The process of becoming mature in our walk with God and mature in our knowledge of God is the "strong current" flowing through these three verses.

The next two verses in the same chapter verify this truth:

> *"That we henceforth be no more children, tossed to and fro, and carried about with every wind of doctrine, by the sleight of men, and cunning craftiness, whereby they lie in wait to deceive;*
> *But speaking the truth in love, may grow up into Him in all things, which is the head, even Christ."*

(Ephesians 4:14-15)

● When every born again member of the family of God reaches this goal of "growing up," then we will emerge in the sight of heaven as **A PERFECT MAN,** or **A MATURE MAN,** as the New American Standard version reads.

This **"perfect man"** is a **corporate man,** comprised of Jesus, who is the head, and all New Covenant believers, who are the individual "cells" that collectively make up His body (the body of Christ).

Fully "growing up" into **Him** involves being perfected in every area of

147

our being: emotional, mental, spiritual and ultimately, even physical. It means every member of the body of Christ coming forth in "the measure of the stature of the fulness of Christ." (Ephesians 4:13)

When this fully takes place, God's original purpose - "Let us make man in our image" - will be brought to its absolute fulfillment.

The first man Adam fell from the matchless beauty of paradise perfection into the gross darkness of carnal imperfection.

The second man, the last Adam, willingly descended to the dreadful depths of carnality in order to lift us back to the brilliant heights of God-breathed flawlessness.

We know this great transformation will never fully transpire until the resurrection. Nevertheless, we are still called to pursue such a lofty goal with patient determination and consistent effort.

"Let us go on unto perfection," the writer of Hebrews concludes...for only those who strive ever complete the journey by the help of God. (Hebrews 6:1)

THE DIFFICULT HURDLE

● The most difficult hurdle to get over in pursuing the goal of perfection is, obviously, the inherent imperfection in our flesh.

Even the righteous patriarch, Job, admitted:

> *"If I justify myself, mine own mouth shall condemn me: if I say, I am perfect, it shall also prove me perverse."*
>
> (Job 9:20)

And King David was very blunt in declaring to God:

> *"I have seen an end of all perfection: but Thy commandment is exceeding broad."*
> (Psalm 119:96)

The sweet psalmist of Israel must have been referring to all those things in this world that pass for perfections. Matthew Henry, in his commentary on this passage, said it excellently:

> *"David in his time had seen Goliath, the strongest, overcome, Asahel, the swiftest, overtaken, Ahithophel, the wisest, befooled, Absalom, the fairest, deformed...in short, he had seen an end of perfection."*

In his own life David had seen a nearly flawless walk with God turn into a muddled mess of sin, failure and resulting judgments...*an end of all perfection.*

And so it is, to one degree or another, with everything and everyone in this world. (See Job 15:29)

In the natural, the most beautiful woman eventually loses her beauty; the most stylish clothing eventually rots; the most impressive building eventually crumbles. And in the spiritual, even the most stunning religious efforts of man, if not correspondent to the Word of God, eventually end up empty and cursed towers of Babel.

Yet even though this world, its flesh-bound inhabitants and its religious pursuits, are subject to such frailty - even though there is *an end to all perfection* - still, God's *"commandment is exceeding broad."*

His demands on Adam's race are great, sobering and difficult to achieve.

They are very *broad* in their influence, covering the entire width and breadth of all that we are, all that we do and all that we can be for the glory of God.

THE GOD OF PERFECTION
DEMANDS PERFECTION

● **The Scripture declares of the Creator that :**
He is "perfect in knowledge" - (Job 37:16).
He is perfect in character - (Matthew 5:48).
His "work is perfect" - (Deuteronomy 32:4).
His "way is perfect" - (II Samuel 22:31).
His law is perfect - (Psalm 19:7).
His gifts are perfect - (James 1:17).
His will is perfect- (Romans 12:1-2).

So it is only to be expected that He commands His people to measure up to standards of perfection as well.

This is not an option. It is an unquestionable and unavoidable demand.

Job 28:3 states that Jehovah "searcheth out all perfection." He searches throughout all creation and into the very depths of our hearts to discover all those areas which have been "taken over" by the perfection of His nature.

● **Even under the inferior Old Will, we find God searching for and demanding perfection in His own.** Though Abraham had already been serving God for twenty-five years, still he received the divine mandate:

> *"I am the Almighty God; walk before Me,*
> *and BE THOU PERFECT."*
> (Genesis 17:1)

When God said *"Walk before Me,"* in essence, He was saying - *"Abraham, live your life as if you are under My continual observation."*

It is interesting, though, that God prefaced His command with the proclamation - *"I am the Almighty God."*

The original Hebrew of this divine entitlement is *El Shaddai* which means *the All-Sufficient God* or *the God who is more than enough.*

God was charging Abraham to reach for perfection, but He was simultaneously assuring this great patriarch that He could supply *more than enough* power to help Abraham achieve such a lofty goal.

● Then in Deuteronomy 18:13 God commanded all of Israel:

> *"Thou shalt be perfect with the Lord thy God."*

(See also I Kings 8:61)

It is quite significant to see that this was the concluding statement of a series of warnings against any involvement in false religious practices.

Just prior to the verse quoted above God gave the strict command - "There shall not be found among you any...that useth divination, or an observer of times, or an enchanter, or a witch, or a charmer, or a consulter with familiar spirits, or a wizard, or a necromancer. For all that do these things are an abomination unto the Lord." (Deuteronomy 18:10-12)

Though the wording is a little different in some cases, these are references to many occult and New Age religious practices prevalent in our society today. Divination is Satan's counterfeit for a true gift of prophecy. An observer of times was a fortune-teller or a soothsayer who used various means, including astrology, to foretell the future. An enchanter was a conjuror or exorcist employing incantations or using magical spells or chants to supernaturally effect certain happenings.

Consulting with familiar spirits is what we might call channeling or being a spirit-medium now. Necromancy is contacting the dead. The word for wizard means "a knowing one" and implies anyone claiming to have esoteric knowledge, especially through contact with evil spirits.

These, along with many other New Age occult practices, never have been compatible with true and undefiled religion and never will be. They are an abomination to God because the supernatural experiences afforded are of a demonic origin.

Those who are seeking to be *perfect* with the Lord will purge everything out of their discipline of worship except that which is Bible-based and acceptable to God.

OLD TESTAMENT EXAMPLES
AND THE MYSTERY OF THE "PERFECT MAN"

● **There are four main individuals in the Old Testament described in terms of perfection.**

"**Noah** was a just man and *perfect* in his generations." (Genesis 6:9)

"**Job**...was *perfect* and upright...one that feared God and eschewed evil"... so that God said there was "none like him in the earth." (Job 1:1,8)

Asa, king of Judah, was spoken of as having a heart *"perfect* with the Lord all his days."* (I Kings 15:14)

And, of course, beloved **David**, the shepherd/king, was described this way as well. (I Kgs. 11:4; 15:3-5, See also I Chr. 28:9, Is. 38:3, I Kgs. 8:61)

Now we know that these men were not absolutely flawless. Noah became drunken after exiting from the ark. Job admitted his sinful attitudes when God spoke to him out of the whirlwind. And Asa allowed certain idolatrous high places to remain in Judah during his reign, as well as making other major mistakes.

So God must have been speaking relatively.

Compared to the rest of the world these men were the most perfect examples of God-fearing, God-loving individuals that could be found.

● **A great deal of revelation, concerning the "mystery of a perfect heart," is found in the life of David.**

Both Solomon and Abijam were spoken of as having a heart that was NOT *perfect* with the Lord as the heart of David their father. (See I Kings 11:4; 15:3-5)

But how could this be?

David rebelled against God's law by numbering Israel without demanding a ransom price.

He committed adultery with Bathsheba.

He purposefully had Uriah, her husband, placed in a dangerous position in battle so he would be killed.

How could this king of Israel possess a *perfect heart* with such gross imperfections in his life?

The answer may well be hidden in the statement that the prophet Samuel made at the onset of David's call - "for the Lord seeth not as man seeth; for man looketh on the outward appearance, but the Lord looketh on *the heart.*" (I Samuel 16:7)

In the psalms we read how David acknowledged his sin, manifested a broken and contrite heart, thirsted for God, pled for a right spirit, and his soul followed hard after the Lord. He was described as being *a man after God's heart.* (See I Samuel 13:14)

Evidently the deepest part of David longed to be pure before the Lord. He desired, above all else, to be in *perfect*, intimate and unhindered communion with the Most High.

So God did not judge him altogether by his surface actions, as evil as they were, but rather, by the prevailing current of what he really was in the very core of his being.

By God's standard - as a man "thinketh in his heart, so is he." (Pro. 23:7)

True lovers of God may have errors in their past that cause great grief, but they have a passion to be right with God that is much stronger and goes far deeper.

Moreover, their trust and faith is not in the flesh, but in God.

Men and women of such spiritual caliber can expect God's favor, blessing, protection, strength and defense:

> *"For the eyes of the Lord run to and fro throughout the whole earth, to shew Himself strong in the behalf of them whose heart is perfect toward Him."*
>
> (II Chronicles 16:9)

THE BRINGING IN OF A BETTER HOPE

Too often under the Old Will, promises like the one just mentioned went unclaimed...for men and women were bound in their carnality and their hearts were not inclined toward God.

Those who received the revelation of God's Word, prior to Calvary, were primarily shown the proof of how depraved human character really is:

> *"For the law made nothing perfect, but the*
> *bringing in of a better hope did."*
> (Hebrews 7:19, See also 10:1)

The New Covenant is that *better hope,* for it opened a "door to perfection" that was, for the most part, closed and sealed until the birth of the church.

● This sixth volume of **OUR GLORIOUS INHERITANCE** revolves around this *better hope* that Jesus came to announce and reveal.

The main passage of Scripture that weaves its way through every chapter is Colossians 1:26-27.

These two verses reveal that "the mystery which hath been hid from ages and from generations...is Christ in you, *the hope of glory."*

Then the next verse goes on to explain:

> *"Whom we preach, warning every man,*
> *and teaching every man in all wisdom; that we*
> *may present every man PERFECT IN*
> *CHRIST JESUS."*
>
> (Colossians 1:28)

So our main *"hope of glory"* is the attaining of ultimate perfection "in Christ."

This scripture is the master key unlocking the door of this perfection-revelation.

No human being can ever achieve perfection by his or her own efforts.

But if we are positioned "in Christ," we inherit His flawless perfection.

Washed in His blood and cleansed by His love, we become just as pure as He - "unblameable and unreproveable in His sight"...because "as He is, so are we in this world." (Colossians 1:22, I John 4:17)

So the perfection of a born again child of God is first inherited and positional.

"In Christ" we are righteous.

"In Christ" we are holy.

"In Christ" we are *perfect.*

And all because of Jesus' death on Calvary.

> *"For by one offering He hath perfected for*
> *ever them that are sanctified."*
> (Hebrews 10:14)

Of course, this did not happen by chance. It was Jesus' purpose in coming and the answer to one of the main prayers He prayed just before leaving.

Outside the Garden of Gethsemane, He spoke to the Father concerning His disciples saying:

152

> *"...the glory which Thou gavest Me I have*
> *given them; that they may be one, even as We*
> *are one:*
> *I in them, and Thou in Me, that they may be*
> *MADE PERFECT IN ONE."*
>
> (John 17:22-23)

The fullness of the Godhead dwelt bodily in Jesus...so that He became the manifestation of all that the Father is.

Now Jesus dwells bodily in us...so that we have inherited the potential of manifesting all that the Son of God is.

> *"For as many of you as have been baptized*
> *into Christ have put on Christ."*
>
> (Galatians 3:27)

The Father now sees us under the canopy of Christ's perfection where His love, His charity, covers "the multitude of sins." (I Peter 4:8)

This is the hidden place where God's *hidden ones* find refuge from the condemnation that pursues us all from the past.

In this secret place, we are no longer under bondage, no longer under the suffocating influence of the law of sin and death.

Instead we are under the soul-healing, liberating influence of "the law of the Spirit of life in Christ Jesus," or as James termed it - "THE **PERFECT** LAW OF LIBERTY." (Romans 8:2, James 1:25)

This law, that provides redemption to erring sinners, is *perfect* because God considers it so.

He found fault with the Old Will.

He is pleased with the New.

The Old Will proved us guilty.

The New Will delivers and justifies the guilty, just as if they never sinned.

THE PRIZE OF THE HIGH CALLING

● **It is extremely important for any Christian to comprehend that perfection is an inherited position. It is just as important, though, that each child of God set the manifestation of perfection as the focus and goal of his or her life.**

Of course, for this to happen believers must necessarily die to self, mortify the flesh, and rise above sin.

The caterpillar must weave a cocoon of a temporary "death" around itself in order to emerge as a beautiful butterfly.

The acorn must fall into the ground and die if the potential of being an oak tree is ever to be realized.

So we must be crucified with Christ in order for this inherited *perfection*, resident in our spirits, to be resurrected and manifested in us to the highest degree possible.

● **Fully reaching this place in God is referred to as "the mark for the prize of the high calling of God in Christ Jesus."** (Philippians 3:14)

Let us review the text from which this key statement is taken, Philippians 3:12-15, in which Paul admits:

> *"Not as though I had already attained,*
> *either were already perfect: but I follow after,*
> *if that I may apprehend that for which also I*
> *am apprehended of Christ Jesus.*
> *Brethren, I count not myself to have ap-*
> *prehended: but this one thing I do, forgetting*
> *those things which are behind, and reaching*
> *forth unto those things which are before,*
> *I press toward the mark for the prize of the*
> *high calling of God in Christ Jesus.*
> *Let us therefore, as many as be perfect, be*
> *thus minded..."*

At first, the two statements in boldface type above seem to be contradictory.

To start with, Paul states that he has definitely **not reached perfection** but he is striving that direction. Then he concludes by exhorting all who **are perfect** to maintain an attitude of mind similar to his.

How can those who are **perfect** be established in **perfection** by admitting their **imperfection**?

The NIV translation of verse 15 provides a suitable answer, saying -

> *"All of us who are **mature** should take such*
> *a view of things."*

So the first use of the word *perfect* carries more of a meaning of *flawlessness,* while the second implies that which is *full grown or mature.*

In other words, if we are *mature* believers, we will first be candid and honest in confessing that we are far from having attained a state of flawlessness.

We will not be haughty in self-righteousness.

We will not be blind to our own need or numb to the convicting influence of the Holy Spirit.

Simultaneously and secondly, though, we will not allow ourselves to swing too far to the other extreme and be swallowed up by grief and condemnation over former failures.

● **We must take the four necessary steps outlined in this challenging passage.**
1. Count not ourselves to have apprehended.
2. Forget those things which are behind.
3. Reach for those things which are before.
4. Press toward the mark for the prize.

As stated already in a previous chapter on *The Called,* the *high calling* is absolute *perfection* in all that we are, all that we say, and all that we do.

The "prize" is the manifold reward that will result from even partially reaching such a goal, and it includes:

Peace - "Mark the *perfect* man, and behold the upright: for the end of that man is *peace."* (Psalm 37:37, See also Isaiah 26:3)

Direction and Protection - "The righteousness of *the perfect* shall *direct* his way: but the wicked shall fall by his own wickedness." (Proverbs 11:5)

Deeper Revelation in the Word - "But strong meat belongeth to them that are of a *full age* (Gr. *teleious,* the word normally translated *perfect*), even to those who by reason of use have their senses exercised to discern both good and evil." Christians who search out deeper truths must be spiritually mature to keep from getting into error. They must be of *"full age."* (Hebrews 5:14)

Paul said - "Howbeit we speak wisdom among them that are *perfect*...even the hidden wisdom, which God ordained before the world unto our glory." (I Corinthians 2:6-7)

Abiding in the Abundant Life in Christ - "For the upright shall dwell in the land, and the *perfect* shall remain in it." (Proverbs 2:21)

This last scripture is a reference to dwelling in the "Land of Promise" both literally and spiritually. For New Testament believers this has a dual meaning, both present and future. Presently, it means abiding in the fulfillment of all the promises of God, living in that spiritual land of bounty and blessing that "flows" with the "milk" of the Word and the "honey" of the Spirit.

Futuristically, it means abiding forevermore in a restored paradise world, reigning with Christ as kings and priests - from Jerusalem, from the Land of Promise itself - throughout the Millennium and the New Creation to come.

SPECIFIC AREAS OF PERFECTION
TO WHICH WE ARE CALLED

● **There are a number of scriptures that either command or encourage perfection in specific and various areas of sonship character development.**

Some of the most choice are as follows:

Perfect Speech - "If any man offend not in *word*, the same is a *perfect* man, and able also to bridle the whole body." (James 3:2)

Perfect Holiness - "Having therefore these promises, dearly beloved, let us cleanse ourselves from all filthiness of the flesh and spirit, *perfecting holiness* in the fear of God." (II Corinthians 7:1)

Perfect Unity - "Now I beseech you, brethren, by the name of our Lord Jesus Christ, that ye all speak the same thing, and that there be no divisions among you; but that ye be *perfectly joined together* in the same mind and in the same judgment." (I Corinthians 1:10)

Perfect Hatred - "Do not I hate them, O Lord, that hate Thee? am not I grieved with those that rise up against Thee? I hate them with *perfect hatred*: [the utmost hatred]: I count them mine enemies." (Psalm 139:21-22 AV,NAS)

Note: this primarily refers to a very godly hatred that should rest in the bosom of a child of God toward the devil and toward his works. If we hate with a *perfect hatred* we will certainly not sit back and unresistingly watch the advance of the enemy as he comes to steal, kill and destroy people's lives. We will rise up with the zeal of the Lord's house and fight until the serpent's head is crushed and he is writhing under our feet. Too many Christians are too passive, too fruitless, and too reluctant to cultivate this area of perfection.

Perfect Love - There are three main scriptures that deal with the development of this area of perfection, all in the first epistle of John.

The first deals with perfecting our love toward God - "But whoso keepeth His Word, in him verily is *the love of God perfected:* hereby know we that we are in Him." (I John 2:5)

The second deals with perfecting our love toward others - "If we love one another [with the same kind of love God has toward us], God dwelleth in us, and *His love is perfected* in us." (I John 4:12)

The third deals with comprehending the love that God has toward us and the greatness of what He has done for us - "Herein is our *love made perfect,* that we may have boldness in the day of judgment: because as He is, so are we in this world." (I John 4:17)

Note: when we realize that God's love toward us has made us to inherit all that Jesus is - His righteousness, His authority, His oneness with the Father, etc. - we will have boldness in the day of judgment. This refers, not only to that time when we each personally appear before the judgment seat of Christ, but also to those times when we come under God's judgment rod and are chastened. Christians who understand God's love know that "whom the Lord loveth He chasteneth." We understand that He sends forth "judgment unto victory" - "that we should not be condemned with the world." (Heb. 12:6, Mt. 12:20, I Cor. 11:32) Such a revelation of God's *perfect love* is very strengthening for it "casteth out fear." (I John 4:18)

Perfect Faith - "Was not Abraham our father justified by works, when he had offered Isaac his son upon the altar? Seest thou how faith wrought with his works, and by works was *faith made perfect?*" (James 2:21-22)

Spiritual works that result from faith are the evidence of faith and, therefore, the perfection of faith.

Perfect Submission to the will of God - Paul urged the Roman church - "I beseech you therefore, brethren, by the mercies of God, that ye present your bodies a living sacrifice, holy, acceptable unto God...that ye may may prove what is that good, and acceptable, and *perfect, will of God.*" (Romans 12:1-2) Also, Epaphras prayed for the Colossian church that they would be *"perfect* and complete in all the *will of God."* (Colossians 4:12)

Perfect Praise - "Yea; have ye never read, Out of the mouth of babes and sucklings Thou hast *perfected praise?"* (Matthew 21:16)

This was the statement Jesus made to the chief priests and scribes who were offended by the jubilant praise of the children during His triumphant entry into Jerusalem. *Perfect praise* is NOT practiced, prideful, professional, programmed, or padded with ulterior motives. Contrary to all of these, the children's worship was *perfect* in God's eyes because it was sincere, pure, spontaneous, free from ceremonialism, and intense with true devotion to God.

● **Furthermore, the Scripture commands, above all other things, that we "put on charity, which is *the bond of perfectness*."** (Colossians 3:14)

Charity should be the uniting principle that *binds* all of these harvested perfection-commands together, like a sheaf of wheat, and presents them unto the Lord of the harvest. Charity - the God-kind of love - is the bond that perfectly unites our hearts to the hearts of others in the body of Christ and it bonds our very hearts to the heart of God.

If our motive is not charity, the result is nothing more than an empty-shelled religious system, an enforced spiritual discipline, an accomplishment goal that begets pride in the heart.

● **Perfection through Suffering** - It should also be mentioned that Jesus, the Captain of our salvation, was made *"perfect through sufferings."* (Heb. 2:10, See also 5:9) What an amazing thing! That the spotless Lamb of God, the incarnation of perfection itself, could even be exalted to a higher degree of perfection! And if this primarily took place in the firstborn Son through the suffering of Calvary, then sharing the cross, being crucified with Christ, will do the same for us.

The death to self that discipleship demands opens up a vacuum within us that the resurrection life of God can then fill. It is usually through these experiences, and not through our most victorious moments in life, that we emerge most Christlike and most perfected. (See I Peter 5:10)

● **God's strength, made perfect by weakness, and also...the perfect work of patience** - It is also true that our weakest moments, our most difficult battles, are times when God's strength can become most evidenced in us. When Paul pled with God to deliver him from a certain thorn in the flesh, God assured him - "My grace is sufficient for thee: *for My strength is made perfect in weakness."* This promise is for us as well. So we can rejoice in the worst of tribulations and dare to say, like Paul, the apostle - "When I am weak, then am I strong!" (II Corinthians 12:9-10)

Through it all, we must be wise, understanding the divine purpose behind trials and thereby, purposing to persevere. Christlikeness is the goal, and when we achieve it, as already discussed in the previous chapter of this volume on *The Patient,* we *"let patience have her perfect work."* (James 1:4)

If we react to tribulation, and even failure, in a humble, patient and positive way, we are not conformed to this world and its attitudes - (hostility, depression, anxiety, fear, etc.). Rather, we are transformed by the renewing of our minds. This renewing takes place, not only by the Spirit, but also by Word - for God has given all of His scriptural commands and promises "that the man of God may be *perfect,* throughly furnished unto all good works." (II Timothy 3:17)

This is the *"hope of the gospel"* and our *"hope of glory"*...every minute, of every hour, of every day. (Colossians 1:23,27)

JESUS' CHALLENGE TO TRUE DISCIPLES

● **There are many other commands to perfection found in Scripture, such as the following:**
"Let your heart therefore be *perfect* with the Lord our God, to walk in His statutes, and to keep His commandments, as at this day." (I Kings 8:61)

"This also we wish, even your *perfection*." (II Corinthians 13:9)

"Finally brethren...Be *perfect*." (II Corinthians 13:11)

To the angel of the church in Sardis, the fiery-eyed Christ exclaimed - "Be watchful, and strengthen the things which remain, that are ready to die: for I have not found thy works *perfect* before God." (Revelation 3:2)

To the rich young ruler Jesus said - "If thou wilt be *perfect*, go and sell that thou hast, and give to the poor." (Matthew 19:21) (Note: this was not a general command for all God's people, but a personal declaration for one man. This was the specific area where this individual was deficient spiritually. Apparently, his riches had become an idol. Others equally well-off may or may not need to follow suit. It all hinges on where priorities are set. All of us, whether rich or poor, should be rich in good works and mindful of the needs of the poor.)

● **The most profound of all the perfection-pleas is found in Jesus' sermon on the Mount:**

> *"Be ye therefore perfect, even as your*
> *Father which is in heaven is perfect."*
> (Matthew 5:48)

In order to fathom the depth of this statement it is necessary to view it in context. Jesus had just spent nine verses worth of teaching exhorting His disciples to have a compassionate, forgiving heart: to love their enemies, do good to those who hate them, bless those who curse them, and pray for those who despitefully use them.

His argument was that the Father "maketh His sun to rise on the evil and on the good, and sendeth rain on the just and on the unjust." (Matthew 5:45)

So if God's perfection is especially seen in His ability to love the undeserving, so will it be for us.

One writer, unknown to the author, said it very well:

> *"Tis a mark of great perfection to bear with*
> *the imperfections of others."*

Too many times, it happens just the opposite. When believers feel they are attaining some high level of perfectness in their walk with God, often they become intolerant toward those who are weak, and judgmental toward those who are bound by errors.

In a very similar passage in Luke, Jesus urged:

> *"Be ye therefore merciful, as your Father*
> *also is merciful.*
> *Judge not, and ye shall not be judged:*
> *condemn not, and ye shall not be condemned:*
> *forgive, and ye shall be forgiven."*
> (Luke 6:36-37)

If Jesus mercifully forgave the very ones who cursed, blasphemed and persecuted Him, then it is only right for us to do the same.

Viewed from this perspective, perfection is not just reaching the goal of being good; it means loving those who are not good.

Such a challenge is not to be shunned, overlooked or ignored by any child of God. For "the disciple is not above his master: but every one that is PERFECT shall be as his master." (Luke 6:40)

Loving in this depth is part of sharing the cross, the sign of a disciplined heart, and one of the highest roads leading to Christlikeness.

THE PERFECT DAY

● Proverbs 4:18 reveals that - "The path of the just is as the shining light, that shineth more and more unto THE PERFECT DAY."

This "perfect day" is the Day of the Lord, God's thousand-year-long Kingdom Era (for "one day is with the Lord as a thousand years, and a thousand years as one day" II Peter 3:8).

From the fall of Adam to the coming of the Lord it appears there will be a sum of six divine days (six millenniums). Then, even as the seventh day of man's week is a sanctified day of rest, so the seventh divine day will be a divine Sabbath, a sacred period of ultimate rest for all who are included.

In biblical numerology, seven is the number of perfection; so it is only to be expected that this choice era will witness the blossoming of perfection in every perfectible arena of existence.

- The human race as a whole will know perfect peace...for wars will "cease unto the end of the earth." (Psalm 46:9)

- The animal kingdom will know perfect harmony...for "the wolf and the lamb shall feed together, and the lion shall eat straw like the bullock." (Isaiah 65:25)

- The governmental structure will know perfect order...for in that day it will be said, "the kingdom is the Lord's: and He is the governor among the nations." (Psalm 22:28)

Angels will walk on the earth, the Most High God will reign from Jerusalem, and perfect love will permeate all things.

We will cease from our labors and become infinite fountains of perfect joy.

We will "know even as also [we] are known." Our understanding of God will be as perfect as His understanding of us. (I Corinthians 13:12)

Yes, all perfectivity will accompany this wonderful blending of heaven and earth...and "when that which is *perfect* is come, then that which is in part shall be done away." (I Corinthians 13:10)

Of course, all this perfection will be directly preceded by the resurrection, translation and glorification of God's offspring.

Jesus used a term in reference to His own bodily resurrection very suitable to this *title-study*. Concerning Herod, Jesus said to His disciples - "Go ye, and tell that fox, Behold, I cast out devils, and I do cures to day and to morrow, and the third day I shall be *perfected*." (Luke 13:32)

So we will also be *perfected* - in spirit, soul, and body - at "the last day" and "the last trump." (John 6:40, 44, 54, I Corinthians 15:52)

When Jesus comes He will present us *"faultless* before the presence of His glory with exceeding joy." Yes, we will be *"blameless* in the day of our Lord Jesus Christ." (Jude 24, I Corinthians 1:8)

As already mentioned in *The Contrite Ones* and *The Humble,* Hosea gave a stirring and mysterious prophecy of this coming event, promising:

> *"After two days [the two thousand year long Church Age] will He revive us: in the third day [the Millennial Kingdom] He will raise us up, and we shall live in His sight."*
>
> (Hosea 6:2)

Both Old and New Covenant saints will be perfected at once. (See Heb. 11:40)

Similar to Jesus, we will be perfected "the third day" (but in our case this means at the beginning of the third millennium since His first coming).

At that time we will inherit all things and reign as kings and priests.

We will worship the One called "a greater and more *perfect* tabernacle" and see Him face to face. (Hebrews 9:11)

● In that day, we will, in an ultimate sense, ascend "unto mount Sion, and unto the city of the living God, the heavenly Jerusalem, and to an innumerable company of angels, to the general assembly and church of the firstborn, which are written in heaven, and to God the Judge of all, AND TO THE SPIRITS OF JUST MEN MADE PERFECT." (Hebrews 12:22-23)

Surely, of both the holy city and the glorified saints who inhabit the city, it will then be said:

> *"Out of Zion, THE PERFECTION OF BEAUTY, God hath shined."*
>
> (Psalm 50:2)

We, the glorious and eternal body of Christ, will then make up that **PERFECT MAN** prophesied of in Ephesians 1:4 and 4:13. We will be "holy and **without blame** before Him in love."

But we are not only represented collectively as a final ideal man. The NAS version of the Song of Solomon 6:9 depicts God's everlasting nation as a perfect woman. ("But My dove, **MY PERFECT ONE** is unique: She is her mother's only daughter...")

The two symbols blend together as one, though, and speak a singular message: that only one thing will ever emerge from this imperfect world infinitely free from the stain of its imperfection - GOD'S COVENANT PEOPLE. Jeremiah said - "in the latter days ye shall consider it *perfectly* ." (Jeremiah 23:20)

Therefore, since these are the latter days, let us *perfectly* consider how wonderful and miraculous all these promises are - promises that have been foreshadowed from the very beginning of God's dealings with men.

Even as the blood-sprinkled ark of the covenant was formerly placed in a room, the holy of holies, that was a PERFECT CUBE (10 x10x10 - 1000 cubits square), so the eternal ark - the abode of God's Word and God's glory - will be permanently positioned in hearts that have been brought into perfect order by the sprinkling of Jesus' blood.

This 1000 square cubit holy of holies, filled with Shekinah glory, also speaks of the 1000 year long Kingdom Reign when the knowledge of the glory of the Lord will fill the earth. (Habakkuk 2:14)

Furthermore, it foreshadows glory-filled New Jerusalem, the capital city of the New Creation, which will also be **foursquare** - as well as the sainted, bloodwashed, perfected throng who will reside there eternally.

O, beloved, this is our destiny - the outcome of God's perfect plan toward us - something we never could have reached by our own merits or strength.

Ezekiel 16:14 plainly concedes that the beauty of the bride of Christ is *"perfect* through [His] comeliness."

So let each one of us delight to declare, both now and forevermore:

- "It is God that...maketh my way *perfect."* (Psalm 18:32)

- "The Lord will *perfect* that which concerneth me." (Psalm 138:8)

- "Looking unto Jesus the author and the finisher [the pioneer and *perfecter]* of our faith." (Hebrews 12:2 AV, Mon)

THE PERFECT ENDING

● As we make one final search of all the perfection-scriptures, we discover a *perfect* way to end this chapter - the quoting of two New Testament prayers that express God's *hope* for the church:

> *"But the God of all grace, who hath called us unto His eternal glory by Christ Jesus, after that ye have suffered a while, MAKE YOU PERFECT, stablish, strengthen, settle you."*
> (I Peter 5:10)

> *"Now the God of peace, that brought again from the dead our Lord Jesus...MAKE YOU PERFECT in every good work to do His will, working in you that which is well-pleasing in His sight, through Jesus Christ; to whom be glory for ever and ever..."*
> (Hebrews 13:20-21)

THE MYSTERY OF
PERFECTION

Perfection..how it presently seems,
 A lofty, unreachable goal!
Yet it is merely just retrieving
 Man's possession, Satan stole.

If we had it once, we can have it twice
 God hasn't changed His mind.
And the thief who took it from us,
 He forevermore will bind.

Our God delights in restoration,
 And when this miracle takes place,
Those He restores are better off
 For having known His grace.

So imperfection must yield its rule
 To the greatest perfection of all.
And we'll find ourselves in yet a higher place,
 Because of Adam's fall.

This is the wonder of our Father's plan,
 And the promise of His Word.
For all things will work together for good,
 To them that love the Lord.

PRISONERS OF HOPE

HIS PRISONERS

---

*"As for Thee also, by the blood of Thy covenant I have sent forth **THY PRISONERS** out of the pit wherein is no water.*

*Turn you to the strong hold, ye **PRISONERS OF HOPE**: even to day do I declare that I will render double unto thee."*

(Zechariah 9:11-12)

*"For the Lord heareth the poor, and despiseth not **HIS PRISONERS.**"*

(Psalm 69:33)

PRISONERS OF HOPE

> *"As for Thee also, by the blood of Thy
> covenant I have sent forth THY PRISONERS
> out of the pit wherein is no water.*
> *Turn you to the strong hold, ye
> PRISONERS OF HOPE: even to day do I
> declare that I will render double unto thee."*
> (Zechariah 9:11-12)

● To comprehend the above passage, the "person" in which it is spoken must first be understood.

It is the Everlasting Father speaking to His eternal Son.

"The blood of the covenant" is a sure reference to the precious blood of the Lamb of God that was shed for us.

"The pit wherein is no water" is a fit description of this world. There is no "water" here that can sufficiently quench the thirst of men's souls for truth and for fellowship with God. (See Psalm 40:2)

"The strong hold" is Jesus. He is our high tower and our place of defense. He is an impenetrable wall of salvation surrounding His submitted offspring.

"Prisoners of hope" is a *title* describing all of God's people. We may be *prisoners* of time and *prisoners* of these carnal bodies, but we have committed ourselves to Jesus in the *hope* that He will deliver us. Now we are *prisoners* of His will and His love, *fellowprisoners* in Christ Jesus. Such an imprisonment is excellent in nature and certainly to be desired. (See Philemon 23)

"I will render double unto thee" is the Saviour's pledge to those who surrender to His purpose and power. Because we have given Him our lives, He has given to us "the promise of the life that now is, and of that which is to come." (I Timothy 4:8)

We give Him a natural life and offer our hearts as *His habitation*; He gives us spiritual life now and eternal life in that world yet to come.

This could also be a revelation that the redeemed of Adam's race, in the end, will be *"doubly blessed"* for having faced this world and its woes. Adam was only a "lord" over the garden of Eden. We will reign with Christ over the vastness of a New Creation. Adam was in the image of God, yet he was of the dust and had a potential of falling. God's glorified saints will be brought forth in God's image to such degree that we will shine like the sun in His kingdom. We will no longer be of the dust. We will be sealed into our inheritance, never to fall again. Moreover, we will have experienced many facets of God's character and learned many valuable lessons in this valley of death's shadow that we never could have learned in a perfect, celestial state. (Review the revelation of the name **Ephraim** - which means *doubly fruitful* - in the chapter entitled *His Afflicted*.)

This must have been the *hope* that rested in God's bosom when He picked up that first handful of dust - and the *hope* that compelled the Son of God to walk to the peak of a hill called Calvary.

FURTHER EXPLANATION OF
THE "PRISONER" STATUS

● All who are born into this world are to be labeled *prisoners,* for through no choice of their own they are "locked" in a realm ruled by sin and cloaked in death. Lucifer dominates this place of pain and, in the end, we will find that he "opened not the house of *his prisoners."* (Isaiah 14:17)

Understandably such have cause to despair, but we who have been born again have *hope.* We have received the revelation of God's love. Moreover, we have the blessed assurance that:

> *"He doth not afflict willingly nor grieve the children of men.*
> *To crush under His feet all the prisoners of the earth."*
>
> (Lamentations 3:33-34)

> *"For He hath looked down from the height of His sanctuary; from heaven did the Lord behold the earth;*
> *To hear the groaning of the prisoner; to loose those that are appointed to death."*
> (Psalm 102:19-20)

Jesus came to execute this divine desire...to "proclaim liberty to the captives, and *the opening of the prison* to them that are bound." (How symbolically significant it was that a *prisoner,* Barabbas, was set free on the day of Jesus' death - and his name means *son of Abba!*) (Isaiah 61:1, See 42:6-7; 49:9, Psalm 146:7, Romans 8:15, Galatians 4:6)

Once we came out of sin's prison, though, we became, in a very positive, good and beneficial sense, *prisoners* of the very One who liberated us: *prisoners* of His love, *prisoners* of His purpose, *prisoners* of His keeping power.

We are not our own any longer.

We have been bought with a price.

Our choices in life now are not to be made independent of His will.

And if it takes presenting our bodies a living sacrifice just to "know" the perfect will of God, how much more will it take a total crucifixion of self to fulfill that will. (See Romans 12:1-2)

This is the inescapable demand of sonship.

If we run from such a responsibility or if we willfully stray from the Shepherd, we can expect chastisement - that "we should not be condemned with the world." (I Corinthians 11:32)

One way or the other God intends to keep us in His grip!

He even promised that nothing can pluck us out of His hand!

● As we consider these truths, it becomes all the more comforting to know that - "the Lord...despiseth not HIS PRISONERS" (those who are bound to Him in a covenant relationship: spiritual, blood-bought bondslaves who are committed to His service and His care). (Psalm 69:33, See I Peter 4:19)

We know that the will of God will never take us where His grace cannot keep us. If His plan for our lives carries us through fiery trials, it is so that our faith will be found "unto praise and honour and glory at the appearing of Jesus Christ." (I Peter 1:7)

Though it may seem, at times, that we are locked inside of adverse circumstances we cannot avoid, we know that "all things work together for good to them that love God, to them who are THE CALLED ACCORDING TO HIS PURPOSE." (Romans 8:28)

So let us "hold fast the confidence and *the rejoicing of the hope* firm unto the end." (Hebrews 3:6)

Let us ever consider that Jesus is not only our Lord and Master; He is "our *hope*." (I Timothy 1:1)

So for *prisoners of hope,* our *hope* is not a concept; it is a person - one who was both God and man - *the God of hope* who fills us with all joy and peace in believing.

LITERAL "PRISONERS OF HOPE"
CHOICE BIBLICAL EXAMPLES

There are many characters in biblical history that were literal prisoners of hope. As we turn our attention toward three of them - Joseph, Paul and Jesus - we are sure to learn valuable "hope-lessons" very applicable to those who suffer in a similar, though spiritual sense.

■ Joseph - the patriarch in prison ─────────────

Joseph, the eleventh son of Jacob, received two dreams that clearly indicated his older brethren would one day bow down to him. God had ordained that he be their leader, deliverer and strength during a time of severe famine yet to come. These prophetic insights became *hope-seeds* planted in Joseph's spirit even when his brethren totally rejected him.

As a slave in Egypt he was once again wrongly judged and falsely accused. He was thrown into prison, into the king's dungeon. Through it all, God was working out His intricately detailed plan. Pharaoh's dreams had to be interpreted. Joseph had to be brought out of prison and appointed prime minister. Grain had to be stored in huge deposits, and all the Israelites had to move to Egypt.

Afterward, Joseph comforted his brethren by saying - "Fear not...as for you, ye thought evil against me; but God meant it unto good...to save much people alive." (Genesis 50:19-20)

Joseph realized he was never a prisoner of his brethren, of the Ishmaelites, or of the Egyptians. **He was a prisoner of the ordination of his God.**

167

In a similar way, some of you who are reading this chapter may have been placed by God in the midst of a family, a church, a ministry, a business or a job where there is a great deal of misunderstanding, conflict, rejection, persecution or opposition.

You may want to run from the pressure.

It may even feel like a prison to you. But if you are chosen of God and in His will, you can look to the future with hope. We are not prisoners of our circumstances. We are prisoners of God's purpose - and this is cause to rejoice. In the end, His perfect purpose will bring forth much fruit. Others may intend evil against us, but God is very capable at making it all turn to our benefit.

■ Paul - the apostle in prison

Paul is an excellent example of a person fulfilling this *title-calling*. He even referred to himself several times as either *the prisoner of Jesus Christ* or *the prisoner of the Lord.* (Ephesians 3:1; 4:1, Philemon 1:1,9)

This was the apostle's way of publicly explaining and affirming the primary reason that he was in jail. It was not so much the Jewish authorities, nor the Roman government, that put him behind bars. Rather, it was the God of heaven who had ordered his steps and ordained it to be so.

Numerous believers had warned Paul, by the Spirit, that if he went to Jerusalem, bonds, afflictions and imprisonment awaited him there. Some of them apparently presumed that, this being the case, he should not go. (See Acts 21:10-14)

Paul, though, sensed that it was God's will and should therefore not be feared. He even confessed to the elders of the church at Ephesus:

> *"And now, behold, I go bound in the spirit unto Jerusalem..."*
>
> (Acts 20:22)

This passage especially reveals that Paul was a *prisoner* before he was ever locked up in literal manacles and chains.

He was *the Lord's prisoner*...a willing and submissive *prisoner* to the will and purpose of God.

He was *bound in the spirit* to something that certainly he would have preferred not to face.

He was *bound* by a sense of duty.

He was *bound* by his covenant commitment to God. (See Ezekiel 20:37, Numbers 30:2)

But he was surely *bound,* most of all, by His love for the Master.

The love of Christ constrained him.

He possibly could have gotten out of it and been relatively blessed and fruitful serving God in some other capacity (in what might be termed God's permissive will). Instead, Paul courageously chose God's perfect will: the place of greatest suffering, yet also, the place of greatest joy, victory and reward.

Paul, to a degree, must have realized this for he asserted - "that the things which happened unto me have fallen out rather unto the furtherance of the gospel; so that my *bonds in Christ* are manifest in all the palace, and in all other places; and many of the brethren in the Lord, waxing confident by my *bonds*, are much more bold to speak the word without fear." (Ph. 1:12-14)

Quite possibly the greatest fruit born of Paul's forced time of solitude were the epistles which have since blessed multiplied millions.

If he had not had so much extra time on his hands, they may never have been written. Paul probably never knew the vast importance nor the far-reaching impact that these epistles would eventually have, but God did.

All Paul could do was sow in whatever capacity possible under the adverse circumstances, and trust God to bring the increase. He was a *prisoner* in chains "for the *hope of Israel*": his belief in the Messiah and the resurrection of the dead. (Acts 28:20)

So also, our faith may carry us into extreme commitments to the will of God. We may even feel *bound in the spirit* to something that others consider improbable, illogical, avoidable or undesirable. But follow through we must, knowing that God reserves the best for those who leave the choices to Him.

■ Jesus - the Saviour in prison

Jesus is the finest example of this particular concept. Isaiah 53:8 prophesied that He would be "taken from *prison* and from judgment...for the transgression of [His] people."

When He could have walked away from it all, love constrained Him to submit to the will of the Father in Gethsemane. When He could have called ten thousand angels to rescue Him, instead He submitted to the cruelty of man on Calvary.

He was both a *prisoner* of the election of God and a *prisoner of hope*!

Though He walked willfully into the horrid, ruthless, gaping mouth of death, His *hope* was to rise above it all, and become "the *hope* of all the ends of the earth." (Psalm 65:5 NIV)

This divine desire was fulfilled, so much so that now He can extend His nail-scarred hands to all who are crucified with Him (*His prisoners* in this world) promising:

> *"I am the resurrection, and the life: he that believeth in Me, though he were dead, yet shall he live."*
>
> (John 11:25)

This is the ultimate *hope* of *prisoners of hope*.

If we know Him in the fellowship of His suffering, we will also know Him in the power of His resurrection.

If we suffer with Him, we shall also reign with Him.

We know that He will one day open the house of *His prisoners* and set us free - never to bear this *title* again.

To receive such a promise and finally see it come to pass is *the hope of our calling, our blessed hope* and *our hope of glory*...something so wonderful that earth-bound words can never sufficiently describe it!

HIS REST

HIS RESTING PLACE

AN HOUSE OF REST

● THE PLACE OF HIS REST ●

HIS REST FOR EVER

*"Arise, O Lord, into **THY REST;** Thou, and the ark of Thy strength."*

(Psalm 132:8)

"Now therefore arise, O Lord God, into **THY RESTING PLACE,** *Thou, and the ark of Thy strength..."*

(II Chronicles 6:41)

"Then David the king stood up upon his feet, and said, Hear me, my brethren, and my people: As for me, I had in mine heart to build **AN HOUSE OF REST** *for the ark of the covenant of the Lord, and for the footstool of our God..."*

(I Chronicles 28:2)

"Thus saith the Lord, The heaven is My throne, and the earth is My footstool: where is the house that ye build unto Me? and where is **THE PLACE OF MY REST?"**

(Isaiah 66:1)

"For the Lord hath chosen Zion; He hath desired it for His habitation.
This is **MY REST FOR EVER:** *here will I dwell; for I have desired it."*

(Psalm 132:13-14)

HIS REST

*"Arise, O Lord, into THY REST; Thou, and
the ark of Thy strength."*

(Psalm 132:8)

● All of the five *title-scriptures* quoted at the beginning of this chapter refer first to a literal structure, building or location provided for the ark of the covenant at different times under the Old Will. On a second and higher level, they refer to all those under the New Will who have become God's *abode*..the new dwelling place of His covenant and His glory.

Let us inspect each of these scriptures individually.

1. In Psalm 132:8 David pled - *"Arise, O Lord, into THY REST; Thou, and the ark of Thy strength."* This prayer of the psalmist was uttered when the ark was to be removed from Obededom's house and set up in the tent David had erected for it on mount Zion.

2. In II Chronicles 6:41 Solomon prayed a very similar prayer - *"Now therefore arise, O Lord God, into THY RESTING PLACE, Thou, and the ark of Thy strength..."* This was part of the petition recited when the ark was in transit from the tabernacle of David to the newly constructed temple of Solomon.

3. In I Chronicles 28:2 David spoke of how he originally desired to build this temple of worship, but was prevented by Jehovah from doing so. He called it - **"AN HOUSE OF REST."**

4. In Psalm 132:13-14 David spoke of Zion, the mountain where the tabernacle for the ark was set up, and he quoted God as saying - *"This is MY REST FOR EVER: here will I dwell; for I have desired it."*

5. Finally, Isaiah 66:1-2 is God's declaration that all of these other physical locations were insufficient in meeting His need; and that a poor-in-spirit, contrite individual is actually His prime choice for a temple-dwelling. Let us examine these two verses closely. (This passage of Scripture has already been emphasized in previous chapters entitled *The Contrite Ones* and *The Humble* and will yet be emphasized in *The Temple*):

> *"Thus saith the Lord, The heaven is My throne, and the earth is My footstool: where is the house that ye build unto Me? and where is THE PLACE OF MY REST?*
> *For all those things hath Mine hand made, and all those things have been, saith the Lord: but to this man will I look, even to him that is poor and of a contrite spirit, and trembleth at My Word."*

So God was very plainly stating that the tabernacle of Moses, the tabernacle of David, the temple of Solomon, and mount Zion itself had never provided

His Spirit a suitable *resting place*. They were only temporary stopping points on a divine journey leading to something far better.

God has always desired living sanctuaries: humble, repentant and believing hearts that would yield to His influence and indwelling. So Jesus went to the cross to provide the blood that would wash us clean.

Not only that we might find *a place of rest* in God.

But that God might find *a place of rest* in us.

Because of this, we have even inherited the names that God gave His temporary Old Will dwelling places.

We are called **THE TABERNACLE OF DAVID** and **THE TABER-NACLES OF THE MOST HIGH**. (See Acts 15:16, Psalm 46:4)

We are called **THE TEMPLE OF GOD**. (See I Corinthians 3:16)

And spiritually speaking, we are even referred to as **ZION**. (See Zechariah 2:7, Psalm 102:16)

Therefore, it is both logical and reasonable to assume that we can also refer to ourselves as **HIS REST, HIS RESTING PLACE, AN HOUSE OF REST** and **HIS REST FOR EVER**.

If the Old Will **temple of God** - inferior, insufficient and temporal - was called **His resting place**, how much more should the New Will **TEMPLE OF GOD** - superior, sufficient and eternal - be entitled **HIS RESTING PLACE!**

And if the original ark of the covenant in the holy of holies was glorious (being a type and shadow of that which was to come)...how much more glorious is the antitype, the fulfillment of the symbol.

As we will yet see more clearly, that fulfillment involves:

God's nature,
God's holiness,
God's power,
God's glory,
God's name,
God's provision,
God's authority,
God's life,
God's law,
God's Word,
God's mercy,
God's covenant,
God's throne,
And the privilege of high worship,
Residing in the heart of every redeemed child of God.

WHY DID GOD NEED A RESTING PLACE?

The answer to the above question has already been partially answered in the chapter entitled *His Abode.*

When Adam and Eve fell in the beginning, sin laid a death-grip on the whole world and the gentle, grieving Spirit of God rushed away in departure. From that time onward, neither man nor God could truly be at *rest* in this realm. (See Psalms 38:3, 39:12, Jeremiah 14:8)

● **The great dilemma and the seemingly unsolvable problem can be summed up in three simple statements.**
1. God could not dwell with sin.
2. Man could not free himself from sin.
3. Therefore, God could not dwell in man.

God was offended and repelled. Man was rebellious and unworthy.

Because the flesh constantly lusts against the Spirit, and the Spirit constantly strives against the flesh, heaven and earth became quite incompatible.

There was no peace, no harmony, no contentment, no fulfillment - *no rest* - in the Creator's relationship with this prime portion of His creation.

But thank God, He did not forsake us in our miserable plight!

Instead, the Most High formulated, and began implementing, a step-by-step plan that would ultimately restore a portion of Adam's seed back to this calling of being *His abode - His resting place.*

Reaching such a renewed state of harmonious coexistence would be no easy task; it would take centuries and even millenniums to accomplish. On the way that direction, though, God purposed, in His curious and mysterious way, to prophetically foreshadow the highest expression of His plan in lesser expressions of symbolic truth.

THE DOVE SYMBOL
THE HOLY SPIRIT SEEKING A RESTING PLACE

● **Two main biblical symbols bring forth this concept of "God seeking *a place of rest"*: the dove symbol and the ark symbol.**

We will explore the dove symbol first (already touched upon in *His Abode*).

Toward the end of the flood, Noah (whose name means *rest*) sent forth a dove from the ark, but she "found no *rest* (Heb. *manowach - a settled spot or home*) for the sole of her foot." The dove returned to Noah only to be sent forth again. This time she came back with an "olive leaf pluckt off." This was the sign that the waters had abated from off the earth. The dove was then sent forth a third time and never returned again. (See Genesis 8:8-12)

In this story, the dove is representative of the Holy Spirit.

After the fall of Adam, the enemy came in like a flood and ungodliness flooded the world. Under the Old Will, our heavenly "Noah," the Father of *rest,* sent forth this *"dove of the Holy Spirit"* to aid and bless His people, but again, the dove found no *"rest* for the sole" of His foot: no *settled spot,* no *home,* no heart in which He could continually and peacefully *abide.*

The Spirit of God would "move on" or *"rest* upon" certain individuals temporarily, but He never took up residence within them permanently. (See Numbers 11:25-26, II Kings 2:15, Judges 6:34; 15:14)

Far too often, God's covenant people "rebelled, and vexed His Holy Spirit" and the dove was compelled to return back to God. (Isaiah 63:10)

But then Jesus came.

In advance Isaiah foresaw that the Spirit of the Lord would *"rest* upon Him, the spirit of wisdom and understanding, the spirit of counsel and might, the spirit of knowledge and of the fear of the Lord." (Isaiah 11:2)

175

When this Son of man/Son of God was baptized, (representing His iden-
tification with us in death) the following phenomenon took place:

> *"And John bare record, saying, I saw the*
> *Spirit descending from heaven like a dove,*
> *and it **abode** upon Him.*
> *And I knew Him not: but He that sent me*
> *to baptize with water, the same said unto me,*
> *Upon whom thou shalt see the Spirit descend-*
> *ing, and **remaining** on Him, the same is He*
> *which baptizeth with the Holy Ghost."*
>
> (John 1:32-33)

For the first time in human history, the dove found a *resting place,* a
permanent residence on earth, a place of quiet and constant communion. But
then, like an "olive leaf pluckt off," the Messiah was cut off in the midst of His
days. He was "put to death in the flesh, but quickened by the Spirit" - and by
the "dove" of the Spirit He was carried back to heaven. (I Peter 3:18)

Parallel to the Noahic symbol, at that point the "flood waters" of judgment
and death, to a great degree, abated from off the earth - and man could be
reconciled to God. Fifty days later the dove-symbol was completed, for on the
day of Pentecost the Holy Spirit was sent forth from heaven into the upper
room - and into the hearts of believers - **never to return again.**

THE ARK SYMBOL
THE SON OF GOD SEEKING A RESTING PLACE

Just as the dove in its journeys represented how the Holy Spirit would seek
a place of rest in the hearts of men, so the ark of the covenant in its journeys
represented how the Son of God would seek for a similar place of quiet
communion and covenantal relationship.

In order to support this claim, let us inspect all the details of this divinely
designed and sacred piece of furniture.

● **There were five main parts to the ark itself:** the chest, the lid (which also
served as the mercy seat), the cherubim, the staves and the rings. (Refer to the
cover of this volume.)
● **Four items were contained in the ark:** the law on tablets of stone, Aaron's
rod that budded, the golden bowl full of manna, and the book of the law.
● **The most significant aspect of the ark was the Shekinah glory that rested
between the cherubim just above the mercy seat.**

Because of this last feature especially, the ark was all-important in the faith
and worship of the Israelites. This was the their contact with heaven, God's
footstool on earth. This was the connection, the bridge between time and
eternity, the place of salvation, redemption and reconciliation under the former
era. **To God's New Covenant offspring, though, the ark is merely a biblical
symbol, albeit an extremely important one, foreshadowing the Christ
which was, at that time, yet to come.**

From the moment the glory of God descended upon Jesus in the Jordan river,

He began fulfilling to perfection all that the ark symbolized.

Instead of the ancient, gold-overlaid acacia wood box, Jesus became the container of God's covenant and of the bread which comes from above. He became our "mercy-seat": the "place" of atonement, the sole source of hope for erring sinners seeking to be reconciled to God. (See Isaiah 42:6; 49:8, I Timothy 2:5, Hebrews 8:6; 9:15; 12:24)

But not only does the ark represent the *Christ in His glory*, it also speaks of *the glory of Christ in His church*: what Jesus is in the heart of every believer.

The uniqueness and importance of the ark is seen in the fact that it was the first piece of sacred furniture constructed and the only article used in all three of the Jews' "worship structures": the tabernacle of Moses, the tabernacle of David and the temple of Solomon.

Without the presence of the ark, these religious structures would have been relatively meaningless and powerless. And so it is also, that without the personal presence of Jesus Christ in our lives, all of our religious strivings are in vain. Therefore, let it be emphasized again:

The ark of the covenant represents two things:
First, it is a symbol of all that Jesus is.
Second, it is a symbol of all that Jesus can be in us.

Let us keep this dual application constantly before us as we study the following details of the ark. And let us rehearse the theme passage of this volume over and over in our hearts - *Christ in us, the hope of glory.*

A DETAILED STUDY OF
THE ARK OF THE COVENANT
(A symbol of the presence of God seeking a place of rest)

(Note: in each of the following divisions, a certain symbolic aspect of the ark is first described, then the interpretation is given. Usually, italicized words are employed to connect the symbol and the truth it reveals).

THE HEBREW DERIVATION ───────────────────

Symbol - The Hebrew word translated *ark* is *arown*. This came from a primary root word *arah* which means *to pluck (in the sense of gathering).*

> *Interpretation* - It is possible that this word was used because by means of the ark - and by means of what the ark symbolized - a harvest of souls would be *"gathered"*...reaped from the human race..."*plucked*" out of the fire of eternal damnation. *Arown* has also been translated *chest* and *coffin*. In II Kings 12:10-11 it was used in reference to a *chest* containing offering money for the repair of the temple. In Genesis 50:26, it was used in reference to the *coffin* that contained Joseph's remains. So *arown* speaks also of a container for that which is valuable, as well as preservation in death. Jesus is both to us and we are possessors of both...in His name.

177

Symbol - **The following is a list of twenty-three names given to the ark, twenty-two from the Old Testament and one from the New Testament:** 1. *the ark* (Ex. 25:21) 2. *the ark of the testimony* (Ex. 25:22) 3. *the ark of the covenant* (Jo. 3:6) 4. *the ark of the covenant of the Lord* (Jer. 3:16) 5. *the ark of the covenant of God* (II Sam. 15:24) 6. *the ark of the covenant of the Lord of hosts* (I Sam. 4:4) 7. *the ark of God* (I Sam. 3:3) 8. *the ark of the Lord God* (I Kgs. 2:26) 9. *the ark of the Lord, the Lord of all the earth* (Jo. 3:13) 10. *the ark of the God of Israel* (I Sam. 5:7) 11. *an ark of shittim wood* (Ex. 25:10) 12. *the holy ark* (II Chr. 35:3) 13. *the ark of Thy strength* (Ps. 132:8) 14. *the ark of the Lord God of Israel* (I Chr. 15:14) 15. *the ark of our God* (I Chr. 13:3) 16. *the ark of God the Lord* (I Chr. 13:6) 17. *the ark of the Lord* (Jo. 4:11) 18. *His strength* (Ps. 78:61) 19. *His glory* (Ps. 78:61) 20. *His footstool* (Ps. 132:7) 21. *the footstool of our God* (I Chr. 28:2) 22. *the testimony* (Ex. 30:36) 23. *the ark of His testament* (Rev. 11:19). This last name was used only of the ark in heaven after which the earthly ark may have been patterned. Of course, this could have been the earthly ark assumed into heaven at some point in its history.

Interpretation - Though many of these names are similar, all have their significance. Viewed together they provide a good picture of what happens when "the ark" enters our lives. It brings us into a *covenant* relationship with *the Lord of all the earth* and makes us *holy* and fit containers for His presence. God's *strength* and God's *glory* fill us and radiate out of us toward others. We each become an heir and a witness of the testament which he has established. We become *His footstool* - *His place of rest* and a channel of His authority in this world. (See explanation for *His footstool* at the end of the chapter entitled *The Temple of God.*)

THE DWELLING PLACE OF THE NAME OF GOD —————————

Symbol - I Chronicles 13:6 speaks of "the ark of God the Lord, that dwelleth between the cherubims, *whose name is called on it.*" So the ark was the place where the *name* of God was revealed, manifested, declared and praised.

Interpretation - In Jesus we find the revelation, manifestation and declaration of *the name of God*...and it all redounds to His praise. All of the redemptive names of God revealed in the Old Testament - Jehovah-Jireh, Jehovah-Rophe, El Shaddai, etc - find their ultimate fulfillment in Jesus. It is as if all these various names are melted down and forged into one glorious name that is above every name: **the Lord Jesus Christ.** This is the triune name of the triune God: **Lord** (relating to the Father) **Jesus** (relating to the Son) and **Christ** (which means *Anointed One,* relating to the anointing of the Holy Spirit). So we see the fullness of the Godhead revealed bodily in Jesus who is our "covenant ark" in this Age of grace. Jesus Himself verified this when He said - "Father...I have manifested Thy *name*...and I have declared unto them Thy *name.*" (Jn. 17:1,6,26) Now we have become His holy of holies, the sacred chamber of this ark of God's testament, so over our lives *the name of God* is being revealed, manifested, declared and praised. Because of the miraculous change His *name* has wrought in us, we will ever be *His people for His renown and praise and honor.* (See II Chr. 6:20;7:14, Jer. 13:11 AV, NIV)

THE MATERIALS USED

Symbol - According to Exodus 25:10-11, the ark was made of *shittim wood* (also known as *acacia wood*). It was then inlaid and overlaid with gold. The Septuagint called this material *"incorruptible wood"*...certainly because of its hardness and durableness. The *acacia* tree - a very deep-rooted and gnarled tree - grows in conditions that would prove to be life-threatening to most vegetation - the arid, blistering hot, desert region of Sinai. The original Hebrew word *shittiym* proceeds from the word *shotet* which means *to flog or scourge* (because of its *scourging thorns*). It is also worth mentioning that around the top of the ark was something called *a crown of gold.* This apparently held the mercy seat in place. (Exodus 37:2)

> *Interpretation* - All of the above details are very symbolic. The wood speaks of Jesus' humanity, how He was tempted in all points, yet He was never *corrupted* by sin. He endured the unbelief, the rejection, the persecution, the *scourging* that He received here below...and not only the cruel whiplashes literally laid on his back in Pilate's hall. The tongue-lashing of the Jews who opposed Him must have cut nearly as deep. He was "a root out of a *dry* ground" - for at that time, desert-dry, spiritual conditions prevailed all around Him threatening the very life of the nation of Israel. And not only was He *scourged,* He was *crowned with thorns.* Still He overcame - because He was *overlaid* and *inlaid,* covered over and filled, with the brilliant and lasting gold of the divine nature. This threefold combination - gold/wood/gold - represents the three-in-one nature of the Godhead. The outer covering of gold represents the Father, the wood - the Son, and the inlaid gold - the indwelling Holy Spirit.
> The beauty of the symbolism is enhanced when we realize that Jesus came to share all of this with His own. Those who become *His rest,* His holy of holies dwelling place, receive "an inheritance *incorruptible*" and come forth as *gold.* Having been begotten of an *"incorruptible* seed," we become partakers of both the human and divine nature of the One who was *scourged* for us. "And of His fulness have all we received." (I Pt. 1:4,23, Jn. 1:16) As He was *crowned* with life, righteousness and glory; so have we been *crowned* as well. (James 1:12, II Timothy 4:8, I Peter 5:4)

THE DIMENSIONS OF THE ARK

Symbol - The dimensions of the ark of the covenant are as follows: 2.5 cubits long, 1.5 cubits wide and 1.5 cubits high.

> *Interpretation* - The dimensions of the crown of the ark (also called the mercy seat) speaks of the incarnation of the Son of God: 2 X 1.5 =3 (the number of the Godhead) and 2 X 2.5 = 5 (the number of grace and atonement) - hence, the foreshadowing of how Jesus would be

God manifested on earth, full of *grace* and ready to mercifully *atone* for the sins of men. The full measurement added together 3 + 5 =8 is the number that speaks of *resurrection, new creation and new beginnings*...exactly what Jesus did, what He is doing, and what He will yet perform to perfection. Each end of the ark was 4 X 1.5 =6 cubits in circumference (the number of man). Added together the measurement is 6 + 6 =12 (the number of the perfection of divinely ordered government). So Jesus, the Wonderful Counselor, came to gather all redeemed men of the Old and New Will, (represented by both ends of the ark) under His kingship. He came to sit "upon the throne of David, and upon his kingdom, to order it, and to establish it with judgment and with justice from henceforth even for ever." (Is. 9:7) We will be a part of the perfect governing body that will assist Him in His rule.

THE LOCATION OF THE ARK

Symbol - The ark was placed in *the holy of holies*; first, in the tabernacle of Moses; then, later on, in the temple of Solomon. This inner sanctuary was also called *the holy place* (Heb. 9:12); *the most holy place* (I Kgs. 6:16); *the holiest of all* (Heb. 9:3); *the most holy house* (II Chr. 3:10); *the inner house* (I Kgs. 6:27); *the oracle* (I Kgs. 6:20); *His holy oracle* (Ps. 28:2); *the oracle of the house* (II Chr. 5:7); *the place of the mercy seat* (I Chr. 28:11); and *His place* (II Chr. 5:7). The word *oracle* means *utterance of God*. When used in reference to the holy of holies, in essence it means - *the place of His voice* or *the place from which He speaks*. In the tabernacle, the dimensions of the holy of holies were 10X10X10 cubits, a perfect cube. In the temple of Solomon, the measurements doubled to 20X20X20 cubits, still a perfect cube. Above the holy of holies was another 10 cubit upper chamber used for a *treasury*.

Interpretation - The main emphasis is very plain: the fact that God will only dwell in that which is exceptionally *holy*. The tabernacle of Moses primarily represented Jesus. He was *holy*, undefiled and separate from sinners - the Father's dwelling place on earth. But even as the ark was moved from the tabernacle to the temple, so the glory of God moved from a one-member body in Jesus, to a many-membered body in the church. Now we are a *holy temple unto the Lord*...through the application of the precious blood of Jesus. In our regenerated spirits - which is *the most holy place* of all - *God speaks to us*. Moreover, because the spiritual ark dwells within us, there are times when God may speak out of us. Peter said - "If any man speak, let him speak as the *oracles* of God." (I Peter 4:11)

If we are God's *holy of holies*, then above us is the Headship of Christ, who has also become a kind of *treasury* to us - "in whom are hid all the *treasures* of wisdom and knowledge." (Colossians 2:3)

The perfect cubic dimensions of the oracle in both the tabernacle and temple speak of the perfection of Christ being passed on to us. The doubling of the holy of holies size in the temple speaks of the double portion inheritance being passed on to the church as well as the early and the latter reign. The full measurement of the holy of holies in the temple (20X20X30) equals 12,000, which is a dimension associated with the holy city, New Jerusalem. This city is also foursquare. It is called "the bride, the Lamb's wife" and it is yet to come. (See Revelation 21:9,16)

THE CONTENTS OF THE ARK

Symbol - Contained within the ark were four main items: *the tablets of stone, the golden bowl full of manna, Aaron's rod that budded,* and *the book of the law.* (This last item was placed in the side of the ark.) All of these articles were valuable, sacred, unique and irreplaceable. They were preserved as a testimony to future generations of God's power, God's provision and God's demands toward His people.

> *Interpretation* - Just as these items were hidden in the ark beyond the veil, so their symbolic fulfillment was hidden in the very heart of the Messiah, beyond the veil of his flesh. Jesus was the way (represented by *the stony tablets*) the truth (represented by *the manna*) and the life (represented by *the blossoming rod*). He was also the Word made flesh (represented by *the book of the law*). Because the Son of God now lives within the hearts of His own, these contents of the ark tell the story, not only of what He is, but of what He is in us. This is also valuable, sacred, unique and irreplaceable. We will study each of these items in greater detail individually.

THE TABLES OF THE LAW

Symbol - The tablets of stone were also called *the tables of the covenant* (Heb. 9:4) *the two tables of testimony* (Ex. 31:18) and *the testimony* (Ex. 16:34). These stones contained the ten commandments, *engraved* thereon by the fiery finger of God. They presented the moral standard that Jehovah, the Lawgiver, expected His people to abide by all their days.

> *Interpretation* - These two tables represented two main things. They were first a *testimony* and revelation of Jesus, the Son of God, who would come to fulfill the law and actually be the embodiment of the Old Covenant law. (See Mt. 5:17, Is. 42:6, Ps. 40:8, Heb. 10:7) Second, these tables *testified* of the work that God is presently performing in His New Covenant people. Even as God, with His finger, *engraved* His law on those stony tablets, so has He written, or *engraved*, the law in our hearts: hearts that were also, at one time, as hard as stone. (See Jer. 31:33, Ez. 36:26) Something *engraved* is permanent. God intends that this change of heart in us be a permanent covenant act, something He will watch over to preserve. The law is part of our inner character now, so we should automatically strive for that which is moral and good. (See I Corinthians 9:21)

THE GOLDEN BOWL FULL OF MANNA

Symbol - God provided for the Jews forty years by sending bread from heaven. It was called *manna* (meaning *What is it?* - the Jews first reaction to its appearance). Every man was commanded to take an equal amount - an omer - and none was to be left until the morning. If left over, it would breed worms and stink (except when saved to be eaten on the Sabbath). It was round and small (like coriander seed), white (like bdellium); it came with the dew of heaven, and was described as tasting like fresh oil or sweet as honey. It melted as the sun arose. All of the manna was visible and readily accessible to the Israelites except this small portion that was hidden in *a golden bowl in the ark of the covenant.* (See Exodus 16:13-36, Numbers 11:7-9)

> *Interpretation* - This *manna* definitely represented Jesus who would also descend with the dew of heaven (the Holy Spirit) and who would be the true bread from heaven (the Word made flesh).(See Jn. 6:32-63, Mt. 4:4) Concerning His purposes and truth, carnal minded human beings still say - *"What is it?"* - unable to comprehend on their own. In coming to Him, believers are all equally provided for; there are no children of God that lack sufficient promises or grace. As the Jews were commanded to eat all the manna, so we must be willing to digest into our inner being the entirety of the Word of God. If we eat only a portion, our lives will become a breeding ground for worm-like evil spirits and evil attitudes. **Jesus is the true manna from above.** As it was small, like coriander seed, so He became small, compared to His former glory and greatness, in order to become seed sown in the earth. The whiteness of the manna speaks of Jesus' purity; the roundness, of His perfection; the honey taste, of His sweetness; the oil-like taste, of His calling as the Anointed One. The manna was very easy to gather, laying on the surface of the ground all around the camp of Israel. This relates to those biblical truths that are "on the surface" - easily gathered by believers. The "hidden manna" - contained in the *golden bowl* in the ark - is reserved only for overcomers: those who overcome this world and all of its entrapments, those who are intimate with God, those who truly show His law written on the tables of their hearts, those who manifestly become His holy of holies on earth. (Rev. 2:17) The *golden bowl* speaks of being partakers of the divine nature, being "shaped" into godly individuals. When this happens, we become suitable containers for a certain "bread-like" inheritance. As Jesus was the bread of life, so we are called to be living bread also - nourishing the heart of God, so hungry for fellowship, and the hearts of men, so hungry for truth. (See I Cor. 10:17, also the chapter on *One Bread*, **Our Glorious Inheritance**, Vol. 4)

AARON'S ROD THAT BUDDED

Symbol - In order to still the rebellion begun by Korah and confirm Aaron's priesthood rights, God gave this plan. Twelve *rods*, one from each tribe of Israel, were to be laid up all night before the Lord in the holy of holies. The name of each tribal head was to be written on the *rod*. The name **Aaron** - which means *enlightened* - was written on the *rod* from the tribe of Levi. God promised that by the next morning, the *rod* of the man He had chosen would be changed in appearance. Only Aaron's *rod* was, bringing forth *buds, blossoms* and *almonds.* (Num. 17:1-13) It was preserved in the ark as a token, a reminder of God's purpose.

> *Interpretation* - The *rod* of a tribal head was a token of his authority. God's *rod* of authority in this world is His Word, as well

as those who bear his Word. We are even called *"the rod of His inheritance."* (Ps. 74:2) Isaiah prophesied that the Messiah would be a *"rod* out of the stem of Jesse" and would "smite the earth with the *rod* of His mouth." (Is. 11:1,4) As the quickening power of God resurrected Aaron's *rod* back to life, confirming His position as high priest, so the quickening power of the Spirit raised Jesus back to life, confirming His position as the great High Priest. And so it is, when He comes into our hearts, that we, too, are *enlightened.* He resurrects us from death into life and we are confirmed as His *"holy priesthood,"* - called to minister to God and to man. (I Pt. 2:5) We bring forth *buds, blossoms and fruit* (the thirtyfold, sixtyfold, then hundredfold development of the divine calling within). The original Hebrew word translated *almond* is *shaqed.* It means *the waker* or *the awakening one* - most likely because of its early blossoming (toward the end of January or begininng of February). In the dead of winter, even before its leaves come, the almond tree will produce lovely white blossoms, faintly tinged with pink. This all speaks of how the Word and Spirit of God *awakens* a person to righteousness, fruitfulness and victory from a state of being dead in trespasses and sin. Even after we are saved, when we are hit with death-dealing circumstances, not only can we survive; we can emerge in fruitfulness and glory. Further-more, as priests, we have inherited both the privilege and respon-sibility of *awakening* in others an inner knowledge of the truth. **Such is the sign that God has truly chosen us, that we are His repre-sentatives in this world.**

THE BOOK OF THE LAW ────────────────

Symbol - The *book of the law* was also placed in the side of the ark. This book expanded and built upon the ten commandments inscribed on the tablets of stone. Its numerous laws can be classified under three headings: moral laws, ceremonial laws and civil laws.

> *Interpretation* - This book first represented Jesus who came in *"the volume of the book"* and was "the Word...made flesh." It speaks also of how we, as believers are "under the law to Christ." By hiding God's Word in our hearts, we actually become "the epistle of Christ"...for all time and eternity. The Word of God should permeate every area of our lives. (Heb. 10:7, Jn. 1:14, I Cor. 9:21, Ps. 119:11, II Cor. 3:3)

THE MERCY SEAT ────────────────

Symbol - the lid of the ark was also called *the mercy seat.* Along with the cherubim, it was made of one solid piece of pure gold. On the Day of Atonement this *mercy seat* was sprinkled with the blood of a goat to *atone* for the sins of Israel. This was the most important place in the holy of holies, for above it the Shekinah glory hovered, and from it, God said - "I will *meet* with thee, and...*commune* with thee." (Exodus 25:17-22)

> *Interpretation* - This *mercy seat* relates first to what Jesus has become for every repentant sinner. If we were confronted only with the law, we would discover to our terror, not "the ministration of life,"

but rather, "the ministration of death." (II Cor. 3:7) Certain presumptuous and foolish Bethshemites, who opened the ark out of curiosity, found this to be all too tragically true. Over fifty thousand died as a result. (I Sam. 6:19-20) Thank God, in coming to Jesus we find that *"mercy* rejoiceth against judgment." (Ja. 2:13) What would have been a dreadful and unapproachable throne of judgment has become for us an altar of infinite mercy...and all because of the sprinkling of Jesus' precious blood. How significant it is that the same Greek word - *hilasterion* - translated *mercy seat* in Hebrews 9:5 is also rendered *propitiation* in Romans 3:25! In that verse Paul referred to Jesus - "Whom God hath set forth to be a *propitiation* through faith in His blood." It could have just as easily been worded - "Whom God hath set forth to be a *mercy seat*." For Jesus has become for us a "place" of atonement, propitiation, reconciliation, deliverance, and redemption. He *propitiated* - meaning He appeased and satisfied - the demands of justice concerning the sin debt of the human race. Now we can come to the throne of grace boldly, expecting to obtain mercy. Even as Aaron covered the mercy seat with a cloud of incense on the Day of Atonement, so we should cover it with prayer that is on fire with passion for God. Surely we will then be accepted in His presence. (See Leviticus 16:13)

This mercy seat is an earthly representation of God's heavenly throne. It was made of pure gold which speaks of the divine nature - unerring and unflawed - and so it is with our God. Furthermore, because we are now His holy of holies dwelling place, He has also enthroned Himself in our hearts, and from us, *mercy* should be extended to the world. This is only right! For if we are blessed to *commune* with the Father of mercies in the inner sanctuary of our regenerated spirits, we should then rejoice to give away to others what God has given us. (See Heb. 10:11-12, Is. 16:5, Ez. 43:7 and *Vessels of Mercy* in Volume 2 of **Our Glorious Inheritance**)

THE CHERUBIM OF GLORY ───────────────

Symbol - As already mentioned, the lid of the ark was actually comprised of three parts: the mercy seat and two *"cherubims* of cunning work," all made of *one piece of pure, solid gold.* (Ex. 36:8) The wings of the cherubim touched and the Shekinah glory of God manifested between them. Two larger cherubim were also placed in the holiest in the temple of Solomon. They were made of *olive wood overlaid with gold.* This second set of cherubim were ten cubits high and had a wing span of ten cubits. Their wings touched either wall of the holy of holies and touched each other just above the ark. Together they were both referred to as *"the chariot of the cherubims"* - an apparent connection to the psalmist's statement that God "rode upon a cherub and did fly." (I Chr. 28 :18, Ps. 18:10, See Ez. 10:18-19) The cherubim on the ark were fashioned *facing each other,* as if gazing with deep satisfaction and awe-filled worship toward the glory cloud and the blood-sprinkled mercy seat between them. The two olive wood cherubim were set *facing eastward toward the veil.* Cherubim were engraved on both the walls and the doors of the temple and were embroidered on the veil. Therefore, the depiction of these celestial creatures was seen in EVERY CHAMBER of this palace of worship unto Jehovah-God. (Ex. 25:18-22;37:9, I Kgs. 6:23-28, II Chr. 3:10-14;5:7-8, Heb. 9:5)

Interpretation - We have very little information about these mysterious heavenly creatures and no proof concerning the exact appearance of those cherubim fashioned on the lid of the ark. What little information we have is as follows. The Bible NEVER refers to the *cherubim* as angels. The word **angel** means *messenger* and this role *cherubim* are never seen fulfilling. Nevertheless, they could still be of a very high angelic order. They are almost always connected with the throne of God, the defense of His glory, the vindication of His holiness and the administration of His righteous judgments. The *cherubim* make their first appearance in Scripture when Adam and Eve were thrust out of the Garden of Eden. It was then that God "placed at the east of Eden *cherubims,* and a flaming sword...to keep [to guard] the way of the tree of life." (Gen. 3:24) This could mean that they were positioned there to either prevent man from reentering Eden or quite the opposite, to preserve the pathway that would insure his return. Of course, this would link the cherubim to the guardianship of eternal life, procured through partaking of the tree of life. They may very well be involved in this ministry now.

Cherubim do not conform to any one standard of outward appearance. Some have six wings, some four, and others have just two. (Rev. 4:8, Ez. 1:6, I Kgs. 8:7) The cherubim of Ezekiel's vision (Ez. 10) have four faces, while the cherubim of the Ezekiel's temple have two faces (Ez. 41:18). Those on the ark and in the temple of Solomon seem to have one face, as do the ones beheld by John in his revelation visitation. In this vision they are called *beasts* in the KJV, *living creatures* in the NIV. One has the appearance of a lion - which speaks of fearless dominion, another has the appearance of a calf - which speaks of servitude, another has the visage of a man - which speaks of intelligence and godlikeness, and a fourth bears the resemblance of a flying eagle - which speaks of keen insight and a conquering spirit. All four of these top the list in their species and speak of kingship and lordship. The lion is the king of all wild beasts, the calf - of all domestic animals, the eagle - of all fowl, and man - of all created beings. So the cherubim bearing these images speaks of that which is superior, excellent and Christlike. (See Rev. 4-5, Ez. 10:14) Sometimes cherubim are shown full of eyes...which speaks of great wisdom and revelation (things which are certainly acquired in the high realms of communion with God).

In the holy of holies and on the ark, the cherubim speak especially of both defense and adoration. Being the defenders of God's violated holiness, their sometimes fierce appearance reveals especially the unapproachableness of the Most High. The two olive wood cherubim on either side of the ark were positioned gazing toward the veil, seemingly guarding against any unlawful intrusion. Simultaneously, the cherubim on the ark were ever gazing toward the Shekinah glory in their midst.Thus, they became emblems of the highest degree of enraptured worship. (See Ez. 3:12, Rev. 4:8) Being of *one* piece of gold with the mercy seat, the cherubim reveal especially how we become *one* with God through worship. The wings of the cherubim touching each other typifies eternity itself and an unbroken, unceasing communion with the Almighty God. The wings of the olive wood cherubim touching either wall speaks of the plan

185

of God and the glory of God reaching into the eternal past and the eternal future - an unbroken continuance of God's sovereignty and power. The wings of heaven's cherubim sound, at times, like the very voice of the Creator. (See Ez. 1:24;3:13;10:5) God is often spoken of as dwelling between the cherubim. Apparently, this is not only true on earth, but in heaven itself. (I Sam. 4:4, II Sam. 6:2, Ps. 80:1; 99:1)

The *oil wood* or *olive wood* of the temple cherubim relates to *the oil of the anointing:* the specific application of the Holy Spirit to perform a certain task. At one time Lucifer was *"the anointed cherub that covereth"* - *"the covering cherub"*- but fell from this high calling. (Ez. 28:14,16) Now it is very possible that we, the *anointed* of the Lord, have inherited his former forfeited position...or something very similar to it. Since Jehovah has presently chosen us as His holy of holies and enthroned His glory in our hearts, we are called to daily and eternally *"cover"* Him with the devotion and adoration that He most certainly deserves. **So of all that has been said, this is the sum: the cherubim relate to holiness, revelation, wisdom, intimacy with God, eternal life, the authority of His throne and the highest state of worship attainable. Where you find the glory of God, you find these things.** (See Ezekiel 10:1-20)

THE SHEKINAH GLORY———————————————————

Symbol - Of course, the most significant thing about the ark of the covenant was *the glory of God* that rested upon it. Whether or not this was always visible is up to question, but certainly, it was ALWAYS THERE. As has been mentioned, without this *glory* all the other utensils and pieces of furniture would have been somewhat powerless and meaningless, mere religious paraphernalia. *This glory provided the only light in the holy of holies.* In the outer court they had the light of the sun; in the holy place, they had the light of the lampstand (which was still something man-made that used a supply of earthly oil, though it was lit with fire that came from heaven). In the holy of holies the light was TOTALLY DIVINE IN ORIGIN. This celestial splendor was beheld only by the high priest, who would only enter the holiest if he was crowned with the miter which bore the inscription - HOLINESS UNTO THE LORD. The Jews called this manifestation of God - THE SHEKINAH - meaning *the One who dwells.* They knew as long as the presence of the Most High dwelt with them this way, they were safe; they were secure; and they would somehow emerge victorious against all odds. The Israelites so associated the God of the ark with the ark of God that when the latter was moved, Moses and the people would pray - "Rise up, Lord, and let Thine enemies be scattered." Then when the ark rested, they would say - "Return, O, Lord, unto the many thousands of Israel." (Numbers 10:35-36)

Interpretation: The literal ark and mercy seat were only the temporary abode of the Shekinah glory of God. As our theme scripture states, now it is "Christ in you, *the hope of glory.*" (Col. 1:27) *The One who dwells* has finally found a suitable *dwelling place* and permanent ark-like *resting place* in the blood-sprinkled hearts of His redeemed. Our goal should be to live, not in the light of this world, nor even in the mixed light of the holy place, but in the pure, celestial light of the holy of holies. Our foremost thought and desire should always be HOLINESS UNTO THE LORD, communing with God daily in the deepest part of our regenerated spirit. By doing so we fulfill the call to be *His abode, His glory, His rest* and *His temple.*

THE ARK IN TRANSIT

Symbol - From the time of its creation, the ark was on a journey. *It had no rest.* It was continually changing locations, carried on the shoulders of the priests by means of two gold-overlaid acacia wood staves. These were placed in gold rings on each of the four corners of the ark. **These staves were never to be removed.** God also commanded that three coverings be placed on the ark when it was in transit, lest the people look upon the sacred depository. These were: the veil of the holy of holies, a covering of badger skins, and a cloth of blue. (Num. 4:5-6) At one time, the ark went before the camp of Israel a three day journey - *"to search out a resting place for them."* (Num. 10:33) It turned back for forty years to abide with the children of Israel in their time of backslidings and chastisements (just as God always abides faithfully with His own). Then finally, it went into the midst of the Jordan river, rolling the waters back all the way to the city of Adam. Its presence caused the walls of Jericho to fall and the Canaanite tribes to be defeated. The ark was on a God-ordained journey to a predetermined goal: the conquest of a Promised Land, the establishment of a theocratic kingdom, and the building of a glorious temple. *Until God's people had rest, the ark could not enter into rest.*

Interpretation - We must rehearse in our minds once again that the ark first represents Jesus. From the time the glory came upon Him, He too was on a God ordained journey. The Son of man had no place to *rest* His head. He was a stranger and pilgrim on a holy pilgrimage in the earth. During His journeyings, He also had three coverings. The first covering of the ark was the holy of holies veil made of fine twined linen, blue, purple and scarlet. These colors, in order, speak of Jesus' righteousness, His heavenly origin, His royal nature and His calling to be a sacrifice. The second covering of badger skins relates to the covering of Jesus' flesh: that there would be no beauty that we should desire Him, for the glory would be hidden. (See Is. 53:2, Heb. 10:20) The third covering, a cloth of blue, speaks especially of the heaven-sent anointing of the Holy Spirit that rested upon the firstborn Son. **It behooves us to remember that now these coverings have been tranferred to every member of the body of Christ.** Because He is our covering, the covering that *rested* upon Him, now *rests* upon us. Jesus, our covenant ark, passed through the deep, dark Jordan waters of death and rolled it all the way back to the sin of Adam - that we all might pass through. He toppled the walls of the kingdom of darkness, defeating our enemies for us, that we might inhabit a spiritual "Land of Promise." He accomplished all these things that the New Covenant temple of the Lord might be built out of lively stones. Jesus came to provide *a place of rest for us* ("Come unto me...and ye shall find *rest* unto your souls" - Mt. 11:28-29) that He might find *a place of rest in us.*

It is also worthy of being mentioned that the priests who bore the ark were called **Kohathites.** This name means *assembly* and speaks of the fact that the whole *assembly* of God's people should *bear His* *glory* through this world. This can never be accomplished by means of a Philistine-like wagon of manmade religion, but on the shoulders of those who are sanctified unto the priesthood and sincerely willing to bear the burden of all that the ark represents. If we do not seek God "after the due order" this way, it will surely create a "breach" between us and God...something foreshadowed by Uzzah's tragedy so long ago. (See II Samuel 6:1-11, I Chronicles 15:13)

THE STAVES REMOVED

Symbol - The staves in the ark were *never to be removed* during its "tabernacle years": the years of wandering through the wilderness of Sin and the years of battling the Canaanite tribes. But when *King Solomon - "a man of rest"* - finally ruled over Israel, the people had *rest* from all their enemies round about. (I Chr. 22:9) The temple was then built and the ark finally found its *place of rest*. At that time, the staves were *finally removed* from the rings and laid just within the veil, so as to be visible from the holy place. (I Kgs. 8:8)

> *Interpretation* - The *temple of Solomon* is a predominant biblical symbol of the church, which has become a far more perfect *temple of God* under the New Covenant. Just as the ark had *no rest* until it was placed in that first temple, so the glory of God had *no rest* until it was finally able to enter into the hearts of His offspring, beginning with the day of Pentecost. This was the day when the New Testament temple of God began to be built. Every Old Testament dwelling place for God was temporary, something that He eventually forsook. But when our heavenly *Solomon* - our King of peace and *"man of rest"* - began choosing redeemed, blood-washed men and women as *His abode,* He rejoiced to declare - "I will never leave thee, nor forsake thee." (Heb. 13:5) His days of searching and wandering ceased. Once the ark of His covenant was positioned in our hearts, in a spiritual sense - *the staves were permanently removed.* Now we, too, have *rest* from our enemies round about. Also, it should be emphasized that the staves were not taken away from the temple, but laid to the side, a visible reminder of how far God had brought them. So we still contain a memory, deep inside, of our days of wandering: where we used to be without God. This inner witness - in the "holy place" of our redeemed souls - is a constant reminder of God's mercy and grace.

THE FINAL GLORY
THE MOST EXCELLENT REST

● **God never intended that the literal ark be a permanent expression of his covenant with man.** At the time when it was placed in the temple, certain items were even found to be missing from the ark (Aaron's rod and the golden bowl of manna). Furthermore, Jeremiah even foretold that in the New Will era, the emphasis on this piece of tabernacle furniture would be done away with. (See Jeremiah 3:16)

At some indefinable point in Israel's history, the ark disappeared from the scene. It may have been captured by some enemy or even assumed up into heaven. Irregardless, God must have purposed that this be the case, lest the ark become a religious fetish to the people, as the brazen serpent of old. (See Numbers 21:9, II Kings 18:4)

But even though the original ark passed away, what the ark symbolized NEVER HAS AND NEVER WILL PASS AWAY.

The ark is primarily a symbol of the presence of God. And so it is, that from the fall of man onward, this divine "presence" has also been on a journey - seeking first, *a place of rest* for God's people, and second, *a place of rest* for Himself.

The Jews of the Old Covenant *entered into God's rest* when they occupied the Land of Promise. (See Hebrews 3,4)

We of the New Covenant *enter His rest* when we possess a spiritual "Land of Promise" - a realm containing all the exceeding great and precious promises available to us from the Most High.

When we live in these promises, *we rest on God and in His name.* (See II Chr. 14:11 - Also, compare the latter part of the chapter on *Believers* in Vol. One of **Our Glorious Inheritance.**)

In returning and *rest* we are saved. (See Isaiah 30:15)

Isaiah also prophesied, concerning the infilling of the Spirit - "This is the *rest* wherewith ye may cause the weary to *rest;* and this is the refreshing..." (Isaiah 28:12)

Psalm 16:9 reveals that if we are united to God, our flesh can also *"rest in hope."* This *blessed rest* and *hope* belongs to every child of God. It is that inner knowing that we will finally be lifted far beyond all strife in the realm of time into a place of absolute confidence, eternal contentment and everlasting peace. No wonder the Bible joyously announces of the Messiah that "His *rest* shall be glorious." (Isaiah 11:10)

Again, let it be emphasized - having successfully provided *a place of rest* for His people, God has simultaneously discovered, in us, *a place of rest* for Himself. At present, the spirit of the world strives against its Creator, but for those who repent and believe - "the spirit of glory and of God *resteth* upon" us. (I Peter 4:14)

● **One day, when the resurrection transpires, this glory and *rest* will intensify to such degree that it will overflow with regenerative, recreative power into all creation.**

It will then be said - "the whole earth is a *rest*" - and also - "the whole earth is full of His *glory."* (Isaiah 14:7;6:3)

In that spectacular, heaven-on-earth era, Jehovah God will rejoice to declare over Zion:

> *"This is MY REST FOR EVER: here will I dwell; for I have desired it."*
> (Psalm 132;14)

This scripture speaks of both the eternal city of God, as well as all those who will inhabit the city. The city of God and the bride of Christ are one and the same. (See Revelation 21:9-10)

We will ever be **spiritual Zion** - the eternal *abode* of the Most High God - the place where He will find everlasting contentment, complete fulfillment, the perfection of praise, and the final unveiling of His original plan.

The purpose of deity, at the onset, was to dwell in man, and thus, reproduce Himself in divine offspring. Therefore, it is quite an understatement to say that He was never satisfied with any of the temporary arrangements initiated under the Old Covenant.

King David and King Solomon both prayed - "Arise, O Lord into **THY REST**; Thou and the ark of Thy strength" - but God never affirmed that the tabernacle or the temple would actually provide this *place of perfect rest.*

For the nature of God could never be expressed in a tent made of badger skins...and the image of the Most High could never emerge in a temple made of stones overlaid with silver and boards overlaid with gold.

Only redeemed offspring could become partakers of His divine nature this way, destined to finally emerge in the perfection of His likeness.

When this takes place, more than ever before, the King of kings will rejoice over us with joy, and joy over us with singing.

He will *"rest* in his love"...for His love will have found *a resting place* in us...forever and always. (Zephaniah 3:17)

In that day, we will surely discover, to our great delight, that everything the ark symbolized will find its highest degree of fulfillment in the glorified sons and daughters of God.

And that is...Christ in us, the hope of glory....
both now and evermore!

STRANGERS

SOJOURNERS

PILGRIMS

EXILES

---

*"For we are **STRANGERS** before Thee, and **SOJOURNERS**, as were all our fathers: our days on earth are as a shadow, and there is none abiding."*

(I Chronicles 29:15)

*"Dearly beloved, I beseech you as **STRANGERS** and **PILGRIMS** [**SOJOURNERS** and **EXILES**] abstain from fleshly lusts, which war against the soul."*

(I Peter 2:11 AV, AMP)

"I am a STRANGER IN THE EARTH: hide not Thy commandments from me."

(Psalm 119:19)

"These all died in faith, not having received the promises, but having seen them afar off, and were persuaded of them, and embraced them, and confessed that they were STRANGERS AND PILGRIMS ON THE EARTH."

(Hebrews 11:13)

"The land shall not be sold for ever: for the land is Mine; for ye are STRANGERS AND SOJOURNERS WITH ME."

(Leviticus 25:23)

"And an highway shall be there, and a way, and it shall be called The way of holiness; the unclean shall not pass over it; but it shall be for those: the WAYFARING MEN, though fools, shall not err therein."

(Isaiah 35:8)

STRANGERS IN THE EARTH

STRANGERS AND
PILGRIMS ON THE EARTH

STRANGERS AND SOJOURNERS
WITH HIM

WAYFARING MEN

THE CHOSEN PILGRIMS
OF THE DISPERSION

THE EXILES OF THE DISPERSION

THE SOJOURNERS
OF THE DISPERSION

THE DAUGHTER OF HIS DISPERSED

HIS SCATTERED PEOPLE

HIS DISPERSED ONES

THE OUTCASTS OF ISRAEL

THE DISPERSED OF JUDAH

*"Peter, an apostle of Jesus Christ, to the **STRANGERS** scattered throughout Pontus, Galatia, Cappadocia, Asia, and Bithynia [THE CHOSEN PILGRIMS OF THE DISPERSION, THE EXILES OF THE DISPERSION, THE SOJOURNERS OF THE DISPERSION]."*
(I Peter 1:1 AV, Rhm, RSV, ASV)

*From beyond the rivers of Ethiopia My suppliants, even **THE DAUGHTER OF MY DISPERSED [MY DISPERSED ONES, MY SCATTERED PEOPLE]**, shall bring My offering."*
(Zephaniah 3:10 AV, NAS, NIV)

*"And He shall set up an ensign for the nations, and shall assemble **THE OUTCASTS OF ISRAEL**, and gather together **THE DISPERSED OF JUDAH** from the four corners of the earth."*
(Isaiah 11:12)

STRANGERS

"For we are STRANGERS before Thee,
and SOJOURNERS, as were all our fathers:
our days on earth are as a shadow, and there
is none abiding."

(I Chronicles 29:15)

A stranger is an alien or a foreigner, one residing in a land other than his own. A stranger is one who does not belong to some particular group, or country, or era...an outsider, a misfit.

God warned Abraham - "Know of a surety that *thy seed* shall be a *stranger* in a land that is not their's." (Genesis 15:13)

The natural seed of Abraham were *strangers* over four hundred years in Egypt and then passed through the wilderness of Sin before they entered the Land of Promise.

We are the spiritual seed of Abraham. Therefore, we are also *"strangers in a strange land"*: this world of deception and sin.

We are passing through a terrible wilderness of temptations and tribulations on our way to a wonderful, heavenly kingdom.

This is a *strange* and peculiar land to us, this seething caldron of lust, greed, rebellion, hate and covetousness called the earth, and we just do not fit.

● Certainly it was for this reason that Peter addressed his readers as "the *strangers* scattered throughout Pontus, Galatia, Cappadocia, Asia, and Bithynia." (I Peter 1:1)

Several other translations render this entitlement - *"the chosen pilgrims of the dispersion," "the exiles of the dispersion"* and the *"sojourners of the dispersion."* (Rhm, RSV, ASV)

It seems this was a special reference to the Messianic Jews that were still *dispersed* throughout the world as a result of the Assyrian and Babylonian captivities centuries prior.

On a higher level, this speaks of how we all came from God, but have been *exiled* for a season in this "valley of the shadow of death." Having been *dispersed* throughout the nations, we are being gathered, one by one, back to the bosom of the Father.

Until we found the Lord, we were ignorant of our true origin and blind to our ultimate destiny. The covering cast over all nations veiled our minds in darkness and separation from the glory of the Father. But now, thank God, we have been enlightened know that this world is not our home.

While others are caught up in the "world spirit," we cry - "Vanity of vanities...all is vanity and vexation of spirit." (Ecclesiastes 1:2, 14)

We see past the constant carnal struggle toward goals and achievements that will end in the grave. The indwelling Spirit of truth has enabled us to differentiate between that which is temporal and valueless and that which is eternal and valuable.

We can now declare unequivocally that:

> *"...all that is in the world, the lust of the flesh, and the lust of the eyes, and the pride of life, is not of the Father, but is of the world.*
> *And the world passeth away, and the lust thereof: but he that doeth the will of God abideth for ever."*
>
> (I John 2:16-17)

● Two other scriptures out of the Old Testament, that relate to us in a New Testament sense, tie in beautifully at this point:

> *"And He shall set up an ensign for the nations, and shall assemble THE OUT-CASTS OF ISRAEL, and gather together THE DISPERSED OF JUDAH from the four corners of the earth."*
>
> (Isaiah 11:12)

> *"From beyond the rivers of Ethiopia My suppliants, even THE DAUGHTER OF MY DISPERSED [MY DISPERSED ONES, MY SCATTERED PEOPLE], shall bring My offering."*
>
> (Zephaniah 3:10 AV, NAS, NIV)

Jesus is the *ensign* lifted up for the nations.

We were *outcasts* from His presence, *dispersed* throughout the world.

But now, we are returning to Him with the *offering* of worship for the change He has wrought in our lives.

REFLECTING GOD'S FEELINGS

● This *"sense of non-belonging"* is a gift from God. It comes with the entrance of grace into our lives. It is also a reflection of the way that God Himself feels when expressing Himself in this realm.

The perfection of His holiness is so often insulted and the gentle Holy Spirit is so easily and often grieved by this wayward and rebellious human race.

This is so true that when God manifests Himself here, it is called a *visitation*.

Jeremiah lamented this sad condition, saying - "O *the hope of Israel*, the saviour thereof in time of trouble, why shouldest Thou be as *a stranger in the land*, and as *a wayfaring man* that turneth aside to tarry for a night?" (Jer. 14:8)

The following Old Testament ordinance, given to the Jews concerning the Land of Promise, shows God's attitude on the matter:

> *"The land shall not be sold forever: for the land is Mine; for ye are strangers and sojourners with Me."*
>
> (Leviticus 25:23)

In other words, God was saying - *"Even though the land is Mine, and will be forever, still, I feel somewhat out of place in this world right now. And you My people, should feel the same. You are strangers and sojourners with Me. NEVERTHELESS - HOLD ON TO WHAT I HAVE GIVEN YOU! DO NOT SELL YOUR INHERITANCE FOR ANYTHING THE WORLD MAY OFFER! MY HOPE IS THAT ONE DAY THE LAND WILL BE PERMANENTLY AND GLORIOUSLY IN YOUR POSSESSION!!"*

● This *"sense of non-belonging"* was very apparent in the Son of God during His years of ministry. One time, He was unwittingly called *"a stranger in Jerusalem"* and He even announced concerning His disciples - *"They are not of the world, even as I am not of the word."* (Luke 24:18, John 17:16)

Every true disciple of Jesus Christ must fit this description, for it is obvious that Jesus set the pace before us, then commanded us to follow. I John 2:15 further challenges- *"Love not the world, neither the things that are in the world"* for *"if any man love the world, the love of the Father is not in him."*

We are *strangers* here, so how can we find fulfillment pursuing the same things the world pursues for enjoyment? If we do so, we are only cheating ourselves and deceiving ourselves! And we end up only superficially religious!

Only those who shun the world ever come in contact with heavenly things and only those who fall in love with heavenly things tend to shun the world.

The old saying is so very true:

> *The things of earth must be known to be loved, but the things of heaven must be loved to be known.*

If we truly and deeply love the unseen things of eternity, we will be far more prone to reap the full benefits of salvation, and thus, walk in this *stranger/sojourner/pilgrim title-calling* every day of our lives.

THE POTTER'S FIELD

● Parallel to all these simple yet profound truths, it should be noted that Jesus' death-price (thirty pieces of silver) was never placed in the Jewish treasury.

Instead, the silver, which represents redemption, was used to purchase the *"potter's field, to bury strangers in."* (Matthew 27:7)

Because of this, the field was called **Aceldama,** which means - *"the field of blood."* (Acts 1:19)

There could well be a subtle, symbolic and prophetic message from heaven contained in this peculiar transaction.

For the wonderful and valuable effects of Jesus' death could not be contained in the empty and aged "treasury" of a dead and passing religious system.

Instead, that "blood money" bought a field in which to bury *strangers.*

In a spiritual sense, we are those *strangers.*

If we have been truly born again, we do not fit in this sad world with all of its senselessness and hopelessness. Instead, we choose to die to the world and be buried in *Aceldama...*buried deep in the very hope that Jesus procured through all the rejection and *bloody* persecution He suffered.

197

This plot of ground was also called *"the potter's field,"* so we assume that it was originally owned by potters. These craftsmen either obtained suitable clay for their trade from that place or it was the location where they discarded their broken and cracked vessels.

Either way the analogy fits, because those who are spiritually buried in this field always become "clay in the Master's hand." He molds and shapes their lives into something of eternal and lasting value.

Furthermore, what the world rejects, He accepts and mends. The outcasts, the ostracized, the "broken and marred vessels," can all find a place of rest, redemption, healing and acceptance in Him.

THE PRAYER OF DAVID - THE PILGRIM CALLING

When receiving an offering for the erection of the temple, and when Solomon, his son, was being anointed to reign in David's stead, this King of Israel prayed a prayer to Jehovah containing the following words:

> *"For we are **strangers** before Thee, and **sojourners**, as were all our fathers: our days on the earth are as a shadow, and there is none abiding.*
>
> *O Lord God of Abraham...keep this forever in the imagination of the thoughts of the heart of Thy people, and prepare their heart unto Thee."*

(I Chronicles 29:15, 18)

● How it keeps our affections set on heavenly things when we realize we are only *strangers* and *sojourners* in this world! This definitely prepares our hearts to seek God...but even more so when we realize we are *pilgrims* as well.

*A **pilgrim** is one who journeys, usually a long distance, to some sacred place as an act of devotion to diety. A **pilgrim** is a traveler, a wanderer, a wayfarer, one who not only stays in a place temporarily, but who normally has a set destination.*

We recognize the fact that we are only in this world temporarily...so we have begun a holy *pilgrimage*, a journey from time into eternity. Right now, we are rejected and scorned by this world below, but we expect to be accepted and received by that kingdom which is above.

In Exodus 6:4 God spoke of His Old Testament people, saying:

> *"And I have also established My covenant with them, to give them the land of Canaan, **the land of their pilgrimage**, wherein they were STRANGERS."*

So God will cause us to inherit the earth, *the land of our pilgrimage*, during the Kingdom Age to come. Then, after reigning with Christ for a thousand years, we will be propelled into the New Creation. There will be a New Heaven, a New Earth and a new capital city over all creation, New Jerusalem.

All *strangers, sojourners* and *pilgrims* in Christ are joyously awaiting the fulfillment of this stage in God's great plan.

But like the ark of God in transit through the wilderness of Sin, so we are in transit, searching for our place of permanent rest. As the patriarch, Abraham, we are looking "for a city which hath foundations, whose builder and maker is God"...an eternal city of celestial excellence. (Hebrews 11:10)

In the interim, we must be full of zeal for God.

Similar to the Jews, on the night of their providential delverance from Egypt, we are partaking of the Lamb (the living Word) with our loins girded, shoes on our feet and staffs in our hands (the universal sign of *pilgrims*). (See Ex. 12:11) We are "eating in haste," for we sense the seriousness of the hour in which we live, the swift passing of time and the nearness of our departure.

The Lord is about to "pass over" this world again with great judgments and awesome fury, so we must stay under the cleansing influence of the blood, ready at all times to respond to Jesus' slightest command.

● Moreover, we must ever remind ourselves that sin will deaden our minds, bankrupt our souls, and ultimately carry us away like floodwaters into destruction and perdition. For this cause Peter sternly warned the church of God:

> *"Dearly beloved, I beseech you as STRANGERS and PILGRIMS [SOJOURNERS and EXILES] abstain from fleshly lusts, which war against the soul."*
>
> (I Peter 2:11 AV, AMP)

We must cultivate this God-pleasing self-discipline if we are to reach the place where our desert blossoms as the rose and our parched land becomes a pool of living waters. In describing conditions such as this, Isaiah prophesied:

> *"And an highway shall be there, and a way, and it shall be called The way of holiness; the unclean shall not pass over it; but it shall be for those: THE WARFARING MEN, though fools, shall not err therein."*
>
> (Isaiah 35:8)

Again, it must be emphasized - *wayfaring men (strangers* and *pilgrims)* - are those who shun this world and its ways, for they realize their true citizenship is in another world, a heavenly world of indescribable splendor.

Only those who have a "made-up-mind" will ever find this "better country."

So let us persevere on this pilgrimage - through failures and successes, through disappointments and victories - until we reach the bosom of eternity, the throne room of the King of all kings.

● In holy desire, let us join the ranks of those who "died in faith, not having received the promises, but having seen them afar off, and were *persuaded* of them, and *embraced* them, and confessed that they were **STRANGERS AND PILGRIMS ON THE EARTH."** (Hebrews 11:13)

In order to be included in this holy number, we must not only be *persuaded* of the integrity and validity of God's Word; we must fall in love with the promises of God. We even *embrace* these promises.

If this is true, we will not dread God's demands; rather, we welcome them and find great joy in discovering and obeying them.

In our hearts there will be an echo of the psalmist's plea - "I am a *stranger* in the earth: hide not Thy commandments from me" and also - "Thy statutes have been my songs in *the house of my pilgrimage.*" (Psalm 119:19, 54)

So let us sing the songs of Zion and rejoice on our journey.

And let us declare that God is not ashamed to be called our God, for He has prepared for us a city. God would be ashamed if He could not live up to our expectations, but He always has and He always will. (See Hebrews 11:16)

DESCRIBING THE SPLENDOR

It is so difficult to explain to others the splendor of the heavenly home to which we are bound. How can we satisfactorily describe in earthly expressions something that is presently seen more with the heart than with the eyes?

Different *pilgrim-prophets* painted various pictures with their words, sometimes literal, sometimes metaphorical, as they sought to offer suitable descriptions of the heavenly state, the eventual entrance of the Kingdom of heaven into this earth-realm and the New Creation beyond.

How poetical, how picturesque are their inspired communications!

Streets of gold, walls of jasper, trees of the field clapping their hands, mountains dropping down new wine, a tree of great renown, a city with twelve foundations - all of these revelatory glimpses into the coming blissful state are so precious, so heart-warming, so stirring to the spirit. And yet...they are only feeble attempts to describe that which is celestial and eternal by comparing it to that which is terrestrial and temporal.

Heaven, the goal of our *pilgrimage,* will certainly be far more than just a crystal sea mingled with fire or a river of life flowing from the throne of God... for mere things do not constitute the deep reality of what heaven is.

Heaven will be heaven most of all because of the full, manifest presence of Jesus, our Saviour, and the overwhelmingly beautiful, spiritual atmosphere that will prevail as a result. If we are to understand heaven, we must find a more perfect way of capturing, with our minds and hearts, a true witness of what this blessed supernal atmosphere will really be like.

The following is possibly one of the best means that could be chosen.

■ **What is heaven? What will paradise really be like?**
Look at it this way.

Certainly the apostle Paul went to heaven, though at one time he was nothing more than a misguided and ruthless Jewish zealot, murdering and torturing those who called on the name of Jesus. But then he received his celebrated visitation on the Damascus road. Jesus revealed Himself and Paul repented.

He found the gracious Lord, who graciously found him.

From then on, Paul spent his life in sacrifical service to the Master.

In his latter years, he openly confessed - "I have fought a good fight, I have finished my course, I have kept the faith: henceforth there is laid up for me a crown of righteousness..." (II Timothy 4:7-8)

History tells us that Paul was beheaded, martyred during one of the great imperial persecutions. In light of these things, we can be certain that Paul, the apostle and *pilgrim*, made it *all the way home.*

● Stephen was the first martyr of the church.

As this highly-anointed, angel-faced prophet preached against the way that stiffnecked Jewish traditionalists had resisted the Holy Ghost, they added to their sin by resisting once again. Cut to the heart by Stephen's words, they gnashed on him with their teeth, then cast him outside the city and stoned him.

Saul, later known as Paul, consented unto his death and was apparently the recognized leader of the angry mob who executed Stephen that day.

As Stephen stood accused before the council, he suddenly cried aloud - "Behold, I see the heavens opened, and the Son of man standing on the right hand of God." As the stones were hurled through the air, he prayed "Lord, lay not this sin to their charge." (Acts 7:55-60)

Surely, this martyr and *stranger in the earth* made it *all the way home* also.

So we ask the question again...**What is heaven? What is the nature and essence of this place called paradise?** Heaven is a place where Paul, the murderer , and Stephen, the very man he helped to kill, will be able to walk together in perfect communion...united in the love of God forever...with no bitterness on Stephen's part, nor any guilt or depression on Paul's part.

It is a true and faithful statement that only heaven could bring to birth *a love as deep as that.*

■ Consider another example.

King David committed adultery with Bathseba. She became pregnant.

In an attempt to hide his sin, David called Bathseba's husband, Uriah the Hittite, back home from the warfront. Foiling David's cover-up plan, this valiant and devoted soldier refused to spend the night with his wife. With fervor he cried - "The ark, and Israel, and Judah, abide in tents; and my lord Joab, and the servants of my lord, are encamped in the open fields; shall I then go into mine house, to eat and to drink, and to lie with my wife? As thou livest, and as thy soul liveth, I will not do this thing." (II Samuel 11:11)

In one last desperate attempt at deception, David had Uriah killed...by purposefully commanding him to be sent into the most dangerous area of a certain battle zone, then abandoned. Uriah died that day, but he was later listed, at the will of God, among the thirty-seven mighty men of David. (II Sam.23:39)

Because of these and other scriptures, it is apparent that Uriah was a courageous man, full of righteousness and integrity, deeply committed to the Almighty God and deeply loved of God in return. We can, therefore, easily make the assumption again that this man, Uriah, was a true *stranger and pilgrim in the earth,* and that he, too, made it *all the way home.*

We also know that David was grief-stricken with remorse and that He begged God to blot out all his iniquities. The prophet Nathan prophesied certain judgments to David, but he also declared - "The Lord also hath put away thy sin." The erring king of Israel was forgiven. He was definitely restored. In thankfulness to God, David penned the words of praise..."He brought me up also out of an horrible pit, out of the miry clay, and set my feet upon a rock." (II Samuel 12:13, Psalm 40:2)

According to certain significant prophecies (Ezekiel 34:24 and 37:25) it seems quite plausible that David will reign as a prince over all the world during the Kingdom Age, subordinate only to the King of kings Himself.

By these scriptures and others we assume that David, *the sojourner* and *exile*, also made it...*all the way home.*

● **Now once again we ask for a definition. What is the nature and essence of this celestial, heavenly realm called paradise?**

First, we must consider David, the adulterer and the murderer, and then Uriah, the man against whom these abominable sins were committed.

Heaven is a place of such selfless love and such perfect mercy and understanding that these two men will be able to eternally dwell side by side. They will be united forever in a oneness just as deep and full as that oneness which Jesus Himself will possess with His eternal offspring, for we will love one another as He loves us.

There will be no grudge or desire for revenge boiling in Uriah's heart. There will be no lingering grief or haunting misery lodged in David's spirit.

Only the greatness of the love of God will prevail, producing a realm of such undisturbed peace and such unfailing forgiveness, that one of the best and only ways of suitably describing it now is just to say the word - *heaven.*

We conclude and reiterate that the perfection of God's nature, the pervading presence of the personality of deity, is exactly what will make the heavenly city what it is...not the walls of jasper or the streets of gold.

And is this not the reason we feel so out of place in this world so full of enmity, strife and discontentment?

The love of God within is constantly wooing us to faithfully continue our pilgrimage toward the realm where it will finally blossom in us to the absolute.

Daily it whispers to our hearts the glorious *hope* that there really is a place and a time where and when this will all rapturously come to pass.

Therefore, we cannot be satisfied with anything the earth affords. In fact, we never will be satisfied until we complete our journey.

David, one of our main examples, confessed to His God:

> *"I shall be satisfied, when I awake, with
> Thy likeness."*
>
> (Psalm 17:15)

We can all say "Amen" to this statement.

So until this *hope of glory* causes us to graduate from *hope* to *glory*, we intend to loudly, clearly and boldly declare our dissatisfaction.

We do not fit in this world. We do not even care to look back.

We want nothing that it has to offer. We have set our faces like flints.

We are as unyielding and resolute as the very purpose and plan of God that lives within us.

Even as the needle of a compass stubbornly refuses to point any direction but north, so we refuse to waver as we journey toward infinity.

No one should be offended if we hastily rush on by.

You see, we really can not help ourselves.

WE ARE SOJOURNERS WITH HIM!
WE ARE STRANGERS! WE ARE PILGRIMS!
We are on our way home!

THE TEMPLE OF GOD

*"Know ye not that ye are **THE TEMPLE OF GOD**, and that the Spirit of God dwelleth in you?"*
(I Corinthians 3:16)

*"And what agreement hath **THE TEMPLE OF GOD** with idols? for ye are **THE TEMPLE OF THE LIVING GOD;** as God hath said, I will dwell in them, and walk in them; and I will be their God, and they shall be My people."*

(II Corinthians 6:16)

*"What? know ye not that your body is **THE TEMPLE OF THE HOLY GHOST** which is in you, which ye have of God, and ye are not your own?"*

(I Corinthians 6:19)

*"...Behold the man whose name is **THE BRANCH;** and He shall grow up out of His place, and He shall build **THE TEMPLE OF THE LORD."***

(Zechariah 6:12)

*"For we are labourers together with God: ye are God's husbandry, ye are **GOD'S BUILDING."***

(I Corinthians 3:9)

**THE TEMPLE OF
THE LIVING GOD**

**THE TEMPLE OF
THE HOLY GHOST**

THE TEMPLE OF THE LORD

GOD'S BUILDING

● LIVELY STONES ●

LIVING STONES

● A SPIRITUAL HOUSE ●

THE HOUSE OF GOD

THE FORMER AND LATTER HOUSE

**AN HOLY TEMPLE
IN THE LORD**

● HIS TEMPLE ●

*"Ye also, as **LIVELY STONES,** are built up **A SPIRITUAL HOUSE,** an holy priesthood, to offer up spiritual sacrifices, acceptable to God by Jesus Christ."*

(I Peter 2:5)

*"And having an high priest over **THE HOUSE OF GOD;***
Let us draw near with a true heart in full assurance of faith..."
(Hebrews 10:21-22)

"The silver is Mine, and the gold is Mine, saith the Lord of hosts.
*The glory of this **LATTER HOUSE** shall be greater than of the **FORMER,** saith the Lord of hosts: and in this place will I give peace, saith the Lord of hosts."*

(Haggai 2:8-9)

*"In whom all the building fitly framed together groweth unto **AN HOLY TEMPLE IN THE LORD."***

(Ephesians 2:21)

THE PLACE OF
HIS SANCTUARY

THE PLACE OF HIS FEET

THE HABITATION
OF HIS HOUSE

THE PLACE WHERE HIS
HONOUR DWELLS

THE STONES
OF THE SANCTUARY

THE DESIRED OF ALL NATIONS

A BRAND PLUCKED
OUT OF THE FIRE

THE PLACE OF HIS THRONE

The following related *titles* are also found in this chapter:
**The Sacred Stones, The Sacred Gems, The Hallowed Stones
of the Temple,** and **A Firebrand Plucked Out of the Burning.**

"...and the Lord, whom ye seek, shall suddenly come to HIS TEMPLE..."

(Malachi 3:1)

"I will glorify the house of My glory...to beautify THE PLACE OF MY SANCTUARY; and I will make THE PLACE OF MY FEET glorious."

(Isaiah 60:7,13)

"Lord, I have loved THE HABITATION OF THY HOUSE, and THE PLACE WHERE THINE HONOUR DWELLETH."

(Psalm 26:8)

"How is the gold become dim! how is the most fine gold changed! THE STONES OF THE SANCTUARY (THE SACRED STONES, THE SACRED GEMS, THE HALLOWED STONES OF THE TEMPLE) are poured out in the top of every street."

(Lamentations 4:1 AV, NAS, NIV, AMP)

THE TEMPLE OF GOD

"Know ye not that ye are THE TEMPLE
OF GOD, and that the Spirit of God dwelleth
in you?"

(I Corinthians 3:16)

In two previous chapters of this volume - *His Abode* and *His Rest* - we laid the foundation for the revelation found in this chapter.

We concluded that God was never satisfied with any of His temporary dwelling places under the Old Will. Then Jesus came and "the dove" found a resting place. He became the first flesh-and-blood habitation of the Most High God. Though they tried to destroy this firstborn *temple of God* - by a cruel crucifixion and burial - still, He raised Himself up again the third day just as He had promised. (See John 2:20-21)

And when He came out of the grave, He established a new order.

Under the Old Will, God definitely did dwell in a natural temple made of gold, silver, brass, iron, stone, timber and precious stones. Now, under the New Will, He chooses to dwell in the hearts of men, making their fleshly bodies His grace-filled tabernacle. In this dispensation, "the Lord of heaven and earth, dwelleth not in *temples* made with hands." (Acts 17:24)

In the Old Testament, ordinary men were not even allowed in the manifest presence of God. Now, through the miraculous application of the blood of Jesus, every believer actually becomes a dwelling place for deity... *"an habitation of God through the Spirit."* (Ephesians 2:22)

● We become the temple of God, both singularly and collectively, both individually and corporately.

In the light of this statement, it is understandable that we are also spoken of as being "LIVELY STONES" - "LIVING STONES" - that "fitly framed together groweth unto AN HOLY TEMPLE IN THE LORD!" (Ephesians 2:20-21, I Peter 2:5 AV, NIV)

This entire temple, in its absolute celestial perfection, will ultimately be comprised of all the redeemed of the Lord: all the individual *lively stones* inseparably joined together as one.

Throughout eternity we will be a living and sacred sanctuary...a palace of worship in which the Father will rapturously dwell.

THE INTERMEDIATE STEP

● From the beginning, God ordained that this would be the ultimate outcome of His plan. But it was also just as much an ordained part of His plan that there be a highly important, highly symbolic, intermediate step: the construction of the Old Testament temple in Jerusalem under the leadership of King Solomon.

Many of the details concerning the erection, the eventual destruction, and the final restoration of this magnificent, historical edifice speak to our hearts right now in a present-truth way.

For it is "a faithful saying and worthy of all acceptation" that the Old Testament temple, chosen as God's temporary dwelling place, was itself a multifaceted foreshadowing of a New Testament temple that He has chosen as His permanent abode.

Therefore, if we are to more fully understand the intricacies of this wonderful and revelatory *title-calling,* it is of the utmost importance that we inspect many of the particulars surrounding the Old Testament type.

To discover such rich typology is supremely enjoyable, for not only do we more fully comprehend "who we are" in God's plan; we also, simultaneously, gain great insight into the very way that the mind of God works.

THE GRAND CORRELATION

Note: In each of the following sections, the first statement - *the symbol* - refers to the natural temple of the Old Testament; the second statement - *the interpretation* - speaks of the spiritual temple of the New Testament. Major corresponding points are, at times, emphasized in italic print.

KING DAVID - A TYPE OF CHRIST

Symbol - King David, whose name means *beloved* and who was himself a type of Christ, purposed initially to build an house of worship unto Jehovah-God, but was commanded not to do so. The word of the Lord came to him saying, "Thou hast shed blood abundantly, and hast made *great wars:* thou shalt not build an house unto My name, because thou hast *shed much blood upon the earth* in My sight." (I Chronicles 22:8)

> *Interpretation* - In like manner, Jesus, the *beloved* Son of God and King of all kings, did not personally, physically oversee the construction of the spiritual temple of the New Testament. He ascended into heaven before its erection began. It is certain, though, that He made it all possible by fighting and winning *great wars* against the powers and principalities that rule the darkness of this world. This warfare reached a climax when Jesus *shed much blood on the earth.* The main difference is quite obvious: the blood was His own.

THE SPOIL OF WAR

Symbol - Though he could not personally *oversee* the building of the temple, still, David laid up much goods, often *the spoil of war,* to be used in its construction. The Bible said that David "prepared abundantly before his death." He stored up huge deposits of gold, silver and timber as well as iron and brass "in abundance without weight." He also provided and commissioned expert workers in stone and in timber. (I Chronicles 22:3,5)

> *Interpretation* - Similarly, Jesus supplied, in advance, all the necessary "building materials" for the construction of the New Testament church. Much of this could also be termed *"the spoil of war"...*for He *"spoiled* principalities and powers" through the cross. (Col. 2:15) He provided, in great abundance, the gold of His divine nature, the silver of His redemptive love, the burnished brass of His substitutionary death, and the solid, dependable iron of all His iron-clad commands and iron-sure promises. During His three-and-a-half

year ministry, He also trained and commissioned an expert apostolic "construction team" to begin the project.

THE USE OF WROUGHT STONES

Symbol - David "set masons to hew *wrought stones* to build the house of God." These stones were, in a sense, *"ordained"*...cut to perfection and set aside, long before they were ever placed one upon the other in the walls of the temple. Later on, "the house, when it was in building, was built of stone made ready before it was brought thither: so that there was neither hammer nor axe nor any *tool* of iron heard in the house, while it was in building." (I Chronicles 22:2, I Kings 6:7)

> *Interpretation* - Parallel to the thought contained in these two passages, every person filling the role of a *"lively stone"* in God's spiritual temple was actually *"ordained"* and set aside for this purpose long ago. We were given a "purpose and grace...in Christ Jesus before the world began." (II Tim. 1:9) The advance of the gospel in this world is effecting the building of the New Testament *house of the Lord.* (Ps. 134:1) The success of this work never has, and never will, depend on mere theology, rituals, or promotional programs utilizing carnal methods or secular means. It must be a move of the Spirit and a work of God. Such truth God strove to communicate, far in advance, when He commanded that the sound of *men's tools* not be heard irreverently defiling the temple construction area.

DAVID'S CHIEF CONCERN

Symbol - David's chief *concern* and his final commands, given right before His death, dealt with the eventual erection of the temple of God. This was his consuming passion, a pressing burden and a vision that burned in his heart to the very end. (See I Chronicles 28)

> *Interpretation* - Jesus' main concern just before His departure was instructing those who would be filled with His Spirit, to perpetuate His message, and thus, build *His temple.* He especially emphasized the attitude His disciples should have toward one another that they might be "fitted together" effectively, functioning as a unit. This was also His burning passion to the very end.

DIVINELY INSPIRED

Symbol - David received the architectural design of the temple through *divine inspiration.* (See I Chronicles 28:12)

> *Interpretation* - In the same vein, Jesus said - "I came down from heaven, not to do Mine own will, but the will of Him that sent Me." The words He spoke, that brought about the construction of this spiritual temple, were all Spirit-filled, *divinely inspired.* (John 6:38)

SOLOMON, THE BUILDER ─────────────────

Symbol - Solomon, who *proceeded forth* from David's loins and whose name means *peace*, was ordained by David, and by God, to begin and complete the work of the original temple. He did little to secure the necessary building materials; he just reaped the benefits of all his father's labors.

> *Interpretation* - The Holy Spirit, who *proceeds forth* from the Father and the Son, and who is called the Comforter and *the Spirit of peace*, was ordained to begin and to ultimately complete this spiritual, New Testament temple. He started the work on the day of Pentecost. He did little to secure the necessary "building materials." He merely administers what Jesus secured through His vicarious sufferings.

THE TEMPLE SITE ───────────────────────

Symbol - Solomon's temple was *built on Mount Moriah*, approximately the same location where Abraham obediently offered Isaac, his son, on an altar of sacrifice. This was itself a figure of God offering up His only begotten Son on the cross. This was also the site of the *threshing floor* owned by Ornan, the Jebusite (also called Araunah), that David purchased to rear an altar of repentance. It was here that the ark was temporarily stored. (See II Sam. 24, I Chr. 21; 22:1, II Chr. 3:1)

> *Interpretation* - The spiritual temple of the New Testament was, in a spiritual sense, *built on Mount Calvary* and the salvation work that transpired there. When anyone goes to Calvary sincerely, they go to a spiritual kind of *"threshing floor"* where the chaff (the carnal part of us) is separated from the grain (the son of God part of us).

THE FOUNDATION ────────────────────────

Symbol - The *foundation* stones of Solomon's temple were called - *"great stones, costly stones...hewed stones."* (I Kings 5:17)

> *Interpretation* - Isaiah prophesied of the New Covenant temple saying - "Behold, I lay in Zion for a foundation a stone, a tried stone, a precious corner stone, A SURE FOUNDATION: [the one who trusts will never be dismayed]." (Is. 28:16 AV, NIV) Later on, in I Cor. 3:9, Paul referred to sons of God as **GOD'S BUILDING**, then emphatically stated - "other foundation can no man lay than that is laid, which is Jesus Christ." But Eph. 2:19-20 gives a little different slant, calling us "the household of God...built upon the *foundation* of the apostles and prophets, Jesus Christ Himself being the chief corner stone." All truly anointed prophets and apostles - past, present and future - are definitely *"great stones, costly stones...hewed stones"* for by means of their relationship with the Holy One of Israel (who was the greatest stone of all) they have become a part of the spiritual foundation He laid. Jesus Christ is still the only foundation, but what He has performed in the apostles of the New Testament and the prophets of the Old and New Testaments has manifestly produced the

foundation laid for the building of the church. All such individuals are *great stones* because of the greatness of the work God has done in their lives; they are *costly stones* because of the purchase price that was ultimately paid to secure them (the precious blood of Jesus); they are *hewed stones* because God, the Rock of our salvation, hewed them out of Himself in the very beginning. He chiseled out their character and shaped their peculiar abilities, well in advance, to perfectly fit the demands of the position in which they were placed. (See Is. 51:1)

THE WALLS OF THE HOUSE

Symbol - The walls of the house of the Lord were made of *white marble stone*. These were apparently overlaid with *silver*, and then plastered together with silver, so that *no stone could be seen*. They were then covered by gold-overlaid, cedar boards ornamented with carvings of *knops, flowers, chains, palm trees*, and *cherubim*. To add a final touch of beauty, the walls were garnished with *precious stones*. (See I Kgs. 6, I Chr. 29:4, II Chr. 3:5-7)

> *Interpretation* - Not everyone can be a foundation stone, but all believers can potentially be *lively stones* in the wall of God's temple. The *white marble* speaks of righteousness, the *silver* of redemption. The work of redemption will finally complete its course in us so that *"no flesh" will be seen*. The *knops* were possibly small, round-shaped gourds and speak of the fruit of the Spirit. The *flowers* tell of maturing in the beauty and fragrance of Christ who was represented Himself as the rose of Sharon and lily of the valleys. He plants the seed of His Word in us, then we blossom in His image. The *palm trees* represent uprightness, victory over this wilderness world, and spiritual stamina. The *chains* speak of the "linking together" of all God's covenants and promises. God's wise counsel, His commandments, should be as an ornamental *chain of gold* worn about the neck of the bride of Christ. (See Pro. 1:9, Song 1:10) The *cherubim* seem to always be connected with the holiness of God, His throne, His demand of atonement for sin and the highest expression of worship. Because they are seen "guarding" the tree of life, the entrance to the holy of holies, and "hovering" over the blood-sprinkled mercy seat, their carved images seem to imply a "guarded" and proper return to the holiness of God and the fellowship with God that was lost in Eden.
>
> The *precious stones* speak especially of the gifts of the Spirit and the good works of believers. (See Is. 61:10, I Cor. 3:9-15) Lamentations 4:1 even refers to God's people as **THE STONES OF THE SANCTUARY** or, as several other translations render this *title*, **THE SACRED GEMS, THE SACRED STONES**, or **THE HALLOWED STONES OF THE TEMPLE**. (NIV, NAS, AMP, Compare Lam. 2:19, Is. 51:20) How touching it is that God would show how greatly He values His people with such a symbol as this!

THE TEMPLE OVERLAID WITH GOLD

Symbol - "And the whole house [of God was] *overlaid with gold*...and the floor of the house he *overlaid with gold, within and without.*" (I Kgs. 6:22, 30)

Interpretation - Gold is symbolic of the perfection of the divine nature. Job, in using this particular symbol, asserted - "When He [Jehovah] hath tried me, I shall come forth as gold." (Job 23:10) The temple being *overlaid with gold* relates to the church receiving the covering of God's righteousness, the impartation of His divine nature, the perpetual luster of perfection "in Christ"...revealed both *within and without*...in our attitudes and our actions.

THE TWO PILLARS

Symbol - On either side of the main entrance to the temple, *two impressive pillars* were erected made of scoured brass. One pillar was named **Jachin**, which means *He will establish*. The other was called **Boaz**, which means *In Him is strength*. These stately pillars were eighteen cubits high and twelve cubits in circumference (probably about twenty-seven feet tall by eighteen feet around). The capitals (or chapiters) were five cubits (about seven-and-a-half feet) higher still. Both were crowned with an oil basin and lampstand, and very likely bore the appearance of a huge fire altar. There was certainly a divine purpose behind the placement of these sacred columns. One commentator said it beautifully - "They doubtless caught the first glint of the Jerusalem sunrise or were wrapped in the mists of the Kidron valley. With their blazing, smoking wicks they recalled to worshippers the fiery, cloudy pillar that led Israel of old through the wilderness." *1

Interpretation - If we are God's living temples, then flanking the entrance of our Spirit-filled hearts there should always be *two pillar-like attitudes*. The main upward thrust of our faith should be the dual confidence that "He which *stablisheth* us...is God" and that God alone "is our refuge and *strength*." (II Cor. 1:21, Ps. 46:1) These revelations should be, as it were, a fire altar crowning our worship and burning before the Most High constantly. **Brass represents God's judgment against sin.** The *scouring process* especially speaks of divinely-imposed chastisements and self-imposed afflictions of the soul that are sometimes necessary in order to bring sin and the flesh under subjection. Though the scouring may bring temporary pain - emotionally, mentally and spiritually - still, "the God of all grace, who hath CALLED US UNTO HIS ETERNAL GLORY by Christ Jesus, after that ye have suffered a while, make you perfect, *stablish, strengthen,* settle you." (I Pt. 5:10) Notice the words *"stablish"* and *"strengthen,"* associated with the pillars, are included in this beautiful promise. Also, it is important to note that on top of each of the pillars there were "nets of checker work, and [seven] wreaths of chain work." On these were hanging two hundred pomegranates, making four hundred altogether. Lily work also adorned the chapiters. (I Kgs. 7:17-22) **All of this is symbolic.** Nets speak of the church's commission to be fishers of men. Chains speak of authority. Pomegranates are "a Promised Land fruit" with a rich, red pulp, harboring many seeds. It speaks of fruitfulness in God through the blood of Jesus. Lilies speak of purity and a sweet fragrance toward God. *Four hundred* is the number of suffering, affliction and exile. God forewarned Abraham that his seed would be a "stranger in a land that is not their's...and they shall *afflict them four hundred years*." But God also pledged that "afterward shall they come out with *great substance.*" (Gen. 15:13-14) So we may pass through times of great suffering during our time of exile here below, but we also will come out with *great substance.* The fiery-eyed Christ of the book of the Revelation promised - "Him that overcometh will I make A PILLAR IN THE TEMPLE OF MY GOD." (Rev. 3:12) This is part of the *hope* that is laid up for us above.

THREE SECTIONS OF THE TEMPLE

Symbol - There were three main sections of the temple: *the outer court, the holy place* and *the holy of holies.*

> *Interpretation* - There are three main corresponding aspects to every son of God who becomes **a temple of the Lord:** the flesh (*the outer court*), the soul (*the holy place*), and the regenerated spirit (*the holy of holies*). What literally took place in *the outer court* relates to how God deals with our flesh; what took place in *the holy place* deals with the activity of God in the soul realm; and what transpired in *the holy of holies* reveals what should be taking place in the regenerated spirit, the hidden man of the heart. So it follows also that there are three kinds of Christians: fleshly, soulish and spiritual. According to the level of commitment, they bear fruit either thirtyfold, sixtyfold or hundredfold.

THE DOORS OF THE TEMPLE

Symbol - We are not told very much about the doors to the outer court, but we know they were *overlaid with brass.* (II Chr. 4:9) The doors leading to the holy place were folding doors made of *fir* (two two-leaved doors - four panels in all). The doors leading to the holiest of all were made of wood from *olive trees* (also called *oil trees*) and were also folding doors (*four panels* altogether). The doors of the holy place and the holy of holies were *overlaid with gold* and bore carved images of *flowers, palm trees* and *cherubim.* (See I Kings 6:32)

> *Interpretation* - **Doors speak of opportunity, entrance and advance in the kingdom of God.** All of the doors in the temple are revelations of the Messiah who said - "I AM THE DOOR!" (Jn. 10:9) We must all pass through Him to enter a relationship with God and to advance in the kingdom. *Brass* speaks of judgment. (Dt. 28:23, Num. 21:6-9) So the *brass doors* of the outer court declare that in coming to the Father we must first judge ourselves and our sins must be brought under judgment. (I Cor. 11:31, I Tim. 5:24) The *fir tree,* being an evergreen, speaks of that which is eternal. The *fir tree doors* of the holy place communicate that newborn believers must leave behind that which is temporal and progress in that which is eternal...especially through the Word and through prayer. The *olive tree,* or *oil tree,* relates to the anointing of the Holy Spirit. The word translated *olive* is *shemen,* also translated *anointing, ointment* and *oil.* The *oil tree doors* of the holy of holies speak of entering a Spirit-filled, Spirit-led walk with God where the *anointing* of God manifests in us. **Now we see the steps that each child of God should take as he or she progresses in God.** After receiving salvation (represented

215

by the *doors* of the outer court) believers should sanctify their lives by the Word, by prayer and by fellowship with that which has eternal value (represented by the *doors* of the holy place). We then should go on to the Baptism of the Holy Spirit and an anointed walk with God (represented by the *doors* to the holy of holies). Each set of *doors* leads to a deeper place of service and worship, and a more fulfiling, more fruitful place in God. In passing through these successive *doors* we mature in Christ. In passing through the *gold doors* of the holy place and the holy of holies we grow in *flowerful* glory and flourish as the *palm tree*. We also dwell in heavenly places in Christ, surrounded by a host of *cherubim* that indicate God's holiness, protection and atonement. They also speak of the realm where adoration reaches its highest expression. The *four panels* could relate to the four gospels or the four aspects of Jesus' nature - Son of Adam, Son of Man, Son of David and Son of God.

FURNITURE IN THE OUTER COURT

Symbol - In the outer court of the temple of Solomon there were *the altar of sacrifice, the molten sea, and ten lavers.* The molten sea, supported by twelve bronze oxen, contained about 15,000 gallons of water. It was used for the cleansing of the priests. The ten lavers contained about 300 gallons of water a piece and were used for the cleansing of the sacrifices. All these articles of furniture were made of *brass.*

Interpretation - The altar of sacrifice relates first to the sacrifice of the Son of God on Calvary, then how we must also present our bodies living *sacrifices,* holy and acceptable to God. The altar, being the first article of furniture encountered in the outer court, speaks that the attitude of being crucified with Christ must be our first priority. Both *the molten sea* and *the lavers* speak of being cleansed by the "washing of water by the Word". (Eph. 5:26) Being sanctified by the Word renders us fit *priests* and acceptable *sacrifices* to God. *Brass* speaks of judgment. When likened to the church and its individual members, *brass* speaks of the necessity of self-judgment, keeping the flesh under subjection. *The twelve oxen* pointing north, south, east and west relates to the *twelve apostles* and possibly to the *twelve tribes* of spiritual Israel, ordained to bear an abundant supply of the water of the Word to all the world.

FURNITURE IN THE HOLY PLACE

Symbol - The furniture in the holy place consisted of *ten golden lampstands* and *ten golden tables of shewbread*. This *shewbread* was also called *the bread of presence, the continual bread, the bread of God,* and *the bread of His face.* (Num. 4:7, II Chr. 2:4, Lev. 21:21, orig. Heb. *paneh* means *face,* thus *the bread of His face*) This bread was *unleavened. Twelve loaves* were placed on each of the *ten tables. The golden altar of incense* was also placed in the holy place just before the veil. All of these - the tables, lampstands and altar - were made of *pure* gold.

Interpretation - The ten golden lampstands speak of the calling

216

Jesus has transferred to the church to be the light of the world. The single lampstand in the tabernacle represented Jesus in this calling. These ten lampstands in the temple speak of the church, the bride of Christ, for we are called to emerge in His likeness. In both cases, the fire that lit the lamps was taken off the brazen altar, having originally fallen from heaven. **So there are three parts to be considered:** the **lampstand** itself - which speaks of being conformed to the image of the **Word**; the **oil** - which speaks of the anointing of the **Holy Spirit;** and the **fire** - which speaks of God-given fervency, **a passion** for eternal things. All three work together to produce light. Each lampstand had seven lamps, full of oil, which doubtless represent "the seven Spirits of God." (Rev. 4:5) Ten times seven equals seventy and so we have the original "seventy disciples" that were sent forth with the anointed Word. The lamps were to be continually burning. So there should never be a time or an age when the light of God fails to shine forth through His people or any time when the light ceases to shine in our individual lives. The lamps were made of beaten work, which relates to the sharing of the suffering of Christ. They were each made of one piece of gold, a type of the unity of all true believers. They primarily typify the anointed Word that should enlighten our way. ("Thy Word is a lamp unto my feet, and a light unto my path." Psalm 119:105)

The ten golden tables of shewbread relate, not only to our privilege of eating that living bread which comes from above, but also, our calling to become *the bread of God.* According to I Cor. 10:17 - "we being many are *one bread...*for we are all *partakers of that one bread.*" In fulfilling this calling we nourish the heart of God, so hungry for fellowship, and the hearts of men, so hungry for truth. Being *unleavened* speaks of the need for believers to live a life free from sin, pride and false doctrines. *Twelve loaves* were on each of the *ten tables. Twelve times ten equals one hundred and twenty* - a sure reference to the upper room disciples. The *table of shewbread* being called *the pure table* in Lev. 24:6 speaks that "the words of the Lord are *pure words*" and that, like Job, our doctrine should be *pure.* (Ps. 12:6, Jb. 11:4) Also, the bread was eaten by the priests in the light of the corresponding lampstand. So the Word must be eaten in the light of the spirit of revelation. The *shewbread* being called *the bread of presence* speaks of the Spirit of God being present in His Word. The *shewbread* being called *the continual bread* (offered *continually* before the Lord) speaks that we should partake of the Word *continually* and become so one with the Word that we are a *continual* offering of the bread of God...earthward and heavenward. It is the *bread of face* because as we eat of the Word and digest it into our inner being, we do so under the affectionate gaze of the Father above.

The *golden altar of incense,* positioned before the veil, speaks of prayer being the way into the holy of holies: that deeper and more intimate relationship with God. The incense altar was anointed and the incense was also lit with fire from off the altar. So effectual prayer must be anointed with the Spirit and on-fire with a passion for Calvary. It was offered *daily.* So the incense of prayer should ascend *daily* from every member of the church. (See Ps. 141:1-2, Rev. 8:1-5)

All of these pieces of furniture in the holy place, being *pure gold,* speaks of *the purity of the divine nature* being imparted to us: through the Word, by the Spirit, and because of a disciplined commitment to prayer. Concerning the *ten* lampstands and the *ten* tables, it should also be remembered that biblically, *ten is the number of divine order.* In the outer court, believers are washed and sanctified by the Word. Then, in the holy place we are enlightened by the fiery light of the Word and nourished with the living bread of the Word. All of this is a preparation, though, for prayer, which then allows us to enter the realm of the Spirit. The Spirit-led, glory-filled life is typified by the holy of holies, that lies just beyond the veil.

THE VEIL

Symbol - At the entrance to the holy of holies hung a veil. There is only one Old Testament verse describing this veil - II Chronicles 3:14. "And he made the vail of *blue*, and *purple*, and *crimson* and *fine linen*, and wrought *cherubims* thereon."

Interpretation - The veil represents what Jesus was, and what we all must "pass through" in order to enter that ultimate relationship with God symbolized by the holy of holies. (Heb. 10:19-22) Blue speaks of that which is heavenly and peaceful. First it tells of the heavenly origin of the Prince of peace and second, that if we are to have peace, we must set our affection on things above. *Purple* speaks of royalty, dominion and power; first, of the Kings of kings, and second, of those who are called to rule and reign with him. *Scarlet,* being the color of blood, speaks of self-denial and sacrifice, especially the sacrifice of Calvary...something that we, too, are called to share. *Scarlet* and *blue* mixed together produce *purple* - and so it is, when we mix heavenly-mindedness and a willingness to sacrifice, we emerge with regal glory and dominion, walking in our kingship calling as sons of God. *Fine linen* speaks of the righteousness of God - first, that which Jesus possessed, and second, that which we inherit from Him and manifest in His name. (Rev. 19:7-8) *Cherubim* are always connected with the throne of God, the holiness of God, atonement and the highest expression of worship attainable. All of these things must be very evident in us if we are going to fulfill the call to be *the temple of God, the place where His honour dwells.* Of course, within ourselves we could never achieve such a goal - so the veil represented something that prevented our forward progress. **But when Jesus died, the veil was rent, so that all men can not only enter the holiest, but actually become this dwelling place of the glory of God.**

THE ARK IN THE HOLY OF HOLIES

Symbol - The most important item in Solomon's temple was *the ark of the covenant in the holy of holies.* This sacred depository was made of shittim wood, also called acacia wood, and overlaid with gold. Within the ark were the tablets of stone that Moses received from Jehovah. On these tablets *the law was written,* engraved with the fiery finger of the Almighty God. The ark also contained *Aaron's rod that budded* and *the golden bowl full of manna. The book of the law* was placed in the side of this divinely designed chest. Immediately above was the lid, also called *the mercy seat.* The ark upon which it rested was also called *the footstool of our God.* (I Chr. 28:2) **Between the cherubim on the lid, the Shekinah glory of God manifested and from the midst of this glory cloud God spoke.**

Interpretation - The most important aspect of becoming New Testament temples is the fact that *the spiritual ark of the covenant now resides in a new type of holy of holies* - our regenerated hearts. This covenant ark is Jesus Himself (humanity overlaid with divinity) and within our hearts, He has again, with His fiery finger, *"written the law."* (See Jer. 31:31-33) The other three items - *the book of the law, Aaron's rod that budded,* and *the golden bowl full of manna* - represent the threefold truth that through Jesus' indwelling we have become *living epistles*; we have been *resurrected* from death unto life; and we have an everlasting supply of *bread from heaven,* an inward source of revelation into God's Word. The rod that budded was also proof that Aaron was chosen by God to be His representative priest. So every believer is chosen to be a priest of God as well.

The lid on the ark was called *the mercy seat;* on either side there were two *cherubim.* Originally, all three items (the cherubim and the lid) were made of one piece of beaten, pure gold. The lid was sprinkled with the blood of both a bullock and a goat on the Day of Atonement, the latter being for the remission of Israel's sin. **This mercy seat was never sat upon by any priest or leader of Israel for it was reserved for God Himself.** This seat represented the angel-thronged throne of God where full atonement was made for us by the sprinkling of the precious blood of the Lamb. It also speaks of the fact that God has *mercifully enthroned* Himelf in the heart of every believer. Though we are yet to enter fully into heaven, right now we are seated with Christ in heavenly places, surrounded by a heavenly host that ceaselessly praise His name. In our hearts, the Shekinah glory now resides for we are **THE HOUSE OF HIS GLORY.** (Is. 60:7) Out of us, at certain blessed moments, God speaks and communicates His will to this world.

The day when Jesus' blood was sprinkled on our hearts, it was our personal *"day of atonement."* Since that day, in a sense, we, too, have become *His footstool* for we are connected to His throne; we are channels of His authority, and He finds rest residing within us. This is our *hope of glory* now and forevermore. (See Lam. 2:1, II Chr. 9:18) **Note: More information is contained on the ark especially in the cover explanation at the beginning of this book and in the previous chapter entitled *His Rest.***

A PERMANENT DWELLING

Symbol - The ark in the tabernacle had *staves* that remained in the rings on its sides because it was ever changing its location. It was borne on the shoulders of the priests through the wilderness. When the ark found its resting place in the temple, though, *the staves* were finally removed. **The temple was meant to be its permanent abode.** (Exodus 25:15, II Chronicles 5:8-9)

Interpretation - The tabernacle in the wilderness primarily represents Jesus. The temple primarily represents the church. *The staves remaining* in the tabernacle ark speaks of Jesus' earthly pilgrimage. The Son of man had no place to lay his head. He was not satisfied with the covenant relationship available in that era, but was on a journey to something far better. After He ascended on high, He made a way to dwell personally in the heart of every believer. When He comes in, the "staves" are removed...for He is finally satisfied and we become **His permanent abode.**

THE PRESIDING HIGH PRIEST

Symbol - The presiding *high priest* ruled over the temple and directed all of its functions. **Aaron**, whose name means *enlightened,* was the first high priest who officiated in the tabernacle of Moses. For many years, it was only his direct offspring who inherited the position. Among many other duties, the high priest would enter the *holy of holies* one time a year to make atonement for the children of Israel.

> *Interpretation* - Hebrews 10:21-22 explains that we, too, have "an *high priest* over **THE HOUSE OF GOD**" and can "draw near with a true heart in full assurance of faith." It is Jesus, the *enlightened* One who *enlightens* us so that we have "boldness to enter into the *holiest* by the blood of Jesus, by a new and living way, which He hath consecrated for us, through the veil, that is to say, His flesh." (Hebrews 10:19-20)

THE NUMBER SEVEN

Symbol - The temple is connected in many ways with the number *seven*. It was completed in *seven* years. The people and the altar were prepared for its dedication *seven* days. The temple itself was dedicated *seven* days during the Feast of Tabernacles in the *seventh* month. (See I Kgs. 6:1, 37-38, II Chr. 7:9-10, Lev. 23:39-44)

> *Interpretation - Seven is the number of completion and spiritual perfection.* So the completion of God's spiritual temple is the sign of His plan coming to *fullness.* This will take place in the last days when the symbolism of the Feast of Tabernacles will be fulfilled in the church - just as Passover and Pentecost have already been fulfilled.

DEDICATION DAY

Symbol - On the day of the dedication of Solomon's temple, *a hundred and twenty priests* were jubilantly sounding *trumpets*. It is also significant that the priests and Levites were all arrayed in *white garments*. (II Chronicles 5:12)

> *Interpretation* - There are four main correlations here. First, on the day of the dedication of this living temple of the New Covenant, there were about *one hundred and twenty believers* gathered. Second, they lifted their voices like trumpets, speaking in tongues and jubilantly

declaring the wonderful works of God. Third, the moment they were born again, surely all of the upper room disciples received the spiritual status of being *priests*. And fourth, as they were washed in the blood of Jesus, they received *white robes* of God's imparted righteousness. (See Acts 2)

THE UNITY OF PRAISE

Symbol - On that consecration day in the temple at Jerusalem, - "It came even to pass, as the trumpeters and singers were as *one*, to make *one* sound to be heard in praising and thanking the Lord...that then *the house was filled* with a cloud, even *the house of the Lord.*" (II Chronicles 5:13)

> *Interpretation* - On the consecration day of the New Testament temple (the day of Pentecost) - "they were all with *one* accord in *one* place. And suddenly there came a sound from heaven as of a rushing mighty wind, and it *filled all the house.*" The disciples then fully became *the house of the Lord.*(Acts 2:1-2)

THE GLORY OF THE LORD

Symbol - The priests in Solomon's temple "could not stand to minister by reason of the cloud: for *the glory of the Lord* had filled the house of God." O, what an awesome and wonderful display of God's power!! (II Chr. 5:14)

> *Interpretation* - The disciples in the upper room were apparently acting a similar way: swaying and falling, like drunken men and women, because *the glory of the Lord* had filled not only the house, but their hearts as well. Our *hope of glory* is that this awesome display revealed in the beginning will certainly be repeated in the end.

FIRE FALLS FROM HEAVEN

Symbol - At the end of Solomon's prayer of dedication over the temple *"fire* came down from heaven, and consumed the burnt offering and the *sacrifices."* It is significant that 120,000 sheep were offered that day. (II Chronicles 7:1,5)

> *Interpretation* - The upper room believers were, in a spiritual sense, presenting themselves as living *sacrifices* on the altar when they were baptized with "the Holy Ghost and *fire"* that fell from heaven. Acts 2:3 states that -"there appeared unto them cloven tongues like as of *fire,* and it sat upon each of them." Again, the 120,000 sheep relate to the 120 disciples, who became "the sheep of God's pasture" consumed with His holy fire.

THE BLESSED PROMISE

Symbol - The night after the completion of the dedication feast, God appeared to Solomon in a dream and gave the promise concerning the temple - "Now *Mine eyes* shall be open, and *Mine ears* attent unto the prayer that is made in this place. For now have I chosen and sanctified this *house*, that *My name* may be there for ever: and *Mine eyes* and *Mine heart* shall be there *perpetually."* (II Chronicles 7:15-16)

> *Interpretation* - In a similar fashion, God certainly hears the prayers of those who comprise His *spiritual house,* far above all other petitions uttered in this earth. Irregardless of where they were in the world, the Jews would always face the temple when they prayed. They believed that their prayers first went to the temple and then ascended to God, possibly mingled in with the rising smoke of the incense on the golden altar. This could have very well been true. (See Jonah 2:4,7) Now, though, each believer has personal contact with heaven. We need not face the temple, WE ARE THE TEMPLE OF GOD. He has chosen us. He has sanctified us. *His eyes* are on us continually. *His heart* pulsates toward us constantly. *His ears* are open to our prayers. We are the focus of His attention and desire. *His name* abides within our hearts and is spoken with devotion every day. One day *His name* will be written on every son of God...a *perpetual* sign of divine ownership. (Revelation 3:12)

THE QUEEN OF SHEBA'S COMMENT

Symbol - Sometime after the completion of the temple, the queen of Sheba came and saw the greatness of Solomon's kingdom, heard the depth of his wisdom, saw the beauty of the temple, "the meat of his table...the sitting of his servants, the attendance of his ministers, and their apparel...and his ascent by which he went up unto the house of the Lord" so that "there was no more spirit in her." She exclaimed - *"the one half of the greatness...was not told me."* (See I Kings 10:1-7)

> *Interpretation* - Corresponding to this statement, surely *the one half of the greatness* of the original New Testament church has never been told...their visitations from God, their exploits and their fervency. And how *great* is the miraculous work that God has wrought in all of our lives: eating and drinking at His table, being clothed with the spiritual garments of praise and robes of righteousness that only He can give! Concerning the King of peace who has gloriously ascended into the heavenly temple and His servants who serve Him, the Queen of Sheba's words could also be echoed - *"Happy* are Thy men, *happy* are these Thy servants, which stand continually before Thee, and that hear Thy wisdom." Yes - *"Happy* is that people, whose God is the Lord." (I Kings 10:8, Psalm 144:15)

THE WARNING

● God warned Israel, in advance, that if they ever forsook His statutes, or worshipped other gods, He would pluck them up by the roots out of their land and cast the house of God out of His sight. They would then become a "proverb and a byword among all nations." (II Chronicles 7:19-20)

It is such a tragedy that they did not hearken to God's counsel and suffered the heart-rending consequences. The Chaldees under Nebuchadnezzar "burnt the house of God, and brake down the wall of Jerusalem, and burnt all the palaces thereof with fire, and destroyed all the goodly vessels thereof. And them that had escaped from the sword [were carried away] to Babylon." (II Chronicles 36:19-20)

But God gave a gracious restoration-promise in the very beginning to those He knew would fail to keep their covenant-commitment. This oft-quoted pledge is for us as well as them:

> *"If My people, which are called by My name, shall humble themselves, and pray, and seek My face, and turn from their wicked ways; then will I hear from heaven, and will forgive their sin, and heal their land."*
>
> (II Chronicles 7:14)

THE BABYLONIAN EXILE

The Jews spent seventy years in bondage in **Babylon** before God miraculously restored them to that goodly land, the Land of Promise.

Including this period of exile in our symbolic comparison is of the utmost importance if we are to comprehend the fullness of the mystery, for Babylon represents moral, social, political and spiritual apostasy (departure from truth).

Such a peculiar correlation is traceable all the way back to **Babel**, one city of a seven-city kingdom established sometime shortly after the flood. The originator was **Nimrod**, whose name means *Let us rebel.*

By the founding of such a city, those involved were rebelling from the start. They were exalting themselves against God's command to replenish the earth and gravitating around an infamous leader intent on building his own kingdom. Their prideful purpose and misled motive becomes clear when we read the biblical record of what the founders said one to another:

> *"Go to, let us build us a city and a tower, whose top may reach unto heaven; and let us make us a name, lest we be scattered abroad upon the face of the whole earth."*
>
> (Genesis 11:4)

Whether or not the tower was actually a ziggurat to be used for astrological purposes and/or false religious practices is up to question. God's reaction certainly indicates the likelihood of such an assumption. The Most High, purposing to thwart their plans, declared His severe judgment:

> *"Let Us go down, and there confound their language, that they may not understand one another's speech. So the Lord scattered them abroad from thence upon the face of all the earth."*
>
> (Genesis 11:7-8)

Hence, the name of the city was called **Babel** which means *confusion.* Later on, from out of the small and seemingly insignificant root of the city

223

of **Babel** grew the poisonous, wild vine of that vast empire called **Babylon**, constricting the inhabitants of the earth with its dominating, tentacular grip.

Because the Babylonians overcame the Jews, burnt their temple to the ground, and carried God's Old Covenant people away captive, they became a very logical symbol for all that would eventually, similarly and tragically captivate the church of the New Covenant.

To pursue this particular portion of this *title-analogy* in depth would prove to be far too lengthy and time-consuming. Let it suffice to say that **Babylon-like bondage** has resulted whenever segments of the professing church have emphasized religious externalism, ceremonies and theology, instead of a personal relationship with the Lord Himself!

Babel-like confusion has reigned over Christendom, as well, whenever denominational allegiance has been stressed above and beyond the experience of the "new birth." Yet this spiritual experience is infinitely more important, for it alone indicates inclusion in the family of God.

In far too many instances, a glorious risen Saviour has been replaced by a mere historical Christ as men attempted *to make themselves a name* by erecting a man-made, doctrinal *tower* that would reach heaven.

But now, thank God, the true church is profoundly and progressively coming out of the darkness of deception. More extensively than ever, we are returning to the glory of the original.

Believers are realizing that denominational names and titles really matter little and that, on the contrary - *"the name of the Lord is a strong tower: [and] the righteous runneth into it, and is safe."* (Proverbs 18:10)

Blessed be the Lord, we are now being united in His name!

This is the tower of defense and worship that God has built, a tower that can alone provide a safe haven from the effects of sin...a tower that will ultimately become a stairwell leading to the splendor of heaven itself.

This is that ecumenical movement, authored by the Holy Spirit, which is successfully binding Christians together, not so much by the discarding of differing interpretations of the Word, but by the emphasis of a common spiritual experience.

Praise be to the Most High! "By the rivers of Babylon, we wept, when we remembered Zion" and God graciously heard us from on high. (Psalm 137:1)

Yes, a great portion of the professing church is, in a spiritual sense, returning to Jerusalem, returning to the faith of our fathers, returning to the place where it all started, returning to our spiritual roots.

Of course, simultaneously, the *"Babylon spirit"* will become more blatantly evident, in these last days, as the unbelieving portion of the professing church whorishly sells her inheritance to blend in with the world-system. The epitome will be that **great whore, Mystery Babylon,** who will be allied with the Antichrist of the last days. (See Revelation 17.18)

Most likely, this group will sacrifice key biblical principles in order to unite all the religions of the world in the name of love, tolerance and understanding. They may even be steeped in that counterfeit brand of **New Age, Gnostic Christianity** that will accept and promote outlandish occult doctrines, such as reincarnation, astrology, spiritualism and channeling.

Such a doctrinal overflow from ancient Babylonian religions presented a serious challenge to the early church. It will pose a similar threat to the true church of the last days.

THE RESTORATION OF ISRAEL
AND THE RECONSTRUCTION OF THE TEMPLE

● The Medo-Persians eventually conquered the kingdom of Babylon. Shortly thereafter, in order to accomplish the rebuilding of Jerusalem and the restoration of the temple of Solomon, God - "stirred up the spirit of Cyrus king of Persia, that he made a proclamation throughout all his kingdom." (Ezra 1:1)

> *"The Lord God of heaven hath given me all the kingdoms of the earth; and He hath charged me to build Him an house at Jerusalem, which is in Judah.*
> *Who is there among you of all His people? his God be with him, and let him go up to Jerusalem...and build the house of the Lord..."*
> (Ezra 1:2-3)

Approximately one hundred and seventy-six years in advance, Isaiah foretold the way God would eventually use this great Gentile ruler:

> *"That saith of Cyrus, He is My shepherd, and shall perform · all My pleasure: even saying to Jerusalem, Thou shalt be built; and to the temple, Thy foundation shall be laid."*
> (Isaiah 44:28)

● One of the main points to be stressed in this particular prophecy is the fact that God described the restoration of the holy city and the temple of God as being *all His pleasure*...or, in other words, *His supreme delight.*
If this was true naturally, how much more is it true spiritually!
The restoration of God's spiritual temple to her former glory could even more correctly be termed *all His pleasure.* For that which is permanent far exceeds in importance that which is only temporary!
Many reformers have done their part in bringing this to pass, men and women like John Wycliffe, John and Charles Wesley, Dwight Moody, Charles Finney, W.J. Seymour, F.F. Bosworth, William and Cathryn Booth and a host of others. In some cases, their preaching exposed truth that had been hidden for centuries. Overall, it began a progressive revival that will ultimately lead the church to a place of unprecedented effect in this world.
It is quite thrilling to see that many details concerning the restoration of the Old Testament temple were amazing prophetic foreshadowings of how this living temple of the New Testament is being, and will yet be, restored to the fullness of glory that God has ordained.
Some of the main correlations are as follows:

THE IMPORTANCE OF UNITY ─────────────────

Symbol - Ezra 3:1 says - "the people gathered themselves together as *one man* to Jerusalem."

Interpretation - Believers, in a parallel way, must forget their non-essential differences and become as *one* before true restoration can transpire in this hour. The body of Christ is to be *one* body, to have *one* heart, *one* mind, *one* spirit and to emerge as *one new man*. (Col. 3:15, Jer. 32:39, II Cor. 13:11, Ph. 1:27, Eph. 2:15)

THE RESTORATION OF TRUE WORSHIP ———————————

Symbol - Before the temple was reconstructed *true worship* needed to be *restored.* The first thing the Jews rebuilt was *the altar.* Soon after, they kept the Feast of Tabernacles...just as they had done in the beginning. (Ezra 3)

Interpretation - In like manner, many man-made rituals and ceremonies must be either de-emphasized or set aside altogether, and the present revelation of *true worship reinstated,* before the reconstruction of the New Testament temple can effectively go forward. We must *re-erect the altar* and go back to Calvary, where we share in Jesus' self-denial and sacrifice, if we are to know Him in the power of His resurrection. The word **altar** means *a place of slaughter.* So we must mortify the flesh and thus, place our lives on the altar, to have the visitation from God we need. The *Feast of Tabernacles* celebrated the latter rains and final harvest; so in these last days we will see a spiritual "latter rain" outpouring of the Holy Spirit and the final harvest of the souls of men. It was also a feast in which the children of Israel spent a week living in booths to emphasize two things: that they were strangers and sojourners in Egypt and in the wilderness, and that this life is but temporary. In like manner, before true revival can come we must realize we are *strangers and pilgrims in the earth* and that we will soon put off these *tabernacles.*

THE FOUNDATION LAID AGAIN ———————————

Symbol - On the day that the *foundation of the temple* was laid - "many of the...ancient men, that had seen the first house, when the *foundation* of this house was laid before their eyes, wept with a loud voice; and many shouted aloud for joy: so that the people could not discern the noise of the shout of joy from the noise of the weeping..." (Ezra 3:12-13)

Interpretation - When the *foundation* is laid again spiritually and the professing church makes a grand departure from Babylonian apostasy, there is much cause for rejoicing and tears of gratitude (especially among those who understand the former glory). *The foundation spiritually* is Jesus Christ and an emphasis on His power and reality. *The foundation governmentally* is the apostles and prophets, the message they have promoted and are yet declaring. *The foundation doctrinally* is spoken of in Hebrews 6:1-2 as "repentance from dead works, and of faith toward God, of the doctrine of baptisms [and this includes the Baptism of the Holy Ghost], and of laying on of hands [and this includes the administration of healing and deliverance], and of resurrection of the dead, and of eternal judgment." When believers return wholeheartedly to these simple yet powerful truths, heaven-sent revival is bound to break loose, accompanied, as it normally is, by expressions of deep emotion.

RESTORATION THROUGH PROPHETIC MINISTRIES ─────

Symbol - There was much persecution against the Jews from those who wanted to see the restoration work stopped. The people, discouraged as a result, slackened their efforts and began concentrating on building their own houses. They were spurred back into action by the ministry of certain oracles of God. The Bible says that they - *"prospered* through the *prophesying* of Haggai the prophet and Zechariah the son of Iddo."* (Ezra 6:14)

> *Interpretation* - Similarly, God has raised up a great number of truly anointed prophets, through the centuries, to guide the church successfully to her restoration-goal. In the last days especially, God has promised to pour out His Spirit on all flesh and many of His sons and daughters will prophesy. True prophetic vessels always stir God's people from lethargy, discontentment, discouragement and deception...and for this we pray. The command is still the same to God's people - "Believe in the Lord your God, so shall ye be established; believe His *prophets,* so shall ye *prosper."* Of course, we must be willing to hear what the Spirit has to say to the church, and we must be sensitive to what is being said. **For this very reason let us inspect the prophecies of Haggai and Zechariah and discover their relevance to the elect of this hour.**

HAGGAI AND ZECHARIAH ──────────────────

Haggai, whose name means *born of a festival day,* and **Zechariah,** whose name means *Jehovah remembers,* were contemporaries. They prophesied to the same generation during a spiritually *festive* time when *Jehovah remembered* the affliction of His chosen people. Little is known about Haggai except that he began preaching during the captivity, in the second year of Darius. The younger Zechariah was of a priestly family, being the son of Berechiah and grandson of Iddo. Both of them gave significant prophecies to the Jews who were restored to their homeland from Babylonian bondage. Some of those which are most relevant to God's latter day church are as follows:

THE PROPHECIES OF HAGGAI UNVEILED

CONSIDERING OUR WAYS ─────────────────

Symbol - Haggai first scolded the Jews who had lost their restoration vision with the stinging words - *"Consider your ways."* (Haggai 1:5,7)

> *Interpretation* - Similarly, before true restoration can come to the church we must also *"consider our ways."* We must prepare the way of the Lord with the kind of introspection that mortifies the flesh with its affections and lusts.

227

REMEMBERING THE FORMER GLORY ─────────────

Symbol - Then the prophet questioned the Jews - "Who is left among you that saw this house in her *first glory?* and how do ye see it now? is it not in your eyes in comparison of it as nothing?" (Haggai 2:3)

> *Interpretation* - Parallel to this inquiry, any seeker for truth, especially several centuries ago, could have easily said, - "Who is left among us who remembers *the first glory* of the early church (the sweeping moves of salvation, whole cities stirred, evil spirits cast out, the sick healed, Peter's shadow with its miraculous results, angelic visitations, supernatural deliverance from jails and so on) and how do we see it now? Is it not *in comparison almost nothing?"*

GOD PROMISES GREATER GLORY ─────────────

Symbol - God promised to supply the need. He declared - "The silver is Mine, and the gold is Mine, saith the Lord of hosts. THE GLORY OF THIS LATTER HOUSE SHALL BE GREATER THAN OF THE FORMER, saith the Lord of hosts: and in this place will I give *peace."* (Haggai 2:8-9)

> *Interpretation* - In like manner, God could easily say to the church of the last days - "All grace, all righteousness, all miracle working power, all authority, and all spiritual gifts are Mine. I impart all this spiritual substance anytime I choose, to whomever I choose. When the fullness of time arrives, therefore, I can easily make THE GLORY OF THE LATTER HOUSE EXCEED THE GLORY OF THE FORMER." As this more fully transpires we can be sure that God will also pour out *peace* that passes understanding on His own.

THE PROPHECY FULFILLED ─────────────

Symbol - This *glory-prophecy* was definitely fulfilled, for the restored temple was finally made at least one-third larger than Solomon's, and by the time of the incarnation, Herod the Great was beautifying the temple to such degree that it was more spectacular in appearance than ever.

> *Interpretation* - This *glory-prophecy* will also be fulfilled spiritually. For the body of Christ is swelling in size, growing more rapidly than ever, and the supernatural displays of *the glory of God* are also increasing. This trend will certainly reach a peak as the second coming of the Messiah draws nigh.

THE DESIRE OF ALL NATIONS ─────────────

Symbol - God promised that just prior to this great restoration taking place, He would first - "*shake* the heavens, and the earth, and the sea, and the dry land; and...*shake* all the nations, and *the desire of all nations* shall come: and I will *fill this house with glory,* saith the Lord of hosts." (Hag. 2:6-7) The first part of this prophecy was fulfilled under the Old Will through the emerging of the Roman empire, *shaking the nations* with its ironfisted rise to imperial prominence. The second portion was fulfilled by the subsequent incarnation and visitation of the Messiah - *the desire of all nations.* Surely, *the glory of the Lord filled the house* when Jesus ministered in the temple under the power of the anointing.

> *Interpretation* - This prophecy will now be perfectly fulfilled in the heavenlies as God *shakes* principalities and powers, and throughout the earth, as God *shakes* His anointed people loose from every dependency other than Himself. Every realm, every arena of life, will be *shaken* - the spiritual world, nature, the social order, the political order, the world's monetary systems, the religious order, and every individual's personal life. The Antichrist will rise to imperial prominence and rule with an ironfisted control over mankind. But then the *"desire of all nations* shall come." This phrase, in its highest sense, could well be speaking of the second coming of Jesus and the establishment of the kingdom of God on earth. In that day God's living, spiritual temple will be utterly *filled with His glory.* We will be glorified in Him, changed in a moment, in the twinkling of an eye. [Note: Many reputable sources claim that this phrase out of Haggai 2:7 refers to something plural, not singular. The NIV translates it - **"THE DESIRED OF ALL NATIONS."** If so, instead of being a reference to Jesus, this could well be a reference to the gathering of God's people in the last days. Of all the people of the world, those most desired by God are His redeemed. They will be gathered to Jerusalem at His coming, to reign with Him in splendor forevermore.]

THE PROPHECIES OF ZECHARIAH UNVEILED

THE STONE WITH SEVEN EYES ————————————

Symbol - Zechariah described the chief cornerstone of the restored temple as *a stone with seven eyes* that would "remove the iniquity of that land *in one day."* (Zechariah 3:9)

> *Interpretation* - For those who count themselves a part of the New Testament temple, the *chief cornerstone* is Jesus. The *seven eyes* in that stone are surely the *"seven Spirits of God* sent forth into all the earth."* (Compare Rev. 5:6) And it is so true, that for believers in this Age of Grace, the sum total of all of our sins, past, present, and future, was potentially removed *"in one day"*...the day Jesus died on Calvary.

ZERUBBABEL CAUTIONED TO TRUST IN GOD ——————

Symbol - Zerubbabel was the governor of Judah during the days of restoration. Through Zechariah, God cautioned him not to trust in His own abilities or to judge the strength of the restored Jews by natural standards, saying **"Not by might, nor by power, BUT BY MY SPIRIT,** saith the Lord of hosts." (Zechariah 4:6)

Interpretation - In like manner, the living temple of the New Testament never has been, and never will be, built and/or kept from harm by the power of mere human effort. This temple began as a work of the Holy Spirit. It will come to completion the same way. Moreover, as the Jews were cautioned through this scripture not to fear their enemies, so also it similarly speaks to us. Even if we feel overwhelmed by the enormity of the task, the frailty of the flesh, or by the satanic assault that often buffets our minds, still we should daily look up toward heaven, to the Master Architect and Builder Himself, and confess with all of our hearts..."Not by might, nor by power, BUT BY THE SPIRIT OF THE LORD."

THE MOUNTAIN BECOMES A PLAIN

Symbol - Darius commanded at one point that the work of the temple should cease. Zechariah likened this and all the opposition Zerubbabel would receive, to a great, impassable mountain. But he daringly and prophetically declared, in behalf of this great governor - *"Who art thou, O great mountain? Before Zerubbabel thou shalt become a plain."* (Zechariah 4:7)

Interpretation - How often Satan has tried to similarly stop the ongoing work of God in our lives! But we, the church of the last days, can boast under the anointing in a similar fashion. We can daringly, prophetically declare to everything that seems to be in opposition to God's purpose in us - *"Who art thou, O great mountain? Before Jesus (the Governor of the nations who lives in us) thou shalt become a plain, leveled to the ground like the walls of Jericho."*

THE JOSHUA PROPHECY

Symbol - Joshua, the son of Josedech, was high priest during the time of restoration. The following verses concerning him have deep symbolic overtones: "Then take silver and gold, and make crowns, and set them upon the head of Joshua the son of Josedech, the high priest; and speak unto him, saying, Thus speaketh the Lord of hosts, saying, Behold the man whose name is THE BRANCH; and He shall grow up out of *His place,* and He shall build THE TEMPLE OF THE LORD: Even He shall build the temple of the Lord; and He shall bear the glory, and shall sit and rule upon His throne; and He shall be *a priest upon His throne:* and the counsel of peace shall be between them both." (Zechariah 6:11-13)

Interpretation - The name **Joshua** is the Hebrew equivalent of the name **Jesus** and it means *the salvation of God.* The phrase *His place* is a reference to the holy of holies, as if the One who is called THE BRANCH grew out of this sacred chamber. Joshua's coronation represented the resurrected Christ, crowned with the gold crown of divine life and the silver crown of redemptive grace. Jesus is the King/Priest and the Branch who will restore the latter day **temple of the Lord.** The government of God is a perfect blend of authority and love. Our God is both *a King,* ruling over us with supreme authority, and *a Priest,* mediating for us and ministering to us with matchless and unending love.

230

Symbol - Verse 15 of the last prophecy also states - "And they that are far off shall come and build in **THE TEMPLE OF THE LORD...**"

Interpretation - This speaks of the inclusion of the Gentiles - "they that are far off" - working to perfect God's temple, the church of God. How significant it is that when Herod was beautifying the temple just prior to Jesus' first coming (40-4 B.C.) he built two new courts, **the court of the Gentiles and the court of women.** Most likely God allowed this to happen to communicate in a subtle way that the New Will was swiftly approaching, a time when "there is neither Jew nor Greek, there is neither bond nor free, there is neither male nor female: for ye are all one in Christ Jesus." (Galatians 3:28)

THE WALL OF FIRE/THE BRAND PLUCKED OUT

Symbol - Furthermore, Zechariah declared - "For I, saith the Lord, will be unto [Jerusalem] *a wall of fire* round about, and will be *the glory* in the midst." He also showed how God would deliver His own saying - "The Lord rebuke thee, O Satan; even the Lord that hath chosen Jerusalem...is not this *"a brand plucked out of the fire"* (from the Heb. *uwd* - trans. *brand* or *firebrand* - meaning *a poker for turning or gathering embers*). (Zechariah 2:5;3:2)

Interpretation - Yes, we can also say with all confidence that Jesus will be a protective and *fiery hedge* round about us and He will be *the glory* in the midst. Without Him we have no protection and we have no glory. But with Him "in the midst"...exalted above all..."the *glory* of this latter house shall be greater than of the former." This is our *hope of glory!* (Hag. 2:9) We, the church of the last days, will be, as it were - **"A BRAND PLUCKED OUT OF THE FIRE" - "A FIREBRAND PLUCKED OUT OF THE BURNING."** (Am.4:11)

Our God will rebuke Satan and rescue us from *fiery* trials and tribulations, even burning chastisements through which we have passed. He will rebuke the devourer for our sake. When the enemy accuses, our High Priest, our Advocate, will stand in our defense.

A *brand,* or *firebrand,* was something placed in the fire for a purpose, but removed just in time before being totally consumed. So it has been and so it is for God's people, both Old Testament and New, who will make up His everlasting *temple.* Right at the critical moment, God comes through. Just as Jehovah brought the Jews out of Babylon, so has He brought the last days' church out of the grave danger of "Babylonian" religious deception.

● **Moreover, the word of the Lord came unto Zechariah, saying, "the hands of Zerubbabel have laid the foundation of this house; his hands shall also finish it" - "and he shall bring forth the headstone thereof with shoutings, crying, Grace, grace unto it."** (Zechariah 4:9,7)

The basic and literal meaning of this prophetic passage is easy to discern, but there is also a hidden meaning which brings our symbolic analogy to a grand climax. *The hands of Zerubbabel* (whose name means *seed of Babylon*) beginning and finishing the construction of the restored temple reveals spiritually that once restoration begins, there will never be another time when the church falls back into the darkness of gross spiritual captivity.

This present outpouring of restoration will continue growing, moving, advancing, and building until it reaches its zenith. This is the culmination of a spiritual cycle and at its peak the Lord will return, carrying His own into the unutterable glory of the Kingdom Age.

The symbolic overtones of the *headstone* being brought forth with *shoutings* is worthy of our attention as well. For this *headstone - this uppermost cornerstone -* is a prophetic reference to the Lord in His second coming. Certainly this event will be accompanied by great *shoutings.*

The Lord will descend from heaven with a *shout,* and surely we will rise to meet Him with a mighty and united *shout.* We will be completely changed into His wondrous image, filled to overflowing with His supernal presence.

The resurrected Christ was the Chief Cornerstone (the first block laid in this spiritual and everlasting temple); He will also be the Headstone (the Uppermost Cornerstone, the last block laid) when He comes in glory.

This is another way of confirming that He is the Beginning and the End of the purpose of God in this world. He is the Author and Finisher of all the wondrous work that has been performed in the church. He will complete, perfect, beautify and utterly glorify this awesome, spiritual edifice.

During the spectacular "grand finale," surely the angels will be shouting over God's living temple, as the Jews shouted over their natural one - *"Grace, grace unto it"*...for it will definitely not be our own works which procure for us such a glorious destiny.

The full perfecting of the church will be accomplished the same way Solomon's temple was restored...not by works of righteousness which we have done, but by *grace,* beautiful *grace*...the *unmerited love of God.* (See Psalm 118:22-23, Isaiah 28:16, I Peter 2:3-8, Titus 3:5)

THE PINNACLE OF THE TEMPLE-ANALOGY

According to Jewish tradition, during the same week in which the crucifixion took place, the priests and the Jewish worshippers could be heard singing the Hallel Psalms throughout Jerusalem as a part of the Passover feast (Psalms 113-118). How significant this is! For these psalms are full of Messianic prophecies...including the following one quoted so often:

> *"The stone which the builders refused is*
> *become **the head stone of the corner**.*
> *This is the Lord's doing; it is marvellous in*
> *our eyes.*
> *This is the day which the Lord hath made;*
> *we will rejoice and be glad in it."*
> (Psalm 118:22-24) *2

How deeply ironic it is that while the angry "builders" were refusing the

Messiah, they were also unknowingly and rejoicingly singing out a series of psalms that foretold His ultimate triumph. Little did they realize when they shouted - *"This is the day which the Lord hath made"* - they were actually celebrating that *"the day"* of Jesus' death was a God-ordained event. It was *the day the Lord had "made"* to bring redemption to all mankind.

The ignorance displayed by the builders, in rejecting Jesus as the lower cornerstone, did not and could not alter the fact that He was to be the *"headstone* of the corner": the *crowning stone* of a living, eternal temple.

● Quite a few years after the Messiah's death, in retrospect, Peter called this great Redeemer - "a LIVING STONE, disallowed indeed of men, but chosen of God, and precious." Then the apostle pulled the veil back even further, declaring that - "ye also, as LIVELY STONES, [LIVING STONES] are built up A SPIRITUAL HOUSE, an holy priesthood, to offer up spiritual sacrifices, acceptable to God by Jesus Christ." (I Peter 2:4-5, AV, NIV)

In this passage, Peter revealed our present status, as well as the future purpose of God in our lives, by revealing two more of our primary *title-callings.* **He also showed yet another way in which we should emerge in the image of the firstborn Son.**

At the start, Jesus was the only dwelling place of deity, the only true *temple of God* in this world. Now, through identifying with Him, we all become individual *temples* .

When all of God's people are represented as a singular *temple,* Jesus is the original *Living Stone.* He is the first *living stone* laid - *the Chief Cornerstone* - in *a spiritual house* dedicated to the worship of the Almighty. The rest of the body of Christ are those *living stones* that bring the building to completion.

This analogy is somewhat of an enigma, though, for stones and rocks can not and do not "live." They fall under the category of **inanimate nature:** that which has no life or spirit.

To the inspired mind, the hidden message is apparent.

We were once dead in a spiritual sense - "dead in trespasses and sins" - with hard hearts and stiff necks, quite rigid in rebellion.

But then the miracle transpired!

We repented of our sins and Jesus, with His fiery finger, wrote the law in our stoney-hard hearts. When this transpired, dead stones became *living stones...*filled with the enlivening presence of the Most High God.

We passed from death unto life, but in the process, we never lost our *stone-status.* Where before, we were hardened against God, now we are called to be even more hardened in resistance against the flesh, the devil and "the sin which doth so easily beset us." (Hebrews 12:1)

We are called to be just as solid in our commitment to truth as Jesus, the Rock of our salvation, for we are His offspring. We have been begotten of the Rock. Therefore, we have inherited the rock-hard stability of His rock-like character. (Compare Deuteronomy 32:18)

● We have also received the challenge to become stability-imparting, strength-sharing units of a composite whole. We are a spiritual *temple* comprised of self-sacrificing men and women who rejoice to give up their single-rock, independent identity for the good of the entire edifice.

When we each find our place in the body of Christ and yield to His plan of "fitted-togetherness," we discover the value and necessity of serving one another in love. Like the silver-encased stones in the walls of Solmon's temple, we become mutually interdependent.

We undergird one another in compassionate strength.

We watch over one another in tender love. We cling to one another in tenacious faith and persistent, intercessory prayer. We are inseparably fused together with the living, spiritual mortar of a blood-covenant bond.

All of this speaks of our calling, as the body of Christ, to *edify* one another. (The word *edify* - Gr. *oikodome* - means *to build up*. It is even translated *building* in some of our main *title-scriptures* - See Gr. of I Cor. 3:9, Eph. 2:21).

So *lively stones* exist *to edify* the *edifice:* to give away strength, support and "encouragement" to all the other *lively stones* that are a part of this holy and eternal building. (See Ro. 14:19, I Th. 5:11, Eph. 4:12, 16, I Cor. 8:1)

● It is only right that Peter, first known as Simon, should have been the one to promote this *lively stone* revelation , for this was quite conspicuously the very first outstanding revelation given to him.

It came coincidental with his calling, recorded by John in his gospel. When Andrew brought Şimon, his brother, to the Master, Jesus said:

> *"Thou art Simon the son of Jona: thou shalt be called Cephas, which is by interpretation, A stone."*
>
> (John 1:42)

Cephas is an Aramaic word which means *a stone* or *a fragment of a rock.* The actual Greek word translated *Cephas* was *Petros,* translated in 161 other places into the name *Peter.*

Imparting this name was the Lord's way of communicating that *Peter* was to become an integral *stone* in God's everlasting, ever-living temple. God would make him dependable and *rock-sure* as a leader among God's people...unflinching and *rock-hard* in the face of all opposition.

This was also God's way of showing Peter that his life was to become a sacrifice to the service of others. For every temple stone exists only to support, strengthen and "edify" the others stones laid in the temple walls - above, below and on either side. Yes, it is so true that each individual stone serves ultimately to strengthen, or weaken, the entirety of *"God's building."*

This must be the very reason that God spoke through the prophet, Isaiah, saying - *"Judgment also will I lay to the line, and righteousness to the plummet."* (Isaiah 28:17)

The *line* being referred to is that horizontal string drawn from corner to corner on a wall that is under construction. The *plummet* is a vertical string, usually hanging taut by means of a weight on the end. The *plummet* or *plumbline,* is directed, by means of the weight, to the center of gravity of the earth. By using these two lines, which cross each other at a perpendicular angle, a mason can be very exact, very precise, in laying block or brick. Any stone not measuring to the correct standard is thereby easily discerned, and either rejected and tossed aside, or chiseled into shape by expert hands.

This is a necessary process, for a few ill-shaped or wrongly laid blocks can detrimentally affect an entire structure, throwing the whole building out of alignment. Each block, therefore, has either a negative or positive in-

fluence on the whole. And as it is in the natural, so it is in the spiritual.

No wonder God warned that after He laid that first precious, foundation stone in Zion, all subsequent blocks would have to measure up to the standards of *judgment* and *righteousness.* (Isaiah 28:16-17)

This spiritual *line of judgment* is, in a sense, clamped on two opposite corners: the beginning and the end of the creation of God.

The spiritual *plumbline* of righteousness, that every *lively stone* must line up with, is drawn downward toward the irresistible core of unchanging truth existing in the heart of God's Word.

Anyone requesting inclusion in God's New Covenant temple, should automatically expect to come under the scrutiny of the Master Builder Himself, either to be accepted as is, discarded, or sculpted into an acceptable form.

As long as we maintain a yielded, humble and repentant spirit, God will do all He can to "make us fit."

● **Such truth makes Zechariah 4:10 all the more understandable and interesting.** In this portion of Scripture, Zerubbabel, the governor of restored Judah, was depicted as a mason with a plumbline in his hand:

> *"...But these seven will be glad when they see the **plumbline** in the hand of Zerubbabel - these are the eyes of the Lord which range to and fro throughout the earth."*
> (Zechariah 4:10 NAS)

In other words, the *seven eyes* which are in the Chief Cornerstone will gleam with gladness when they behold the leadership in the body of Christ dropping the *plumbline* of God's mandate for righteousness into the hearts of His people.

This is the message of the hour, the key to restoration, and the joy of God's heart. For there are too many professing Christians who are, in Philistine-like-manner, attempting to place Jesus - the true ark of the New Testament - in the inner chamber of an idolatrous heart dedicated to the worship of other gods.

● **In I Samuel 5, we read of the literal Old Testament happening.**
In a decisive battle with Israel, the Philistines captured the ark of God and placed it in the house of Dagon, one of their gods. "And when they...arose early on the morrow, behold, Dagon was fallen upon his face to the earth before the ark of the Lord. And they took Dagon, and set him in his place again. And when they arose early on the morrow morning, behold, Dagon was fallen...and the head of Dagon and both the palms of his hands were cut off upon the threshold; only the stump of Dagon was left to him." (I Samuel 5:3-4)

This startling incident communicates a sobering truth: that if we ever invite Jesus into hearts still steeped in idolatry, the Most High will begin forcefully tearing down all those idols that remain. And if we stubbornly attempt to re-erect those same idols, the second judgment of God is often more severe than the first.

No person, no possession, no pleasure, and no goal in life can ever take His place, and none of these things should ever steal our affection and devotion to Him. These are subtle sins of idolatry and from them we must sanctify our hearts in order to become *living sanctuaries* in which the Most High can comfortably dwell. (See Colossians 3:5, I John 5:21)

For "what agreement hath **THE TEMPLE OF GOD** with idols? for ye are **THE TEMPLE OF THE LIVING GOD;** as God hath said, I will dwell in them, and walk in them; and I will be their God, and they shall be My people. Wherefore come out from among them, and be ye separate, saith the Lord..." (II Corinthians 6:16-17)

Before Calvary, men were *separated* from God by the veil of the temple and the veil of flesh-consciousness. When Jesus died, the temple veil was rent.

This represented the truth that now all men can be received by God for we all have "access" into His presence. Once *accepted* by God we are subsequently called to be *separated* from the world.

Paul expressed this thought so aptly when he exclaimed:

> *"What? know you not that your body is*
> *THE TEMPLE OF THE HOLY GHOST*
> *which is in you, which ye have of God, and ye*
> *are not your own?*
> *For ye are bought with a price: therefore*
> *glorify God in your body, and in your spirit,*
> *which are God's."*
>
> (I Corinthians 6:19-20)

We must become sincerely dedicated to ridding ourselves of all besetting sins and habits that we might be a fit dwelling place for deity. **As there was something heaven-sent in every part of Solomon's temple (the fire that fell on the altar in the outer court, the light on the lampstand in the holy place, and the Shekinah glory on the ark in the holy of holies) so the presence of heaven-sent things should pervade every area of our lives.**

● Moreover, we must fulfill that desire expressed by David concerning the original temple:

> *"...and the house that is to be builded for*
> *the Lord must be EXCEEDING MAGNIFI-*
> *CAL, of fame and of glory throughout all*
> *countries."*
>
> (I Chronicles 22:5)

We know this was fulfilled in the beginning of the symbol, for the people came from far and wide just to view the *magnificent* splendor of God's building during Israel's "golden years." But this will also be fulfilled in the end...in a far greater sense. As we near the completion of the Age of Grace, **THE LATTER HOUSE** will surely emerge in the power of the anointing, and be of "great fame and glory throughout all countries"..."*exceeding magnifical.*"

And how much more *magnificent* the splendor will be when we each receive - "a building of God, an house not made with hands, eternal in the heavens." (II Corinthians 5:1)

We know this grand transformation will transpire with startling swiftness. For "the Lord, whom ye seek, shall suddenly come to **HIS TEMPLE,** even the messenger of the covenant, whom ye delight in." (Malachi 3:1)

When He comes, the church of the living God will become a glorified *palace* of worship forevermore...*exceedingly magnifical.*

236

The shadow of symbolism will then utterly fade away. And the full celestial radiance of once-veiled truth will illuminate our hearts with absolute devotion to the Master Builder. We will be His people and He will be our God.

Not only will the Everlasting One walk *with* us and dwell *with* us, He has promised to walk and dwell *within* us. (II Corinthians 6:16)

Long ago, He gave the gracious and meaningful pledge:

> *"I will glorify THE HOUSE OF MY*
> *GLORY...to beautify THE PLACE OF MY*
> *SANCTUARY; and I will make THE*
> *PLACE OF MY FEET glorious."*
> (Isaiah 60:7, 13)

Blessed be the Saviour who has kindly walked into our hearts and lives, and caused us to confidently walk toward this, His ultimate purpose.

Forevermore we are **THE PLACE OF HIS THRONE, THE PLACE OF HIS SANCTUARY, THE PLACE OF HIS REST** and **THE PLACE WHERE HIS HONOUR DWELLS.** (Ez. 43:7, Is. 60:13; 66:1, Ps. 26:8)

● May we ever be as the restored temple Ezekiel beheld in his spectacular vision - with a river of life issuing forth out of the inner sanctuary of our regenerated hearts bringing life and healing to the nations. (See Ezekiel 47:1-9)

And at the coming of the Lord, may the Most High cry - "Grace, grace unto them" - tranforming us into the **SACRED GEMS** and **HALLOWED STONES** of an eternal, heavenly sanctuary. We will then be perpetually lustrous and precious to His heart. (Lamentation 4:1 NIV, AMP)

Forevermore, the ark of God's covenant will find His *place of rest* in us, and the Shekinah glory will radiate out of us brighter than the sun at noonday.

As the earthly holy of holies was called the oracle - because God's voice was revealed there - so we, His everlasting holy of holies, will be, even more perfectly, His oracles throughout the ceaseless ages - channels of His Word and will. **This, too, is our *hope of glory*, our *blessed hope*, and an anchor of the soul that goes beyond the veil.**

(THE EPITAPH OF DAVID LIVINGSTONE)

May we all have an epitaph over our lives similar to that of **David Livingstone,** that great missionary who so courageously penetrated the continent of Africa with the gospel. In England's Westminister Abbey, his mortal remains were buried and over him were declared the words:

> *Open the Abbey doors and bear him in*
>
> *To sleep with king and statesman, chief and sage,*
>
> *The missionary come of weaver kin,*
>
> *But great by work that brooks no lower wage.*
>
> *He needs no epitaph to guard a name*
>
> *Which men shall prize while worthy work is known;*
>
> *He lived and died for good - be that his fame;*
>
> *Let marble crumble; this is LIVING STONE*

OTHER NAMES FOR THE TEMPLE

Other Old Testament names for the temple, besides those already placed at the beginning of this chapter, are also applicable to the church of the New Testament. Some of these *titles* will be used in other chapters or volumes of OUR GLORIOUS INHERITANCE. Others are scripturally used only in reference to the literal temple of Solomon, so they have not been included in the table of contents for this chapter. It seems very logical to apply them to God's offspring, though, since we have inherited a number of other names that were initially given only to this literal building. For this cause, all of these will appear in our final index, but with a special note indicating their origin. The various temple-names that we can claim are as follows:

HIS REST - Ps. 132:8, HIS RESTING PLACE - Is. 66:1 NIV, THE PLACE OF HIS REST- Is. 66:1, A PLACE FOR HIS DWELLING FOR EVER - II Chr. 6:2, AN HOUSE OF REST - I Chr. 28:2, THE HOUSE OF HIS GLORY - Is. 60:7, THE TEMPLE OF THE HOUSE OF GOD - Dan. 5:3, THE TEMPLE OF THE LORD GOD OF ISRAEL - Ez. 4:1, THE TEMPLE OF THE HOUSE - I Kgs. 6:3, THE LORD'S TEMPLE - Hag. 2:18, HIS HOLY TEMPLE - Ps. 11:4, THE HOUSE OF THE LORD - Ps. 134:1, THE HOUSE OF THE LORD GOD - I Chr. 22:1, THE HOUSE OF THE LORD OUR GOD - Ex. 34:26, THE HOUSE OF THE LORD GOD OF ISRAEL - Ez. 1:3, THE HOUSE OF OUR GOD - I Chr. 29:3, THE HOUSE OF THE GOD OF JACOB - Is. 2:3, AN HOUSE UNTO THE NAME OF THE LORD MY GOD - I Kgs. 5:5, AN HOUSE TO THE NAME OF THE LORD MY GOD - II Chr. 2:4, AN HOUSE UNTO HIS NAME - I Kgs. 5:5, AN HOUSE FOR THE NAME OF THE LORD GOD OF ISRAEL - I Kgs. 8:20, A HOUSE FOR HIS HOLY NAME - I Chr. 29:16, A HOUSE FOR THE NAME OF THE LORD - II Chr. 2:1, AN HOUSE FOR HIS KINGDOM - II Chr. 2:1, AN HOUSE OF SACRIFICE - II Chr. 7:12, THE HOUSE OF THE GOD OF HEAVEN - Ez. 7:23, THE HABITATION OF HIS HOUSE - Ps. 26:8, OUR HOLY AND BEAUTIFUL HOUSE - Is. 64:11, THE HOLY TEMPLE - Ps. 65:4, THE SANCTUARY OF THE LORD GOD - I Chr. 22:19, THE HOUSE BUILT TO THE NAME OF THE LORD - I Chr. 22:19, AN HOUSE OF HABITATION - II Chr. 6:2, THE HOLY HOUSE - I Chr. 29:3, THE FATHER'S HOUSE - Jn. 2:16, HIS HOUSE - Lk. 19:46, THE LORD'S HOUSE - Is. 2:2, THE HOUSE OF THE LORD OF HOSTS - Zec. 14:21, HIS HOUSE OF PRAYER - Is. 56:7, AN HOUSE OF PRAYER FOR ALL PEOPLE - Is. 56:7, THE PALACE - I Chr. 29:1. THE SANCTUARY - I Chr. 28:10, BETH-EL (often the orig. Heb. of THE HOUSE OF GOD), THE PLACES OF THE SOLES OF HIS FEET - Ez. 43:7, and HIS FOOTSTOOL - Ps. 132:7

(The *title* - the footstool of our God - was used specifically of the ark. The last *title* in our list - His footstool - seems to also imply the entire temple. (See also Ps. 99:5) The prophet Jeremiah used the term concerning all of Zion. (Lam. 2:1) Finally, Isaiah and Jesus lifted the symbol even higher saying that "the earth is His footstool." (Is 66:1, Mt. 5:35) In the Old Testament it is from the Heb. *kebes* meaning *something trodden upon.*

Merrill Unger says that a footstool is "an article of furniture, used to support the feet when sitting in state, as upon a throne. (II Chr. 9:18) The divine glory which resided...between the cherubim...is supposed to use the ark as a footstool." To worship at God's footstool speaks of complete submission to God's authority and the depth of awe-filled adoration. One day His glory will not be confined to the holy of holies under the Old Will or the hearts of His redeemed under the New Will. His glory will fill the earth. It will then fill this role and fulfill this *title.*

---

*1 Unger, Merrill F. *Unger's Bible Dictionary* (Chicago, Illinois, Moody Press, 1974) p. 547, under *Jachin*

*2 Unger, Merrill F. *Unger's Bible Dictionary,* (Chicago, Illinois, Moody Press, 1974) p. 354, under *Festivals*

THOU WORM JACOB

A NEW SHARP
THRESHING INSTRUMENT

A THRESHING SLEDGE

DIMINUTIVE ISRAEL

---

*"Fear not, **THOU WORM JACOB, [DIMINUTIVE IS-RAEL]** and ye men of Israel; I will help thee, saith the Lord, and thy redeemer, the Holy One of Israel.*

*Behold, I will make thee A **NEW SHARP THRESHING INSTRUMENT, [A THRESH-ING SLEDGE]** having teeth: thou shalt thresh the mountains, and beat them small, and shalt make the hills as chaff."*
(Isaiah 41:14-15 AV, Sept, NIV)

THOU WORM JACOB

*"Fear not, THOU WORM JACOB,
[DIMINUTIVE ISRAEL] and ye men of Israel; I will help thee, saith the Lord, and thy
redeemer, the Holy One of Israel.*

*Behold, I will make thee A NEW SHARP
THRESHING INSTRUMENT [A
THRESHING SLEDGE] having teeth: thou
shalt thresh the mountains, and beat them
small, and shalt make the hills as chaff."*

(Isaiah 41:14-15 AV, Sept, NIV)

● In this obscure and unique passage of Scripture, Jehovah is not expressing disappointment with, or disdain for His people by referring to them as a *worm*. Neither is He placing upon them what seems to be a degrading, demeaning *title* as a rebuke. He is simply describing what the Israelites' lot would be, in the flesh, without His aid.

Moreover, He is merely echoing their own sentiments, pointing out the lack of esteem they have toward themselves and the similar way they are viewed by their enemies. (Unfortunately, the enemy usually sees us in the same light with which we view ourselves. For instance, the ten unbelieving spies said of the huge inhabitants of Canaan - "We were IN OUR OWN SIGHT as grasshoppers, and so we were IN THEIR SIGHT." Numbers 13:33)

So *"diminutive Israel"* (as this *title* is rendered in the Septuagint) considers herself nothing more than a mere *worm* - small, helpless, boneless, spineless and repulsive - but not so in God's estimation. For the Most High recognizes the many weaknesses of His people, but He also sees their hidden potential, their value to His kingdom, and their ultimate victory.

Furthermore, Jehovah pledges His assistance saying - " I will strengthen thee; yea, I will help thee; yea, I will uphold thee with the right hand of My righteousness." (Isaiah 41:10)

● Three times in this chapter God encourages His people with the simple advice - *"Fear not"*, and three times, in the same verses, He promises - *"I will help thee."* (vs. 10,13,14)

This exhortation is not only for those Israelites who lived in Isaiah's day, but for all who ever have been, or ever will be, in a covenant relationship with the living God.

We may feel insignificant, insecure, defenseless, scorned, and even base because of our error-ridden past. As in the case of a worm, we, at times, may feel quite vulnerable, easily trampled upon by the enemies of our soul.

We may even sound out the prophet's concerned inquiry - "By whom shall Jacob arise? for he is small." (Amos 7:2,5)

Yet, through it all, we are still commanded by God not to fear.

As we search the entirety of the Word, we find specific commands:

1. **Not to fear man** - "The Lord is on my side; I will not *fear:* what can man do unto me?" (Psalm 118:6, See Deuteronomy 3:22, Luke 12:4)

2. **Not to fear their reproach nor their reviling** - *"fear* ye not the reproach

of men, neither be ye *afraid* of their revilings." (Isaiah 51:7)

3. **Not to fear disastrous events of life** - "Therefore will not we *fear,* though the earth be removed, and though the mountains be carried into the midst of the sea." (Psalm 46:2, See Matthew 8:26)

4. **Not to fear suffering** - "*Fear* none of those things which thou shalt suffer." (Revelation 2:10)

5. **Not to fear sickness** - "Thou shalt not be *afraid* for...the pestilence [the plague] that walketh in darkness." (Psalm 91:5-6 AV, RBV)

6. **Not to fear lack of material goods** - "*Fear not,* little flock; for it is your Father's good pleasure to give you the kingdom." (Luke 12:32, See vs 22-32)

7. **Not to fear sudden attacks of fear nor the plight of the wicked** - "Be not *afraid* of sudden fear, neither of the desolation of the wicked, when it cometh." (Proverbs 3:25)

8. **Not to fear especially satanic adversaries** - "And in nothing *terrified* by your adversaries: which is to them an evident token of perdition, but to you of salvation, and that of God." (Philippians 1:28, See also II Kings 6:16)

9. **Not to fear death** - "Yea, though I walk through the valley of the shadow of death, I will *fear* no evil." (Psalm 23:4, See Matthew 10:28-31)

10. **Not to fear the splendor of God's presence** - "And when I saw Him, I fell at His feet as dead. And He laid His right hand upon me, saying unto me, *Fear not,* I am the first and the last." (Revelation 1:17)

All **sons of God** have a right to walk in such courage for our Father has promised to fight our battles. In our *title-chapter,* He even announced:

> "*Behold, all they that were incensed against thee shall be ashamed and confounded: they shall be as nothing...*"
>
> (Isaiah 41:11)

On the highest level, this speaks of the day when Lucifer will be cast into the bottomless pit and then into the everlasting torment of the lake of fire "where *their worm dieth not,* and the fire is not quenched." (Mark 9:48)

Though the accuser of the brethren sought to drive us to such everlasting ruin, the grace of God has prevailed in our behalf. Judgment, like a boomerang, will yet return upon his own head and he will be "as nothing, and as a thing of nought." (Isaiah 41:12)

Though the enemy sought to permanently bind us in the chains of a *worm-like,* deceitful Jacob-nature, our God will loose us and resurrect us into the royal Israel-nature for which we have been chosen.

SPIRITUAL IDENTIFICATION

● Studying the particular *title - thou worm Jacob -* is not too disconcerting when we realize that the Bible used very similar terminology of Jesus.

In that psalm which so graphically depicts and foretells the crucifixion, the Messiah to come is quoted as saying:

> "*But I am a worm, and no man; a reproach of men, and despised of the people.*"
>
> (Psalm 22:6)

242

At Calvary, He remembered us in our low estate and bore our sin in His own body on the tree. He identified with us in our loathesome and fallen condition, so *"man, that is a worm"* could be justified in the sight of God. (Job 25:6)

Now, by identifying with the "redeemer, the Holy One of Israel," who identified with us, we become His redeemed and holy people. We are bought back from the bondage of *worm-like* Adam flesh by the One who became a *"worm, and no man"* for us. Because He went through a grand metamorphosis - and emerged glorious and glorified - we can also.

BECOMING A THRESHING INSTRUMENT

● **The next two verses express God's great *hope* toward Jacob, His flesh-bound people, as well as the *hope* that they have in Him.** Revealing that we are far beyond worthlessness and helplessness, Jehovah declares with intensity:

> *"Behold, I will make thee A NEW SHARP THRESHING INSTRUMENT, [A THRESHING SLEDGE] having teeth: thou shalt thresh the mountains, and beat them small, and shalt make the hills as chaff.*
> *Thou shalt fan them, and the wind shall carry them away, and the whirlwind shall scatter them: and thou shalt rejoice in the Lord, and shalt glory in the Holy One of Israel."*
>
> (Isaiah 41:15-16 AV, NIV)

*Threshing is the process by which the outer husks and stalks of grains such as wheat and barley are stripped away from the pure seed. A **threshing instrument**, or **sledge**, as some call it, is probably one of two things: either some kind of weighted board with stones or bits of iron attached underneath... or a low, sled-like wagon with long cylinders for wheels, covered with sharp spikes or ridges (**teeth** according to the AV).*

Both of these ancient farming contraptions are normally drawn by animals.

The phrase *threshing instrument* is so translated from the Hebrew *morag* which itself comes from an unused root meaning *to pulverize thoroughly by rubbing or grinding.*

On the wagon-type sledge, there is constructed, at times, a seat upon which the thresher can sit. Thus positioned, he guides the animals that pull the sledge and provides added weight, which aids in the performance of the desired task.

THRESHING THE MOUNTAINS

● **Isaiah 41:15 announces that God's people will ultimately *"thresh the mountains, and beat them small."***

This could represent truth on several levels of interpretation. First, *mountains* can be a symbol of the nations and kingdoms of this world. (See Rev.

243

17:9-10) Second, *mountains* can symbolize any enemy opposition or seemingly insurmountable problem that we face in life. (See Zec. 4:7, Mk. 11:23)

For the Jews of the Old Testament, *threshing the mountains* primarily meant overcoming and subduing the heathen nations round about them. (See Jeremiah 51:33, Micah 4:13, Habakkuk 3:12)

For New Testament believers, *threshing the mountains* can mean conquering the nations, in a spiritual sense, through the preaching of the Word.

This is called *threshing in hope* according to I Corinthians 9:10. It is entitled so because the proclamation of the gospel delivers men from their chaff-like carnal nature and presents them, as pure grain, to the heavenly Husbandman. They are then used as either seed or bread to meet both the needs of men and of God.

● *Threshing the mountains* also speaks of the church, ripping and tearing through the hosts of hell that rule this world. Jesus, the great Thresher, sits in the midst of this "family of God *threshing sledge*" and guides it onward to victory. This is something that transpires every day as we confront evil spirits and "beat them small." It will happen in a complete way, at the coming of Jesus, when "the Lord shall punish the host of the high ones that are on high." (Isaiah 24:21; 41:15)

Knowing that such dominion will soon be ours, in advance we can declare, concerning Satan's kingdom - "Who art thou, *O great mountain?*" Before Jesus, the governor among the nations - "thou shalt become a plain." (Zec.4:7)

● Finally, *threshing the mountains* can represent the final conquest of all the battles, weaknesses, sins, lusts and disappointments that we have faced during our flesh-bound sojourn in this world. When God's people are resurrected and glorified - "every *mountain* and hill shall be made low." (Isaiah 40:4)

We will rise above them all. We will overcome them all. We will rule victoriously over all our battles, and over nations and kingdoms during the millennial era. And what looked like unconquerable *mountains* will then be nothing more than chaff, blowing in the wind...utterly consumed by the fire of God's passion for His own.

In that wonderful day, we will never again know fear nor be referred to as *Jacob, the worm.* We will no longer be considered *diminutive* (small and pitiable), but we will emerge a great nation, a multitude no man can number.

We will be *Israel,* God's invincible, princely people who rule with Him in splendor and power. Therefore, let us *thresh in hope* knowing that one day we will be made full *partakers of our hope.*

Let us unceasingly declare the gospel and unflinchingly fight against every satanic foe. And let us offer our hearts as the seat of the Master Thresher that He might hold the reins, guide the sledge, and "perfect that which concerneth" us. (Psalm 138:8)

This is also our *hope of glory*...that because of His help we will "yet praise Him" and eternally "*glory* in the Holy One of Israel." (Ps. 42:11, Is. 41:16)

In the end we will surely shout in confidence - "God has done it. He has blown away the chaff. He has set His people free. He has lifted us from weakness to strength, from lack to abundance, from fear to courage, from uselessness to usefulness, and from self-degradation to a state of wholeness, glory and dominion. **Blessed be the name of the Lord!**

• A WOMAN CLOTHED WITH • THE SUN

A GREAT WONDER IN HEAVEN

"And there appeared A GREAT WONDER IN HEAVEN; A WOMAN CLOTHED WITH THE SUN, and the moon under her feet, and upon her head a crown of twelve stars."

(Revelation 12:1)

"And the dragon was wroth with **THE WOMAN,** *and went to make war with the remnant of* **HER SEED,** *which keep the commandments of God, and have the testimony of Jesus Christ."*

(Revelation 12:17)

"Be in pain, and labour to bring forth, O daughter of Zion, like A **WOMAN IN TRAVAIL...***the Lord shall redeem thee from the hand of thine enemies."*

(Micah 4:10)

● THE SEED OF THE WOMAN ●

A WOMAN IN TRAVAIL

A WOMAN WITH CHILD

THE WOMAN

A COMELY AND
DELICATE WOMAN

THE FAIR AND DELICATE ONE

*"Like as **A WOMAN WITH CHILD**, that draweth near the time of her delivery, is in pain, and crieth out in her pangs; so have we been in Thy sight, O Lord.*

We have been with child, we have been in pain, we have as it were brought forth wind..."

(Isaiah 26:17-18)

*"I have likened the daughter of Zion to **A COMELY AND DELICATE WOMAN [THE FAIR AND DELICATE ONE].**"*

(Jeremiah 6:2 AV, Bas)

A WOMAN CLOTHED WITH THE SUN

*"And there appeared A GREAT
WONDER IN HEAVEN; A WOMAN
CLOTHED WITH THE SUN, and the moon
under her feet, and upon her head a crown of
twelve stars."*

(Revelation 12:1)

There is no more bleak, dark, dismal book in the sixty-six contained in the Bible than the book of the Revelation. Dreadful symbolic creatures, cataclysmic upheavals, inescapable plagues, severe judgments, harsh calamities and caustic curses fill up almost every chapter.

However, it can also be said that there is no book in the Bible providing any greater insight into the wonderful and hopeful future awaiting God's covenant people. So the absolute of hopelessness and hopefulness are blended together in one book, balancing the two extremes.

● **One major theme seems to dominate this apocalyptic portion of Scripture - the great contrast between the false and the true church.**

The **false church** is represented as both a city (Babylon) and a woman (the great whore) destined for destruction.

The **true church** is also represented as both a city (New Jerusalem) and a woman (the bride, the Lamb's wife).

This wife of the Almighty, this "help meet for God," is also depicted as a woman arrayed with sunbeams, with multiple shafts of heavenly light emanating from her on every side.

We will spend little time describing that decadent city and vile woman which typify a brand of powerless, compromising and destruction-bound Christianity that, ironically, even the Antichrist will support for a season. (See Revelation 17, 18)

Rather, let us focus on, and hold aloft in our minds, that beautiful and regal heiress of heaven whose high calling it is to eventually share the very throne of the Almighty God.

What greater or more glorious *hope* could grip our hearts than to see ourselves a part of her?

THE SUN-CLOTHED WOMAN

● We will draw most of the information contained in this *title-revelation* from the twelfth chapter of the book of the Revelation. This unique portion of John's vision opens with a spectacular, celestial scene:

*"And there appeared A GREAT
WONDER IN HEAVEN; A WOMAN
CLOTHED WITH THE SUN, and the moon
under her feet, and upon her head a crown of
twelve stars."*

(Revelation 12:1)

This unique woman is a personification of "Jerusalem which is above...the mother of us all." (Galatians 4:26)

She is "the bride," comprised of all the redeemed of both the Old and New Will: all who ever have been, or ever will be, married to God in a covenant relationship.

"THE SEED OF THE WOMAN" are all the many individuals, in every age, who are the product of this heavenly Jerusalem. (Revelation 12:17)

Under the Old Will this woman is natural Israel; under the New Will she is spiritual Israel. The woman-symbol shifts from natural to spiritual Israel after the man child (Jesus) is caught up to the throne of God.

Because **Israel** means *ruling with God*, the woman typifies all who ever have, or ever will, *rule with God* over sin, circumstance, satanic powers, the flesh, or the world...by the Word, by the Spirit and by the name of our God.

Also we should remember that Eve was "called **Woman**, because she was taken out of man." (Gen. 2:23) So the church can be referred to as a woman for we have been taken out of Jesus, the ideal man. In fact, we were actually chosen in Him before the foundation of the world. (See also the first two pages in *The Bride* - Volume Two of **Our Glorious Inheritance**).

THE MAIN SYMBOLIC POINTS

The following are some of the most important symbolic points contained in this Revelation 12 description:

■ **The woman is clothed with the sun** - From the fall of Adam and Eve onward, the search has been for a proper kind of "clothing" to hide man's spiritual nakedness. The only sufficient covering is a restoration of that which was originally lost: the Shekinah presence of the Most High God!

Notice that the false church is covered in purple and scarlet: earthly materials that appear luxurious, but will eventually rot away. (Rev. 17:4)

On the contrary, the bride is clothed with the sun, the glory of God, an everlasting adornment. Of course, for this to happen she must first be "clothed with humility," "clothed with righteousness" and "clothed with salvation." (I Peter 5:5, Psalm 132:9, 16)

Using the sun in this symbolic passage shows, in no uncertain terms, the greatness of what grace has wrought in our lives. This literal ball of burning gaseous vapors is about 865,000 miles in diameter. Its approximate surface temperature is an intense 11,000 degrees Fahrenheit. Though the earth is ninety-three million miles away from the sun, still, were it not for the protective covering of the earth's atmosphere, all life on this planet would be destroyed, burned beyond recognition.

And so it is concerning we frail, erring human beings and the God who is just as unapproachable. He is the Eternal One, "dwelling in the light which no man can approach unto." He is the "Sun of righteousness," blazing in flawless holiness and irresistible judgment. (I Timothy 6:16, Malachi 4:2)

Because of our inherent sinfulness, we should have received from Him only rejection, damnation and death. But, thank God, the Lord is both "a *sun* and *shield*." (Psalm 84:11)

Not only does He, as the *sun*, shine on us with His incomparable holiness;

He also *shields* us with a covering of His blood and grace. Because of such a covering, we are forgiven and we stand "holy and without blame before Him in love." (Ephesians 1:4)

Without this covering, the holiness and judgment of God would have burned against us and, in a sense, reduced us to ashes!

On an even higher level, it should also be emphasized that the sun is not just shining ON the woman; rather, the sun is shining FROM the woman. God has so draped her with the consuming fire of His divine nature that she and He have become one.

The sun was originally created to "rule the day." So *the sun-clothed woman* is a picture of the manifested authority and dominion of God's people in every age. At the resurrection, this characteristic will be perfected in us. We will then "shine forth as the *sun* in the kingdom of [our] Father." (Gen. 1:16, Mt.13:43)

We will rule and reign with the Bridegroom/King forever.

Considering all of these things, we conclude that this *sun-symbol* primarily speaks of acceptance in God's presence, strength, purity, permanence, authority, invincibility and oneness with God. (See Ju. 5:31, Song 6:10)

■ **The moon is under the woman's feet** - The moon has no light of its own; it can only reflect the light of the sun. This is also true of the flesh. It definitely has no light of its own. Paul admitted - "For I know that in me (that is, in my flesh,) dwelleth no good thing." Yet the flesh, if yielded to God, can reflect the light of God's character, the radiance of His Word and His Spirit. (Ro. 7:18)

Furthermore, the moon has a dark, back side. In like manner, all who are in the flesh, even the most saintly, have a dark, back side to their nature: areas of great weakness, great conflict, great struggle and, at times, even great defeat.

It should be emphasized, though, that in the Revelation 12 vision, the moon is UNDER the woman's feet. In plain language, those who are included in her ranks are believers who have succeeded in bringing the flesh under subjection. Because the flesh is at enmity with God, it is our enemy as well. But praise be to the Most High, through grace, He has made our enemy our footstool!

■ **On the woman's head is a crown of twelve stars** - Stars in the Scripture primarily speak of messengers of God, representatives of heaven in this world. Even as the pulsating stars, scattered like diamonds across the universal dome, send out a message of the greatness and vastness of God, so God's messenger/stars proclaim His glory!

In the beginning of the book of the Revelation, the resurrected Christ appears in the midst of seven golden candlesticks, representing the seven churches. He has seven *stars* in His right hand, representing the "angels of the seven churches." Apparently, these are the presiding pastors or head bishops. (Note: the Greek word translated *angels* is *aggelos*, often rendered *messengers*.) Seven is the number of fullness, so seven stars could be a symbol of ALL who have been God's messengers: channels of the living Word to the rest of the body of Christ.

In reality, every one of God's people are called to shine like *stars* during this dark night of separation from God. (See Gen. 22:17, Dan. 12:3, also Ph. 2:15 NIV) The twelve patriarchs are the "crowning glory" of Old Testament Israel and the twelve apostles are the "crowning glory" of New Testament Israel. The crown of twelve stars could typify either or both of these, or it could be speaking of the twelve tribal divisions that are, in a sense, still in effect spiritually. (See Genesis 37:9)

■ "The woman "being with child cried, travailing in birth, and pained to be delivered" - The true people of God have always known a spiritual kind of travail that necessarily must precede the unfolding of His purpose, the revealing of His power, and the manifestation of His glory. Spiritual travail usually involves deep repentance (anguish over the carnality that causes separation from God) or deep longing (the birth pangs of spiritual desire).

God's people under chastisement are referred to as A WOMAN IN TRAVAIL in Micah 4:10. This is certainly a reference to us all - "for what son is he whom the father chasteneth not." (Heb. 12:7, See Jer. 30:6-7, Jn. 16:21) Concerning the relatively minimal results brought forth by God's people, the prophet Isaiah also declared - "Like as A WOMAN WITH CHILD, that draweth near the time of her delivery, is in pain, and crieth out in her pangs; so have we been in Thy sight, O Lord. We have been with child, we have been in pain, we have as it were brought forth wind..." (Isaiah 26:17-18, See Jeremiah 31:22)

The nation of Israel went through great *travail* for centuries (her times of national failure, captivity and restoration, her seeking of God, her sacrifices, etc.) in order to bring forth "the man child" (Jesus) destined to "rule all nations with a rod of iron." (See Rev. 12:4-5) Every time another son of God is being birthed into spiritual Israel, the *travail* continues; for as soon as Zion *travails*, she brings forth her children. (See Is. 66:8) Moreover, until the nature of Christ be formed in us, we daily *"travail in birth again."* Until the day of our glorification comes, we also *"groan within ourselves,* waiting for the adoption, to wit, the redemption of our body." (Galatians 4:19, Romans 8:23)

■ "Two wings of a great eagle" were given to the woman - "that she might fly into the wilderness, into her place, where she is nourished for a time and times, and half a time, from the face of the serpent." (Rev. 12:14) This verse of Scripture is shrouded in mystery and what it means is subject to numerous and varied opinions. "A time and times and half a time" may mean three-and-a-half years. "Her place" may be referring to a literal, physical location. Then again, it may mean a certain "place" of protection and comfort in the Spirit. The nourishment spoken of may be for the physical body. Then again, it may be a spiritual nourishment given to counteract the spiritual assault of the serpent (a representation of the devil).

Irregardless of how these details should be interpreted, there is one point, far more easily understood, that needs to be emphasized: the woman is given *"two wings of a great eagle."* The *great eagle* is God Himself. His *"wings"* are the Word and the Spirit. By these, believers can nobly and victoriously mount up above the storms of life. They can escape the pressures here below. They can "run, and not be weary...walk, and not faint." (Isaiah 40:31)

In Exodus 19:4, Jehovah reminds Israel - "how I bare you on *eagles' wings,* and brought you unto Myself." In other words, by His Word and His Spirit, Jehovah lifted the Jews out of a degrading state of enslavement in Egypt. Then He carried them, as a father eagle would carry his eaglets, into a land of abundance and victory.

In Revelation 12:14, though, God goes one step further. Instead of just *bearing* His people by the divine nature (the Word and the Spirit) He *gives* us the divine nature. In the New Covenant we are begotten of the Word and born of the Spirit. The *eagle wings* become a part of us.

● About half of the twelfth chapter of Revelation deals with the "great dragon" - a symbol of Satan, the master deceiver who "deceiveth the whole world." (Revelation 12:9)

The devil is first depicted making an unsuccessful attempt to destroy "the man child"; then he wars against Michael and the righteous angels in heaven; then, in the last days, he is cast down to the earth having great wrath because he knows he has but a short time.

Satan and all his host will fight directly against God's people in the spirit-realm, as well as influencing the nations to reject and persecute both natural and spiritual Israel.

● The following verses prophesy the **future** victory that will come to God's own, using words both in the **present** tense *(is)* and the **past** tense *(overcame)*. These word choices signify that, as far as God is concerned, the victory has already been won.

> *"And I heard a loud voice saying in heaven, Now IS come salvation, and strength, and the kingdom of our God, and the power of His Christ: for the accuser of our brethren is cast down, which accused them before our God day and night.*
> *And they OVERCAME him by the blood of the Lamb, and by the word of their testimony; and they loved not their lives unto the death."*

(Revelation 12:10-11)

O what a *blessed hope* this is! And what a fitting way to end this sixth volume of **OUR GLORIOUS INHERITANCE** !

■ THE "SERPENT-BRUISER" SEED ─────────────────

We know that, in these last days especially, the dragon - "that old serpent, called the Devil, and Satan" - will be "wroth with **THE WOMAN"** and will go forth to "make war with the remnant of **HER SEED."** (Note: The phrase - *the seed of the woman* - refers to those who keep the commandments of God and have the testimony of Jesus Christ.) (Revelation 12:9,17)

But we also know that "the Lord will be *the hope of His people,* and the strength of the children of Israel." (Joel 3:16)

WE WILL ULTIMATELY OVERCOME...BY THE BLOOD OF THE LAMB AND BY THE WORD OF OUR TESTIMONY!

And we will be part of the fulfillment of an ancient prophecy - given by the Lord Himself in the garden of Eden - that *"the seed of the woman"* would one day *bruise* the head of the serpent.

This was fulfilled primarily and initially in Jesus who was both *the seed of the woman* and the seed of Abraham. (See Genesis 3:15, Galatians 3:16)

It will be fulfilled secondarily and finally in the whole body of Christ. We are also both *the seed of the woman* and the seed of Abraham. (See Revelation 12:17, Galatians 3:29;4:26-31)

Jesus is the Head, the main victor, but we, as His body, have inherited the right to be *"serpent-bruisers"* as well. We are carrying on the ministry and work that Jesus began.

● Romans 16:20 heralds with gladness that:

> *"The God of peace shall bruise Satan under your feet shortly..."*
>
> (Compare Ephesians 6:15)

We will definitely go through afflictions, temptations and tribulations in this world, for the prophecy has been given that the serpent will *bruise* the heel of "the seed." (See Genesis 3:15)

This was initially fulfilled at the cross where Jesus was *"bruised* for our iniquities." (Isaiah 53:5, See also 53:10) It is secondarily fulfilled in all who are crucified with Christ.

But we have the blessed *hope* and the blessed assurance that Jesus came to:

> *"...set at liberty them that are bruised."*
> (Lk. 4:18, See also Is. 42:3, Mt. 12:20)

In the end, God will definitely bring us forth in victory and power.

Though His plan involves a certain "less-than-glorious" process, it will lead us, and even propel us, toward a glorious end result.

As *clay,* we will go through the molding and shaping process of the Master Potter...but we will emerge as vessels of honor.

As *gold,* we will go through the refining process of the Master Refiner...but we will emerge purified of all dross.

As *fallow ground,* our hearts will often be broken with contrition that the Master Gardener might plant in us the seed of the Word.

As *lively stones,* we will often have to give up self-centered, independent attitudes that the Master Builder might use us to build His holy temple.

In all these things, we are, and ever will be, more than conquerors:

> *"For our light affliction, which is but for a moment, WORKETH FOR US a far more exceeding and ETERNAL WEIGHT OF GLORY."*
>
> (II Corinthians 4:17)

■ OUR ETERNAL DOOR OF HOPE

YES, WE ARE HEIRS ACCORDING TO THE HOPE OF ETERNAL LIFE...AND WE KNOW THAT OUR GOD IS AN EXPERT AT MAKING ALL THINGS WORK TOGETHER FOR OUR GOOD.

We are **THE CALLED ACCORDING TO HIS PURPOSE** and in the end His purpose will prevail.

Everything we face, as sons and daughters of God, is going to ultimately work for us, for our benefit, for our profit.

This is God's genius, His marvellous and remarkable ability, the proof of His sovereignty and the demonstration of His love.

● For His beloved ones, He will make the valley of Achor - *the valley of trouble* - a door of hope.

We will learn valuable lessons here that we never could have learned otherwise.

We will see the fullness of God's character formed within our hearts.

We will come forth from this valley of suffering more in the image of God than Adam was in the beginning.

It is no wonder that we are now considered and will ever be called - **A GREAT WONDER IN HEAVEN!**

For the **wondrous** work God is presently performing in us...and the **wondrous** way He will yet bring us to perfection...will ever cause **great wonder** to gleam in the eyes of even the cherubim and seraphim on high.

We are presently like the tabernacle of Moses, covered over with rough, unsightly badger's skins, yet hiding spectacular heaven-sent glory within.

In a spiritual sense, the ark with its blood-sprinkled mercy seat now resides deep in our hearts. His name is Jesus...and He will abide in those He calls **HIS ABODE** both now and forevermore.

Therefore, we can live without fear...knowing we are His **HIDDEN ONES**, hidden under the shadow of His wings and hidden in the palm of His hand.

We can walk in the utmost confidence knowing we are **THE GLORY OF CHRIST**...and "upon all **THE GLORY** shall be a defense." (Isaiah 4:5)

We know that if we, **THE PATIENT IN SPIRIT**, maintain faith and patience...we will finally inherit God's promises.

And it will definitely be said of us:

> *"Better is the end of a thing than the beginning thereof."*
>
> (Ecclesiastes 7:8)

Adam's beginning was glorious.
Our end will be far more glorious.
Adam was of the dust.
We will shine like the firmament.
Adam had the potential of falling.
We will never fall nor fail again.

We will be sealed into our eternal inheritance and ever celebrate the fact that our God:

> *"...raiseth up the poor out of the dust, and lifteth up the beggar from the dunghill, to set them among princes, and to make them inherit the throne of glory."*
>
> (I Samuel 2:8)

Yes, this is the **great wonder** of it all!
We have been spiritually poverty stricken.
We have been beggars in the dust.

255

We have been God's adversaries, "clothed with shame." (Psalm 35:26)

We will yet make up His eternal bride...**A WOMAN CLOTHED WITH THE SUN.**

We have been "the crown of pride," drunk on the mind-numbing, conscience-searing spirit of this world. (Isaiah 28:1)

We will yet make up that Queen of glory who will be spectacularly crowned with a crown of twelve stars, filled to overflowing with the glory of God.

We have been trodden under foot by circumstances and sin; we will yet bring all things under subjection like the glorious woman with the moon under her feet.

Miraculously, there will be no stain of the world left on us and our status as **A WOMAN IN TRAVAIL** will eternally pass away. Instead we will emerge as **"A COMELY AND DELICATE WOMAN [THE FAIR AND DELICATE ONE],"** the final realization of God's age-old longing. (Jeremiah 6:2 AV, Bas)

Because we have fulfilled the call to be **THE HUMBLE** and **THE CONTRITE ONES,** we will dwell eternally in the high and holy place with the "high and lofty One that inhabiteth eternity, whose name is Holy." (Isaiah 57:15)

As **STRANGERS** and **PILGRIMS** we will make it *all the way home.*

We will be recognized and revered in heaven as being **THE PLACE OF HIS REST** - the final and eternal dwelling place of that spiritual "ark of the covenant": Jesus, the Son of God.

In the end, the wonder of the work God has wrought in us will redound to Him in ecstasy of worship...insomuch we will be called **HIS PEOPLE FOR HIS RENOWN AND PRAISE AND HONOR.**

This is the mercy and the grace of our Creator.

This is the plan, purpose and pleasure of a loving, heavenly Father.

And this is...

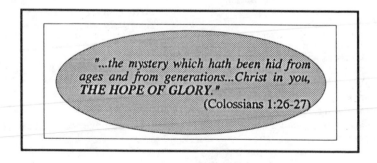

"...the mystery which hath been hid from ages and from generations...Christ in you, THE HOPE OF GLORY."
(Colossians 1:26-27)

Thank God, the mystery is no longer a mystery to us!

THE SUN CLOTHED WOMAN

O, woman clothed with the fire of God,
  Once mortal now immortal be.
Naked couple, and bare offspring redeemed,
  Find holy covering, a part of thee.

A crown of stars adorns thy brow.
  O, wife of God - thy God complete,
And reign with Him from Jerusalem on high,
  The moon (carnality) under thy feet.

O, dragon intent on devouring "manchild,"
  Thwarted you were, and will be and are;
For He now ascended will irresistibly rule,
  With iron rod breaking the nations pow'r.

O, Michael and myriads of angels war,
  Until no place above in heaven remains,
For fierce dragon and his fallen "stars,"
  Till their destiny be - everlasting chains.

So eagle-winged Woman ascend to "your place,"
  And with praise await the Kingdom of Light;
Until the Sun of righteousness envelops you so,
  You will never again know night!

"Christ in you, the hope of glory"

BIBLIOGRAPHY

BIBLE TRANSLATIONS:
King James Authorized Version (AV or KJV)
Phillips Modern English (PME)
Revised Standard Version (RSV)
New International Version (NIV)
New English Bible (NEB)
The Living Bible (LB)
New American Standard (NAS)
Today's English Version (TEV)
Amplified Bible (Amp)
The Septuagint (Sept)

● Unger, Merrill F. *Unger's Bible Dictionary* , 1967,1966. The Moody Bible Institute, Chicago, Illinois, (UBD)
● Vine, W.E. *Vine's Expository Dictionary*, 1984 Bethany House Publishers, Minneapolis, Minnesota, (VED)
● Young, Robert *Young's Concordance,* 1984 McDonald Publications, McLean, Virginia (YC)
● Strong, James *Strong's Concordance,* 1984 Thomas Nelson Publishers, Nashville, Tennessee (SC)
● Dake, Finis *Dake's Annotated Reference Bible ,* 1979 Dake Bible Sales, Lawrenceville, Georgia (DARB)
● Vaughan, Curtis *The Bible from 26 Translations* , Baker Book House, Grand Rapids, Michigan (Bas, Har, Wms, Rhm, Mon, ASV, Nor, etc.)
● Achtemier, Paul J. *Harper's Bible Dictionary,* 1985, Harper and Row Publishers, San Franciso, CA (HBD)
● Smith, William, *A Dictionary of the Bible*, Thomas Nelson Publishers, Nashville, Camden, NY (SBD)
● Conner, Kevin J., *The Tabernacle of Moses*, 1975, Bible Temple Publishing, Portland, Oregon
● Conner, Kevin J., *The Temple of Solomon,* 1988
● Soltau, Henry W., *The Holy Vessels and Furniture of the Tabernacle,* 1971, Kregel Publications, Grand Rapids, Michigan
● Soltau, Henry W., *The Tabernacle, The Priesthood and the Offerings,* Kregel Publications, Grand Rapids, Michigan
● *The Companion Bible*, The Way International, New Knoxville, Ohio
● *Bethany Commentary of the Old Testament* (Bethany House Publishers, Minneapolis, Minnesota 1983)
● *Bethany Commentary of the New Testament* (Bethany House Publishers, Minneapolis, Minnesota 1983)